U.S. pension fund trustees are increasingly recognizin[illegible] long-term value and risk posed by environmental, social, and governa[illegible] tors and move toward a framework that prioritizes long-term value creation. *The Responsible Investor Handbook* provides pension fund trustees with tools and examples on how to shift their governance practices and investment strategies to enhance long-term returns.
Fiona Reynolds, Managing Director, Principles for Responsible Investment (PRI)

Taking account of environmental, social, and governance issues in investment processes is self-evidently an integral part of how investors deliver on their fiduciary duties. It is also essential if we are to deliver a stable, resilient and sustainable financial system that delivers for all in society. *The Responsible Investor Handbook* is not only a call to action but it provides pension fund trustees with the knowledge and skills they need to deliver on their fiduciary duties in the 21st century.
Will Martindale, Head of Policy, Principles for Responsible Investment (PRI)

As a fiduciary of a $90 billion portfolio, I believe Oregon can leverage our investments to accelerate the transition toward cleaner sources of energy. In combination with other investors, we can help build the foundations of what is still an emerging clean energy sector by actively encouraging the development of sound investment opportunities in transitional and renewable energy companies. I am more optimistic than ever that there are opportunities to invest in renewables that meet the high standards we have for all of our investments.
Ted Wheeler, Oregon State Treasurer

Pension funds are long-term investors in the truest sense, responsible for providing retirement security to generations of hardworking and loyal employees. For fund trustees, sustainable business practices—particularly responsible labor, human rights, and environmental practices—are not just moral issues. They are fundamental to creating and protecting long-term shareowner value and sustainable economies. *The Responsible Investor Handbook* provides trustees with an important tool to go from theory to practice.
Scott M. Stringer, New York City Comptroller

Trustees need all the help they can get and a book like this sponsored by the AFL-CIO is one of the tools they can use.
Ed Smith, President and CEO, ULLICO

Managers of pension funds must focus on the long term. Our responsibility is to protect the financial security of Rhode Islanders across multiple generations. We must understand the environmental, social, and corporate governance risks to our portfolios over time, and work to manage them.
Seth Magaziner, Rhode Island General Treasurer

Croft and Malhotra have written a terrific hands-on "how to" and "what it is" book on responsible investment, specifically aimed at trade union pension trustees, and more generally a labor and labor-friendly audience. That said, even those not affiliated with trade unions or involved in labor organizations but interested in the current practice and historical background of responsible investment (with a labor bent) will benefit greatly from reading this well-written, well-informed and very well-documented book.
James Hawley, Ph.D., Transamerica Professor of Business Policy and Strategy, School of Economics and Business Administration, Saint Mary's College of California

There is a vast amount of information here that should be useful to pension fund trustees and others interested in trying to manage pension funds in ways that promote economic development. All too often pension funds have been preyed upon by the financial industry. This book is a great guide to a better path.
Dean Baker, Co-Director, Center for Economic and Policy Research

This is a clear and comprehensive guide for trustees on a topic which is of ever-increasing importance in the realm of investments. Asset owners are increasingly moving towards active ownership and engagement on ESG issues and this guide provides a broad overview of the ways in which trustees can engage and the material impact which they can have.
Ana Lei Ortiz, Managing Director, Relationship Management, Europe, Hamilton Lane

As Roger Urwin (Global Head of Investment Content, Towers Watson & Co.) says, buckle up, trustees. Responsible investment increasingly helps to implement longer investment horizons, greater transparency and ethics in financial markets, reduction of "extra-financial" investment risk, co-alignment of interests of retirement plan investors and investment managers, increased job creation, and sustainable investment returns. This *Responsible Investor Handbook* is a must-read for both trustees and all investors as financial markets increasingly reward responsible investors.
Ron Auer, Executive Director, CORPaTH and Director, Analytic Investors, LLC

The Responsible Investor Handbook

Mobilizing Workers' Capital for a Sustainable World

THE RESPONSIBLE INVESTOR HANDBOOK

Mobilizing Workers' Capital for a Sustainable World

Thomas Croft and Annie Malhotra

Published by Greenleaf Publishing Limited
Aizlewood's Mill
Nursery Street
Sheffield S3 8GG
UK
www.greenleaf-publishing.com

Cover by LaliAbril.com

Printed in the UK on environmentally friendly, acid-free paper from managed forests by CPI Group (UK) Ltd, Croydon

British Library Cataloguing in Publication Data:
A catalogue record for this book is available from the British Library.

ISBN-13: 978-1-78353-555-2 [hardback]
ISBN-13: 978-1-78353-562-0 [paperback]
ISBN-13: 978-1-78353-563-7 [PDF ebook]
ISBN-13: 978-1-78353-550-7 [ePub ebook]

TC—I'd like to lovingly dedicate this book to my wife,
Patricia and my two daughters, Kelsey and Taylor.

AM—To my family.

Contents

Section II:
Pension fund management, governance and fiduciary considerations

Section IV: Implementation and measurement

Figures, tables, and boxes

Figures

Tables

Boxes

Foreword

Richard L. Trumka
President, AFL-CIO (American Federation of Labor and Congress of Industrial Organizations)

How should workers' retirement savings be invested differently? Croft and Malhotra's *Responsible Investor Handbook* answers this provocative question by describing the emerging best practices in responsible investment. I believe that this *Responsible Investor Handbook* should be required reading for all pension plan trustees.

When I was first elected Secretary-Treasurer of the AFL-CIO, I created the AFL-CIO's Capital Stewardship Program based on the premise that pension plan assets are the deferred wages of working people, the fruit of lifetimes of hard work. That money belongs to workers, not Wall Street.

As the stewards of workers' capital, trustees have the responsibility of protecting those assets. As fiduciaries, we are held to the highest standards of loyalty and prudence, committing to promote the interests of our pensioners above all else. With this responsibility comes awesome power, to guide the investment decisions for the hard-earned savings of workers. Those decisions, in turn, affect decision-making in companies at all levels.

Providing workers with a secure retirement—the goal of pension plans—requires a long-term focus consistent with achieving sustainable returns. Today there is a growing recognition that the environmental, social, and governance performance of companies is tied to their sustained success, affecting not only investment returns but workers, jobs, and communities as well.

We have seen what happens when we allow Wall Street to dictate financial practices: pensions destroyed, jobs lost, and deep economic recession. We cannot continue this way, and we need not.

Instead, the stewards of workers' capital have been leading the way by using our rights as owners to encourage companies to address environmental, social, and governance issues. We have also pioneered investments that create good jobs by providing patient capital. But we cannot rest on our past accomplishments. We need to push forward to address new investment challenges to our pension plans and the economy as a whole.

We must reinvest in America's crumbling infrastructure to preserve our economic competitiveness. We need to encourage corporations to allocate capital for new factories, research and development, and workforce training. We should reinvest in our cities, making our housing more affordable and energy efficient for working people. And we must overcome the environmental threat of climate change, create high-wage jobs along the way, while making sure that we don't leave communities behind.

This text will help provide you with the tools necessary to invest responsibly on behalf of all the workers who have contributed their life savings to the pension plan. Together, workers' capital can be invested for a sustainable future. I hope you find this *Responsible Investor Handbook* to be a useful companion for the road ahead.

Richard L. Trumka
President, AFL-CIO (American Federation of Labor and Congress of Industrial Organizations)

Responsible investment in the 21st century

Dr Rory Sullivan

The fact that the Principles for Responsible Investment (PRI) now has almost 1,500 signatories including over 300 asset owners and nearly a thousand asset managers provides evidence that responsible investment is increasingly seen as a standard part of mainstream investment practice. Over the past decade, PRI signatories encouraged improvements in the environmental, social, and governance (ESG) performance of the companies in which they are invested, and they have made significant investments in areas such as renewable energy.

Despite this, the sense is that responsible investment has yet to deliver on its full potential as a positive influence on corporate practice or in society more generally. There are various reasons: outdated or misguided views on fiduciary duty, the perception that a focus on ESG issues does not add value to investment decision-making, the emphasis on short-term investment performance, weak governance structures and processes, the advice being given by investment consultants, the lack of accountability for the negative ESG impacts resulting from with investment decisions, and a lack of attention to the wider interests of workers and retirees. These have resulted in investment practices that ignore long-term risks and that are focused on market timing and short-term gains at the expense of sustainable, long-term value creation.

It is in this context that this book—*The Responsible Investor Handbook: Mobilizing Workers' Capital for a Sustainable World*—is so important. It is not just a how-to guide to responsible investment but also provides a philosophical basis for responsible investment in the 21st century.

Its starting premise is that great change is possible. The book shows how the labor movement and its allies have pioneered long-term investment in the real economy, delivering better corporate governance, strengthening worker rights and protections, and providing capital to build affordable housing, support the manufacturing sector, and grow the clean economy.

It then offers a new vision for responsible investment. Its argument is that responsible investment should reflect the intrinsic interests of workers, not only by generating competitive financial returns, but by contributing to the long-term wellbeing of economies, societies, and the environment. It makes the point that this approach to responsible investment—investing in infrastructure, encouraging corporations to invest in new factories, research and development, and workforce training, making housing more affordable and energy efficient, responding to climate change, creating high-paid and high-quality jobs—clearly aligns with the long-term interests of plan participants and beneficiaries.

It also provides a pathway for action. It highlights the central role of pension fund governance, and the key role that needs to be played by well-informed and socially aware trustees, that are both willing and able to challenge investment strategies that prioritise short-term performance over long-term value creation.

Finally, it concludes that, by leveraging large pools of workers' capital, pension funds can deliver positive ESG outcomes, both for beneficiaries and for society at large. However, to deliver this at the scale needed requires workers and their representatives in the trade union movement to find common cause with other investors (e.g., those that have already made commitments to responsible investment) and with other civil society organisations. If they can find this common ground and work effectively together, there is the real prospect that responsible investment can accelerate our progress toward creating a more liveable, habitable, and hopeful planet.

Dr Rory Sullivan is the General Editor of the Greenleaf Responsible Investment Series. He is an internationally recognised expert on responsible investment, and has advised organizations such as the PRI, UNEP FI, and the UN Global Compact on the law and policy issues around responsible investment. He is the co-author of the PRI and UNEP FI report *Fiduciary*

Duty in the 21st Century (2015), the author of the Global Compact report *Coping, Shifting, Changing: Strategies for Managing the Impacts of Investor Short-termism on Corporate Sustainability* (2014), and the author of *Valuing Corporate Responsibility: How Do Investors Really Use Corporate Responsibility Information?* (Greenleaf Publishing, 2011).

Acknowledgments

The authors would like to extend their deepest gratitude to the AFL-CIO for commissioning this *Handbook*, as well as to a number of additional sponsors that have supported the *Handbook* and the activities of Heartland Capital Strategies (HCS) through the years, including:

- AFL-CIO Housing Investment Trust (HIT)
- United Steelworkers (USW)
- KPS Capital Partners
- ULLICO, Inc.
- Bentall Kennedy (U.S.) LP/MEPT
- NewTower Trust Company
- American Federation of Teachers (AFT)
- Blue Wolf Capital Partners
- Towpath Renewables
- Washington Circle Advisors
- Pegasus Capital Advisors
- Sleigh Strategies
- Robert Samuel
- Steel Valley Authority (SVA)

We would also like to recognize our reviewers who helped tremendously in shaping this *Handbook*: Brandon Rees, Deputy Director, AFL-CIO Office of Investment; Deborah C. Nisson, CRE, Director, Institutional Sales, ULLICO; James S. Beall, Partner, Willig, Williams & Davidson; David Keto, President, Washington Circle Advisors; Tessa Hebb, Director, Carleton Centre for

Community Innovation, Carleton University; Sarah Bernstein, Principal, Pension Consulting Alliance, LLC; Sarah Stettinius, Senior Vice President, Bentall Kennedy (U.S.) LP/MEPT; James Hawley, Professor, Saint Mary's College of California; Tom Powdrill, Responsible Investor Coordinator, ITWF; and Marco Trbovich, Senior Vice President of Strategic Communications, Tricom Associates. Thanks also to Dennak Murphy, former Director of Capital Stewardship, SEIU; Ron Auer, Executive Director, CORPaTH and Director, Analytic Investors, LLC; Goodlow "Geb" Byron, Managing Partner, Potomac Energy Fund; and Chris Cooper, Program Coordinator, Ohio Employee Ownership Center, for their helpful ideas. Kudos to Carrie Mihalko and Rosie Sallinger, Steel Valley Authority; Meghan Holohan, independent book editor; Sabrina Rearick and Kathryn VanDeveer, interns from the Duquesne University Urban Law Clinic; and thanks to Paul Quirk, Pegasus Capital Advisors, in assisting with interviews.

The authors would also like to thank the following participants and contributors for their time in completing interviews and/or surveys—without their expertise and input, the *Handbook* would not have been possible: Christopher Ailman, CIO, CalSTRS; David Blitzstein, Owner, Blitzstein Consulting and former Special Assistant for Multiemployer Funds, UFCW International Union; Stephen Coyle, CEO, AFL-CIO HIT; Allan Emkin, Managing Director, Pension Consulting Alliance, Inc.; Michael Garland, Assistant Comptroller for Corporate Governance and Responsible Investment, NYC; Mario Gianinni, CEO, Hamilton Lane; Jack Marco, Chairman, Marco Consulting Group; Keith Mestrich, President and CEO, Amalgamated Bank; Michael Musuraca, Managing Director, Blue Wolf Capital Management; Ana Lei Ortiz, Managing Director, Relationship Management, Europe, Hamilton Lane; Peter Palandjian, Chairman and CEO, Intercontinental Real Estate Corp.; David Pollak, Director of Marketing and Investor Relations, Pegasus Capital Advisors; Michael Psaros, Co-Founder and Managing Partner, KPS Capital Partners; Therese Schets, Project Manager, FNV/CWC Project; Steve Sleigh, Former Fund Director, IAM National Pension Fund; Edward Smith, President and CEO, ULLICO, Inc.; Sarah Stettinius, Senior Vice President, Bentall Kennedy (U.S.) LP/MEPT; Randi Weingarten, President, American Federation of Teachers; and Janet Williamson, Senior Policy Officer, TUC.

Finally, additional thanks to Ron Auer, Executive Director, CORPaTH and Director, Analytic Investors, LLC, and Jacques Loveall, President of UFCW 8-Golden State and Chair of UFCW Trust, for their gracious assistance. CORPaTH supports objectives covered within the Handbook by providing assistance to those who oversee pension and workers' capital for the benefit of the working men and women who earn and deserve a secure retirement.

Introduction

> Investors have an incredible amount of power. They have the ability to effect huge amounts of change, and they just need to come together and act.
>
> Fiona Reynolds, Managing Director,
> Principles for Responsible Investment

As the sun rose on March 9, 2015, a preposterous-looking solar-powered plane called Solar Impulse 2, with a wing span longer than that of a Boeing 747, took off from the Middle East in a historic record-breaking attempt to fly around the world. "Andre Borschberg and Bertrand Piccard aren't looking to revolutionize aviation with their solar-powered aircraft. Rather, the Swiss duo [said] they want to raise the profile of a suite of technologies on their Solar Impulse 2 aircraft—many commercially available today," showing that alternative energy sources and new technologies can achieve what is considered impossible (Casey, 2015). These pilots, as audacious as any explorer in recent times, had already flown this craft across the continental U.S.A. in 2013. Now, as this *Handbook* goes to print, they have crossed the second of two oceans and, despite snags and delays, the pilots aim to return to the Middle East by late summer 2016. Like the Wright Brothers at Kitty Hawk, their dream will, most likely, not be denied.

American know-how pioneered the early development of modern solar energy, and American workers' pension funds, along with research dollars from U.S. taxpayers, helped make this flight possible. How? U.S. pension funds provided the early capital for the decades-old breakthroughs in solar energy. These investors sourced part of the capital for early corporate inventors of solar technology such as ATT Bell Labs, RCA, ARCO Solar, and GE. (U.S. Department of Energy, 2015). They bet on venture capital funds that launched hundreds of solar entrepreneurs. In so doing, workers' capital—the pension assets and savings of everyday working people such as teachers, steelworkers, firefighters, pilots, and engineers—has seeded and grown innumerable innovative industries that have far-reaching, Earth-changing impacts.

In the U.S.A. and internationally, labor unions were the original "crowdfunders," fighting for the establishment of collective retirement and welfare benefits for their members. Through these pooled assets, workers helped construct the building blocks of advanced economies around the world. For over a century, trade unions and civil society worked together to build housing, finance banks, credit unions, and insurance companies, and capitalize companies. They were among the pioneers of long-term investment in the real economy and in ensuring greater responsible corporate governance. Advancing untold financial design innovations, labor's financial institutions successfully deployed capital to revitalize cities and industries, and, acting as responsible shareholders, pushed "the boss" to be more accountable.

An emerging new generation of responsible investors is mobilizing capital for complex smart buildings and affordable housing, community infrastructure projects, wind and solar projects, electric and hybrid vehicles, and other inventive solutions. These investors are applying a more holistic and integrated investment approach to the challenges facing cities, industries, and our environment, and reaping the financial benefits. They are joining coalitions to pool capital to rebuild cities, make companies more humane and efficient, and address climate change. They are amalgamating resources and investment capacity across borders, as evident from the rapid spread of the UN-launched Principles for Responsible Investment (PRI).

Alongside these developments has been the tremendous growth of pension assets. As the ownership of corporate America began to change hands, from primarily owner-founders in the early 1900s to pension funds and other large institutional investors in the mid-1900s, the latter came to own broad swaths of the public capital markets. As a result, these large institutional investors came to be referred to as "universal owners" (Hawley and Williams, 2000b). In the latter part of the 20th century, pension funds also began to make greater allocations to alternative investments, particularly in private equity and venture capital, hedge funds, and real estate (Leitner *et al.*, 2007).

Today, these assets, *our money*, represent an enormous share of economic and capital market wealth. In 2014, pension assets were valued at over \$36 trillion across 16 major pension markets globally; less than two decades ago, in 1996, pension assets stood at \$11.3 trillion across 11 major pension markets. The U.S. pension assets[1] market has been the largest among these, steadily growing in value from $6.8 trillion in 1996 to $22.1 trillion in 2014. During the same period, U.S. pension assets as a share of gross domestic product (GDP) grew from 87% to 127% (Towers Watson, 2015; Watson Wyatt Worldwide, 2007).

The retirement assets of working people have been instrumental in the development of the U.S. (and the world) economy and its capital markets and those of our global neighbors, fueling the desire for growth and prosperity. While worker representatives were among the most important architects of retirement systems, workers and retirees themselves have little influence on how their assets are used to fuel this growth and whether this growth will cater to their own long-term economic, social, and environmental interests.

Despite important strides made with the investments of workers' capital, trustees who oversee pension funds have been challenged by weak governance structures, increased capital market complexities, the oversized influence of investment managers and external consultants, and a multitude of regulations. They have sometimes succumbed to institutional herd mentality[2] and suffered "disrupted attention to the fiduciary duties of loyalty and impartiality" (Hawley *et al.*, 2011, p. 4). The result has been greater separation between the long-term interests of workers and retirees (plan participants and beneficiaries) and the interests of those who oversee, manage, and/or use pension assets. This agency separation (Stewart and Yermo, 2008) has resulted in the investment of pension assets into approaches that ignore long-term risks and that are focused on market timing and short-term gains at the expense of sustainable, long-term value creation. It has also resulted in little accountability for the negative environmental, social, and governance (ESG) impacts often generated in the pursuit of short-term gains.

1 Including defined benefit (DB) plans, defined contribution (DC) plans, and other assets such as Individual Retirement Accounts (IRAs).

2 "Herd instinct", a form of investor behavior also known as "herding", can "often cause large, unsubstantiated rallies or sell-offs, based on seemingly little fundamental evidence to justify either. Herd instinct is the primary cause of bubbles in finance. For example, many look at the dot.com bubble of the late 1990s and early 2000s as a prime example of the ramifications of herd instinct in the development and subsequent burst of that industry's bubble" (http://www.investopedia.com/terms/h/herdinstinct.asp, retrieved June 21, 2016).

How did we arrive at short-termism as the standard modus operandi in institutional investments (and, indeed, the practice of a large swath of the capital markets)?

> The official inquiries have for the most part identified multiple causes for "short-termism", so almost by definition they must proscribe a set of measures rather than a single solution. One of the most wide-reaching academic analysis of the problem to date (Jackson and Petraki 2011) is quite sobering insofar as it identifies short-termism as a deeply-embedded set of mutually-reinforcing behaviours and expectations on the part of a multiplicity of actors—not only on the part of investors and companies, but also of "gatekeepers" such as auditing firms and rating agencies. This analysis suggests that the incentives and behaviour of all key actors must be changed to break out of the trap of short-termism. (Vitols, 2015, pp. 12-13)

We do not have the space to fully examine the pursuit of short-termism by managers, shareholders, and gatekeepers, except to include the results of some recent reports. However, it is important to understand the drivers of short-termism, so as to be able to counter those forces and reestablish a flight path to long-term investment. While this *Handbook* trumpets the role of workers as shareholders and active owners, we are especially concerned when pension shareholders are found to be among those actors in the investment value chain who contribute to short-termism (Williamson, 2015). Such short-termism has often led to risky financial experimentation, or financialization, leaving working families and communities to absorb the fallouts, as we'll discuss later.

The 2008 financial crisis brought on by the subprime housing market crash bore testament to the explosive negative impacts of short-term, speculative investments "whose risk profiles they [pension funds] did not fully understand" (Antolin and Stewart, 2009, p. 14). These misguided investments impacted not only the financial value of pension assets, but also broader civil society. Nearly $11 trillion in household wealth vanished (Financial Crisis Inquiry Commission, 2011), including $4 trillion in retirement accounts and life savings (Johnson and de Graaf, 2009). In addition, millions of jobs were lost (Galbraith, 2011) and homes were foreclosed (Financial Crisis Inquiry Commission, 2011), and resources were diverted from important environmental issues such as climate change (Finnish Environment Institute, 2014), among many other negative effects.

While some institutional investors recovered, through lawsuits, a small portion of the losses caused by Wall Street's financial engineering mistakes and blatant frauds, the U.S. Government and the Securities & Exchange

Commission (SEC) were famously inept at punishing the illegal actions by banks and investment houses. In all, our federal and state governments recovered a paltry $130 billion from the largest U.S. banks for their actions as of April 20, 2015, according to the Wall Street Journal (Baer and Viswanatha, 2015). For capital stewards, the hard lesson is that there is no higher authority that will recover your losses, and market rebounds may not return all that is lost.

Despite lessons from past crises, "prevailing theories and practices have not been fully adjusted to reflect systemic and long-term risks that threaten to undermine the security of the pension (and other retirement savings) plan "promise'" (Hawley *et al.*, 2011, p. 4). Indeed, in order to close the large funding gaps between plan assets and promised retiree benefits, many pension plans continue to make greater allocations to investments that promise higher returns but that also come with higher risks, further jeopardizing worker and retiree benefits (Oakley, 2014; Barro, 2014).

To push capital markets toward taking a long-term approach to investments, trustees need to take charge. Workers' capital is meant to be held in trust and invested and redeemed as benefits to retirees over long periods of time. The large size of these assets places pension funds in a strong position to influence the behavior of corporations and other capital market participants. In addition, as universal owners, pension funds "have a strong incentive to consider economy-wide economic performance when seeking to improve the returns they receive on their investments" (Hawley and Williams, 2000a, p. 21; see also Zanglein and Clark, 2001).

In this *Handbook*, we encourage pension trustees to realign their governance and investment strategies with the long-term interests of plan participants and beneficiaries by incorporating responsible investment practices into the investment decision-making process for plan assets. We discuss how responsible investors, with their longer-term focus, ESG-based holistic risk assessment, and shareholder activism, are better equipped to preserve and grow retirement capital while maintaining intergenerational equity. This equity represents the idea that "growth should occur while ensuring a certain level of economic, social and environmental security for future generations" (Woods and Urwin, 2010, p. 2)—emphasizing important and inherent links between the goals of workers' capital and those of responsible investing.

Fortuitously, there is a sea change under way in conventional investment philosophy as represented by the UN-backed PRI, which supports the realignment of the stewardship of workers' capital with long-term responsible investing (PRI, 2015). The PRI has been adopted by some of the largest global institutional investors, asset managers, and consultants. This transition did not occur overnight, however. Well-known writers, from Peter Drucker in *The Unseen Revolution,* Randy Barber and Jeremy Rifkin in *The North Shall Rise Again,* and Theresa Ghilarducci in *Labor's Capital,* along with other progressive scholars and analysts, have for decades predicted the eventual investment power of pension funds (Croft and Hebb, 2003).

Seven drivers

The Responsible Investor Handbook is a timely reflection of the momentum that is galvanizing around the financial and nonfinancial impacts of social inequality, climate change, weak corporate governance, and gridlocked political structures. Below we identify seven powerful drivers of this momentum:

1. **The UN PRI.** The PRI, launched in 2006, has inspired investors globally to think long-term and strategically about environmental, social, and governance (ESG) risks and opportunities, and reframes the investment decision to better ensure that investors account for the real risks of their investments. As of May 2016, the PRI had just over 1,500 signatories, representing $60 trillion in assets.

2. **New U.S. DOL guidance on ETIs and ESG.** The U.S. Department of Labor (DOL)'s recently issued guidance—Interpretive Bulletin 15-01—reconfirmed the legality of economically targeted investments (ETIs) and urged that investors consider ESG matters. The new rule, thus, strengthens the responsible investments case. It lays out the legal fiduciary framework by which, under ERISA, pension fund managers and external investment managers alike will have to adhere to responsible investment principles. The bulletin explicitly states that "plan fiduciaries *should* appropriately consider factors that potentially influence risk and return" and that ESG issues "may have a direct relationship to the economic value of the plan's investment. In these instances, such issues are not merely collateral considerations or tie-breakers, but rather are proper components of the fiduciary's primary analysis of the

economic merits of competing investment choices" [emphasis added] (U.S. DOL, 2015).

3. **Responsible investment and financial performance.** As responsible investments gain traction, there is an expanding library of peer-reviewed meta-studies, academic and industry reports, and sustainability data proving the financial advantages (or lack of financial disadvantages) of investing responsibly and of good corporate governance. These reports, along with a plethora of anecdotal references by investors and corporations, are showcasing the positive impact of ESG considerations on both investment portfolios and corporate value, helping investors recognize the merits of responsible investing.

4. **Post-2008 market crash reforms.** The aftereffects of the 2008 financial crisis shed greater scrutiny on unbridled corporate greed at the expense of workers and retirees, whose labor and savings are used to fund corporate growth and shareholder returns in the first place. On the one hand, the crisis resulted in severe negative impacts, not only on the financial value of pension assets, but also on broader civil society. On the other, the crisis has forced investors to question how their savings are invested and to use their voice as shareholders to promote sustainable business practices. For instance, in the aftermath of the crisis, corporate governance practices have been placed front and center in the minds of investors. Supported by investors' concerns, the Dodd–Frank Act of 2010 was enacted to increase corporate board involvement and objectivity and improve accountability to shareholders.

5. **Paris climate change accords and similar developments.** The Paris Agreement enacted by the 21st UN Climate Change Conference of the Parties (COP21) in December 2015 resulted in a landmark commitment from 195 countries to address global climate change. Among its highlights, the legally-binding Agreement calls for participating countries to lower their greenhouse gas (GHG) emissions sufficiently in order to limit the increase in global average temperature. In addition, the Agreement called on the countries to **reach global peaking of GHG emissions** as soon as possible (UN, 2015). Pope Francis' recent encyclical on climate change called for a reversal of the "business as usual" that is greatly contributing to environmental degradation, human exploitation, and

climate change. Domestically, the U.S. SEC now requires disclosures of climate change matters that are material to a company's business and lists several areas that may trigger such disclosures (SEC, 2010).

6. **Endorsement and leadership by the U.S. labor movement.** The AFL-CIO passed Resolution 11 at its 2013 Constitutional Convention in Los Angeles, endorsing the responsible investment of workers' capital and, for the first time, aligning such investments with the global ESG framework. This follows the endorsement of the UN PRI by the Global Trade Unions in 2007.
7. **National movements to pay fair, livable wages and reverse income inequality.** Campaigns such as "Say-on-Pay" votes, aimed at curbing excessive executive compensation, and the "Fight for 15," aimed at increasing low-wage worker pay (particularly within the fast-food industry), are rightfully shifting the focus from "profits at all cost" to more responsible business practices. These follow growing global shareholder campaigns and pressure for corporations and supply chains to adopt core labor standards and international protocols.

Objectives of this *Handbook*

As we elaborate in later chapters, responsible investment is not a new concept. Some forms of responsible investment strategies have been applied since the 16th century (SocialFunds, 2015). Numerous reports by academics and experts in the field, efforts by global bodies such as the PRI and the Committee on Workers' Capital (CWC), and, most importantly, investor experiences have shown that responsible investment strategies can have a positive impact on the value of investor assets, particularly those of pension funds. While these efforts have greatly increased the share of responsibly managed assets, numerous barriers, some discussed earlier, continue to hold back greater integration of ESG practices into mainstream investment strategies. These barriers are summarized below:

- Increasing agency separation brought about by increasing pension assets size and capital market complexities

- Regulatory complexities that leave fiduciaries hamstrung by conflicting or confusing federal and state laws
- Excessive focus on short-term gains at the expense of long-term value creation
- A fear that responsible investing compromises financial returns
- Lack of solid pension fund governance structures and resources that have resulted in greater reliance on other participants in the investment value chain and consequently investment herding
- Lack of capital steward knowledge and in-house staff expertise resulting in less control over investment management decisions
- Limited worker representation on boards of trustees, unless where mandated by law, leaving working people with little say in the investment and ongoing management of their retirement assets
- Lack of inclusion of ESG issues in financial education (PRI, 2013), and consequently, a lack of ESG integration, alongside financial considerations, in investment decision-making
- Lack of collaboration between pension plans, big and small, on responsible investment deals

The purpose of this *Handbook* is therefore to minimize the above-mentioned barriers and enable trustees to realign the investments of their plan's assets with the long-term economic interests of the plan's participants and beneficiaries. Our aim is to empower trustees in challenging the conventional market wisdom and embracing long-term, risk-based responsible investment approaches to investment decision-making. In so doing, we aim to accomplish the following objectives:

- **Highlight good pension fund governance practices** for trustees wishing to gain better control of the investment of workers' capital and embrace responsible investments
- **Discuss and clarify fiduciary responsibilities** in order to minimize agency separation issues that have impaired responsible investments by trustees and fiduciaries along the investment value chain
- **Highlight good corporate governance practices** that trustees should seek from their plan investments and discuss available active ownership strategies to positively influence corporate behavior

- **Show that the investment of workers' capital can be targeted**, across asset classes, and for the long term, **to generate competitive financial and economic returns alongside ESG benefits**
- **Enable trustees to devise a responsible investment policy, and select, engage and monitor service providers**, particularly consultants and managers, in its implementation
- **Empower trustees to ask tough questions** of pension staff, advisors, and managers, and confidently challenge conventional market wisdom and a short-term performance focus
- **Present best practices** to help measure ESG impacts
- **Illustrate our case along the way with practical examples and links to sample governing documents** of pioneer responsible pension investors, consultants, and asset managers, thereby providing capital stewards with peer-to-peer learning opportunities

The *Handbook*'s contents have been organized keeping these objectives in mind. While a majority of the *Handbook* is U.S.-focused, the materials presented are useful to both national and international audiences. As such, Section I begins with a discussion of the momentum toward responsible investments as supported by labor's efforts both in the U.S. and the rest of the world. Section II discusses best practices in pension plan management and governance in the context of responsible investments, and aims to debunk the notion of pension plan fiduciary responsibilities being at odds with responsible investing. Section III explores the available responsible investment approaches and gives trustees an overview on how to invest responsibly within a variety of asset classes, including numerous examples of practitioners who are successfully making such investments. Section IV gives practical advice on how to develop, implement, and monitor a plan's responsible investment policy. Finally, the *Handbook* concludes with an appeal to restore the promised retirement trust and pay the benefits forward to future generations.

We hope that our efforts will help increase trustee knowledge around the why and how of aligning workers' retirement assets and savings with long-term, sustainable, and responsible investment practices, and, most of all, spur action.

A note to trustees

One of the primary audiences for this *Handbook* is pension trustees and other stewards who have been entrusted with the oversight and management of workers' capital.

Pension plans are generally organized as trusts where a board of trustees is responsible for the oversight and investment of pension fund assets.[3] Trustees are the primary stewards of the plan's assets and are the "ultimate decision-makers" in relation to the investment of these assets (OECD, 2013). They have a fiduciary responsibility to invest plan assets prudently, impartially, cost-effectively, in accordance with governing laws and documents, and, most importantly, with loyalty toward, that is, solely in the best interest of, plan participants and their beneficiaries (Hawley *et al.*, 2011).

The immense investment complex that manages workers' capital must be realigned around trust principles, capital preservation and sustainable long-term investment. Investment horizons of pension funds and many other institutional trusts should be tied to the long-term nature of their liabilities. Pension funds, for example, start collecting contributions when individuals enter the workforce and may not pay out benefits until 30–40 years later. As people are living longer, the duration of pension fund liabilities are extended even longer. However, the signs of short-termism in investment decisions are unmistakable and must be altered (OECD, 2013).

As the Organisation for Economic Co-operation and Development (OECD) notes:

> Long-term investors could provide benefits by acting counter-cyclically, engaging as active shareholders, considering environmental and other longer-term risks and by financing long-term, productive activities that support sustainable growth. This requires transformational change in investor behavior, i.e. a new "investment culture," and various major policy initiatives. (Croce *et al.*, 2011, p. 145)

Trustees also need to understand the delicate balance between building shareholder value and maintaining the rights of workers and other stakeholders in business. Otherwise, they can get lured into corporate raids, takeovers, and breakups similar to those by opportunistic activist shareowners such as Carl Icahn, T. Boone Pickens, and KKR, an investment bank that

3 In some cases, the plan may be managed by a single fiduciary rather than a board.

Box 0.1: Characteristics of long-term investments

The OECD has stressed the need for institutional investors to invest for the long term (OECD, 2014). The OECD defines long-term investments as capital that is engaged, patient and productive. The active responsible investment approaches discussed in this *Handbook* support and reflect this three-dimensional approach to long-term investing by pension funds:

1. **Engaged capital.** Long-term capital that "encourages active proxy voting policies, leading to better corporate governance"
2. **Patient capital.** Long-term capital that "allows investors to access illiquidity premia, lowers turnover, encourages less pro-cyclical investment strategies and therefore a higher net investment rate of returns, and greater financial stability"
3. **Productive capital.** Long-term capital that "supports infrastructure development, green growth initiatives, SME financing, etc., leading to sustainable growth"

once used Oregon's teachers' funds to infamously take over and destroy RJR Nabisco.[4]

The stewards of workers' capital have shown that they can make responsible, long-term investments that not only earn a good rate of return, but also yield important collateral benefits. They have also shown that they can positively affect the governance of corporations. Labor's institutions have worked to utilize their savings and assets to build and shape our cities, to fight for fair labor relations and economic democracy, to invest in industrial innovation, and to arrest global warming.

As such, an important takeaway for trustees and fiduciaries is that you are not alone. You have incredible allies in our country and globally who are fighting to reclaim control over the long-term stewardship and responsible investment of workers' capital.

The importance of good capital stewardship

Pension trustees have a duty to protect and grow the trust funds for the trust's participants and beneficiaries. Workers and their family members depend on these assets held in trust to meet their financial goals in retirement. Investments made today have the potential to affect jobs and the quality of life for workers and retirees, the long-term sustainability of

4 This event too was the subject of another book, *Barbarians at the Gate: The Fall of RJR Nabisco* by Bryan Burrough and John Helyar (New York: HarperCollins, 2001), later made into a movie of the same name.

communities, and the overall economy. Thus, this *Handbook* applies the concept of good capital stewardship to trustee actions.

Too often, conventional market wisdom has focused on short-term returns based on quarterly results. This short-termism not only negatively impacts expected returns in the long term, but also ignores the social and environmental costs incurred to society in the process.

Box 0.2: What is good capital stewardship?

Good capital stewardship means that pension fund trustees and other fiduciaries invest workers' retirement savings to achieve the twin goals of realizing the best possible risk-adjusted rates of return on investments while delivering on the long-term interests of plan participants and beneficiaries (Kusnet, 2002).

The resulting herd mentality is more concerned with peer comparisons and relative performance metrics, rather than delivering stable and sustainable risk-adjusted returns appropriate to the plan's goals (Hawley *et al.*, 2011). While such shortcomings can result in poor performance even in good economic times,[5] their impact is exacerbated in times of financial crises such as after the 2008 market crash.

By realigning their governance and investment strategies with the long-term interests of beneficiaries, trustees can regain control of their fiduciary responsibilities and better influence the future of workers' capital. In so doing, trustees can also ensure that "their decision-making processes balance the allocation of capital between near-term needs and future wealth creation and consider the potential transfer of risks between participant generations" (Hawley *et al.*, 2011, p. 8).

Supporting and reaffirming trustees in this realignment of their fiduciary duty are global investor movements such as the PRI, a growing coalition of pension funds and other institutional investors, unions, consultants, and asset managers, who have pledged the incorporation of ESG considerations in their investment decisions. Together, the coalition represents an influential group of aspiring responsible investors who, as of early summer 2015, owned or managed almost $60 trillion in assets (PRI, 2015).

5 For instance, CalPERS sent ripples through the finance community in 2014 when it decided to disinvest in hedge funds, due to, in its view, complexity and costs. Other analysts have questioned the low hedge returns since the 2008 market crash, which liquidated a large number of funds (CalPERS, 2014b).

Similarly, the international labor movement has formed the Global Unions Committee on Workers' Capital (CWC), a joint initiative of the International Trade Union Confederation (ITUC), the Global Unions Federations (GUFs) and the Trade Union Advisory Committee to the OECD (TUAC). With over 200 members from 25 different countries, the CWC seeks to promote the long-term responsible investment of pension assets (CWC, 2015). A statement by the Global Unions on responsible approaches to the stewardship of workers' capital is presented at the end of Chapter 2.

Closer to home, the AFL-CIO has also urged wider adoption of responsible investment practices by pension plans. The AFL-CIO's Resolution 11 is presented at the end of Chapter 1.

The power of workers' capital

Workers' capital represents the retirement assets and savings of everyday working families held in pension funds and invested in the capital markets to provide long-term financial benefits to plan participants and beneficiaries. Some of the earliest pension plans for working people were started by unions (Freeman, 1985). While labor initially fought these battles to help its own members, the goal of labor has always been to help all working families and to build a better society.

Over the years, workers' retirement savings have grown to represent a significant share of global wealth, leading to a transformational change in the world's financial architecture. These assets, along with the assets of other long-term institutional investors, such as insurers, sovereign wealth funds, investment companies, and endowments, controlled over $85 trillion in global capital in 2011 (OECD, 2013).

In the U.S.A., pension assets have grown to represent a significant portion of all institutional assets—from 35.9% in 1980 to 40% in 2009. This growth has resulted in a greater ownership share of pension funds in public and alternative investment markets. For example, as of 2009, U.S. institutional investors collectively owned 73% of the outstanding public equity of Fortune 1000 companies, and pension funds alone held about 30% of this total (Tonello and Rabinov, 2010). U.S. pension fund allocations to alternative investments totaled over $6.4 trillion as of 2014 (Towers Watson, 2015).

The impacts of these sizable pools of workers' capital on the national economy have been immense. As an example, a recent study on defined benefit (DB) plans reported numerous direct and indirect economic impacts of the nearly $477 billion in pension benefits paid to 24 million retired Americans nationally in 2012 (Rhee, 2014). These impacts included, approximately:

- 6.2 million U.S. jobs that paid nearly $307 billion in labor income
- $943 billion in total economic output nationwide
- $555 billion in value added (GDP)
- $133 billion in federal, state, and local tax revenue

At the state level, a similar report demonstrated the vital role that the California Public Employees Retirement System (CalPERS), one of the largest pension plans in the world, plays in California's economy (CalPERS, 2014a). The report noted several direct and ancillary benefits that rippled through the state's economy as a result of $12.7 billion in benefits being paid to 452,750 California residents as of June 30, 2012. These benefits included, approximately:

- $30.3 billion in total economic activity
- 113,600 new jobs in California
- $20.7 billion of investments, supporting 1.5 million jobs
- $800 million in sales and property tax revenue

These numbers present a clear picture of the influence of pension assets in driving the economy as well as the capital markets, both in public and private investments. The funds belong to working families; it is, again, "our money." It should be invested in ways that ensure the long-term viability of our retirement savings and to build a sustainable future for generations ahead. It should be invested in the real economy.

Together, unions, capital stewards, and labor's allies are supporting the mobilization of retirement savings for investments in sustainable development, including affordable housing, poverty reduction, and climate change.[6] These allies include global governments, civil society actors, responsible businesses and finance groups, and academics.

As such, instead of investing in high-frequency trading or asset churning, for example, *our money* could provide the long-term financing essential for the development of critical industries such as (Croce *et al.*, 2011):

6 There are a multitude of international "calls to action" on many aspects of furthering the sustainable development of our world. As a starting point see, for instance, international labor's call in ITUC (2015).

- SMEs, especially young innovative high-growth firms
- Infrastructure, particularly sustainable, community-scale infrastructure
- New, alternative technologies to mitigate or reverse climate change

By leveraging large pools of workers' capital, pension funds can influence companies to uphold human and labor rights, and minimize adverse impacts on the environment, while remaining financially sustainable (CWC, 2015). Most of all, pension assets can enable a shift away from short-term conventional market wisdom toward long-term, responsible investment practices.

Key characteristics of responsible investments

As discussed, there is increasing recognition that the investment of workers' capital should reflect the intrinsic interests of workers, not only by generating competitive financial returns, but also by contributing to the long-term vitality of economies, societies, and the environment. As such, responsible investments are naturally aligned with the long-term interests of plan participants and beneficiaries. In this section, we highlight some important characteristics of responsible investments that will be focused on in greater detail throughout this *Handbook*.

Often used as an umbrella term, responsible investments encompass a range of approaches and investment options, from exclusionary screens to targeted investments to active ownership strategies. Together, these approaches accounted for approximately $6.6 trillion (or 18%) of total assets under professional management in the U.S.A. as of the beginning of 2014 (Kerber, 2014).

Given a plethora of responsible investment terms and approaches, trustees may be confused and/or uncertain about how to incorporate responsible investment strategies in the pension fund's investment portfolio.[7] However, as many experts point out, whether responsible investments are called socially responsible investments, social investments, ethical investments, or more

7 Some experts point out that the different terms often used to define different responsible investment approaches and strategies have resulted in "definitional ambiguities" in defining and adopting responsible investment practices (Woods and Urwin, 2010).

Box 0.3: Growth of impact investments

Another growing field within responsible investments is impact investments. The Global Impact Investing Network (GIIN) defines such investments as those that are "made into companies, organizations, and funds with the intention to generate measurable social and environmental impact alongside a financial return. Impact investments can be made in both emerging and developed markets, and target a range of returns from below market to market rate, depending upon the circumstances" (GIIN, 2016). A significant market opportunity exists for impact investments over the next 10 years, estimated at between $400 billion and $1 trillion. While other institutional investors may be able to choose below-market rate investments, pension investors can only invest in impact vehicles that provide a competitive return (O'Donohoe *et al.*, 2010). As such, capital stewards would generally want to give priority to economic impact investments—investments-at-scale that achieve competitive returns and also emphasize ESG considerations.

recently, impact investments, the main idea is "the integration of certain non-financial concerns in the investment process" (Sandberg *et al.*, 2009, p. 519). In addition, with the successful growth in the number of signatories to the PRI, there is an emerging "degree of standardization across understandings in this area," with signatories "using these terms to refer to the same things: 'integration of ESG criteria into mainstream investment decision-making and ownership practices'" (Woods and Urwin, 2010, p. 2).

The evolution toward the PRI's responsible investment framework also signals a decision to differentiate between investors who have a clear mandate to responsibly achieve a competitive financial return, and investors who are primarily focused on social returns usually for religious or ethical reasons. Financial market skeptics will try to claim that responsible investment practices do not maximize value. But, as this *Handbook* will show, an increasing number of financial and academic studies have found a clear correlation between high ESG ratings and financial outperformance (DB Climate Change Advisors, 2012).

Similar to the PRI framework, we refer to responsible investments as the pursuit of competitive risk-adjusted rates of return alongside the inclusion of material ESG analysis into investment decision-making and ownership practices. Responsible investments are expected to offer opportunities for long-term value creation that benefit not only investors, but also workers and their communities, as well as the broader society (Wood and Hoff, 2008). As such, the key characteristics of responsible investments advocated in this *Handbook* are as follows:

Box 0.4: How long is long-term?

As of May 9, 2014, the Department of Veterans Affairs (VA) was still paying benefits of $73.13 a month to Irene Triplett, a pension payment for her father's military service in the Civil War.

There were 16 widows and children of veterans from the 1898 Spanish–American War and 4,038 widows, sons and daughters still drawing monthly VA pension or other payments.

According to the *Guinness Book of World Records*, the world's oldest pensioner, who passed away in 2008, was 138 years old. He was from India, worked as a clarinet player until 1939, and drew a pension for 69 years (Phillips, 2014; Bidwell, 2013; Vashishti, 2008).

- **Long-term.** As mentioned, pension assets are intended to provide long-term benefits. Social and environmental factors, by their very nature, manifest in the long term, and their inclusion in investment decision-making is thus aligned with the concept of "intergenerational awareness" (Woods and Urwin, 2010).
- **Bridges critical capital gaps.** Such investments support critical economic development by bridging the capital gaps needs of sustainable, productive sectors, from vital infrastructure to the development of energy-efficient initiatives. They support high-growth SMEs and revitalize inner cities and rural economies.
- **ESG integrated.** Though we recognize some investors' desire to screen out certain companies or sectors based on moral or religious concerns, our focus is on engaging capital stewards to undertake a holistic approach to the integration of responsible investments in their pension investment portfolios. Such an approach integrates ESG considerations into investment decision-making from the perspective of generating higher returns while managing risk rather than simply screening out investments or divesting.
- **Material.** Materiality of ESG factors refers to the significance of such factors in terms of their impact on an investment's financial value. Material ESG factors are important drivers of the plan's investment risks and returns. As such, we focus on a framework for responsible investments that is not based on morality or ideology, but rather on the recognition of the dangers of ignoring the impacts of material ESG risks and opportunities on the long-term financial value of workers' capital.

- **Actively owned.** Active ownership refers to the "execution of ownership rights that can influence performance and risk over time" (Woods and Urwin, 2010). Once an investment has been made, capital stewards can use responsible ownership strategies, such as proxy voting and shareholder proposals, to engage constructively with underlying portfolio companies. Such engagements can influence material corporate governance, and environmental and social outcomes, while enhancing the value of portfolio investments.

Responsible investments, good corporate governance and rates of return

Do responsible investment considerations enhance or detract from the financial value of investments? Is there a strong financial and competitive case for corporations to include sustainable practices in the management of their business? Can a corporation positively serve all stakeholders—customers, employees, shareholders, suppliers, communities, and the environment they inhabit—while simultaneously pursuing its business mission? The answer is a resounding "yes," in terms of both responsible investment considerations and good corporate governance. This conclusion is based not only on anecdotal references by investors and corporations, but also an increasing number of strenuous research studies by academics and industry experts in the field.

These studies have found, in the aggregate, overwhelming evidence of the positive impact of responsible investment strategies on a company's operational performance and share price value. Box 0.5 presents a sample of these studies in order to refute a pattern of oft-heard claims that responsible investments, by their very nature, result in concessionary returns. Or, that investors concerned about ESG wrongly trade off financial performance for their social values. As recent research proves, the reality is quite the contrary.[8]

8 The concessionary returns charge may be true for some of the smaller, community-based social and community investors motivated primarily by social benefits goals, such as those made by community development corporations (CDCs), religious funds and endowments. Many of these institutions have not aimed to achieve competitive returns.

Box 0.5: A sample of studies demonstrating a positive link between responsible investments and financial performance

2012 Deutsche Bank study

In a 2012 meta-study of more than 100 academic studies from around the world by the Deutsche Bank Group, every study in the review found a positive correlation between CSR and financial outperformance, while 89% and 85% of the studies found a positive correlation between ESG factors and market or accounting-based outperformance, respectively (DB Climate Change Advisors, 2012).

2014 Arabesque Asset Management Ltd and the University of Oxford

A more recent meta-study (September 2014) of over 190 academic studies by Arabesque Asset Management Ltd and the University of Oxford also highlights results similar to the Deutsche Bank study. The results once again prove that corporate sustainability measures lower the cost of capital (in 90% of the studies) and the incorporation of ESG factors into investment decision-making is positively correlated with market and accounting-based outperformance (in 80% and 88% of the studies, respectively) (Clark *et al.*, 2014).

2011 Harvard Business School study

This study (Eccles *et al.*, 2011) compares 90 "high sustainability" firms—those that voluntarily adopted environmental and social policies—with 90 "low sustainability" firms—those that adopted almost no policies—on the issue of governance, culture, and performance. The study found that a portfolio of high-sustainability firms outperformed a portfolio of low-sustainability firms by 4.8% in stock market performance on an annual basis. The results were statistically significant and outperformance occurred in 11 of the 18 years of the sample period (Caplan *et al.*, 2013). The latter point is of particular significance since the results suggest that the outperformance occurred only in the longer term.

Further, core findings from two meta-studies by Deutsche Bank (DB Climate Change Advisors, 2012) and Arabesque Asset Management (Clark *et al.*, 2014) reveal the following:

- **Companies with high ratings in corporate social responsibility (CSR) and ESG factors** benefit from a lower cost of capital (debt and equity). Such companies are also a lower-risk investment opportunity.
- **Companies with high ratings in CSR and ESG factors** exhibit positive correlation with market and accounting-based outperformance.

2009 Wilshire Associates study

Studies of shareholder activism or "Wall Street Talk" have also shown positive results between responsible investment practices and financial performance. A 2009 study analyzing the impact of CalPERS' corporate governance initiatives (through its focus lists) on the performance of 139 target companies—from the beginnings of CalPERS' engagement in 1987 until fall 2007—found that "for the five years prior to the 'initiative date,' the focus list companies produced returns that averaged 84.2% below their respective benchmarks on a cumulative basis, which is equivalent to an excess return of −30.9% per year on an annualized basis. For the first five years after the 'initiative date,' the average targeted company produced excess returns of 15.4% above their respective benchmark return on a cumulative basis, or about 3% per year on an annualized basis." The 15.4% excess return was roughly the same as since-inception results until 2008 (Junkin and Toth, 2009).

2013 Study on active ownership

This study points to the value of shareholder resolutions, wherein companies conceded to the demands in such resolutions in return for the resolution's withdrawal for fear of any negative publicity. The study also points to the positive effect of successful shareholder engagements (especially on environmental/social issues) on the stock price of target firms (Dimson *et al.*, 2014).

2015 Study of Canadian responsible investment mutual funds

This study examines the relationship between risk and return in Canadian responsible investment (RI) mutual funds (equity, fixed income, and balanced funds), showing that ESG factors, when taken into account, can lower risk in a portfolio. Based on one-, three-, five-, and 10-year observations, the study found that the RI equity mutual funds and the RI fixed income and balanced funds examined outperformed the benchmark 63% and 67% of the time, respectively. Simultaneously, the RI funds were either less volatile than or as volatile as the benchmark, but not more. In particular, the funds were better able to generate excess return at lower risk than the benchmark—72% of the time for RI equity funds and 61% of the time for RI fixed-income and balanced funds—reducing downside risk (Carleton Centre for Community Innovation, 2015).

- **Good corporate governance principles** (such as transparency, board independence, management oversight, and auditor independence), **and management practices** (such as positive employee relations, promotion of job satisfaction, and improved environmental management), lower the cost of capital and are positively correlated with improved operational and stock market performance.
- **Active responsible investment approaches**, such as proxy voting and shareholder engagement, along with the integration of material ESG factors in the valuation of securities, positively impact corporate behavior and performance when compared with passive approaches (such as negative screenings).

While the eventual impact on portfolio performance is dependent on the type of responsible investment strategy employed by investors,[9] below is a compilation of certain insights gleaned from these studies to enable pension investors to focus their responsible investment strategy for optimal performance:

- Focus on the long term to capture the benefits of responsible investment on financial performance
- Focus on material ESG issues relevant to the investment(s) and/or the investors' goals
- Favor active responsible investment approaches over passive approaches (the former have generally outperformed the latter)
- Collaborate with like-minded investors where possible to increase the success rate of shareholder engagements

References

Antolin, P., & Stewart, F. (2009). Private pension and policy responses to the financial and economic crisis. *OECD Working Papers on Insurance and Private Pensions*, 36. doi:10.1787/224386871887.

Baer, J., & Viswanatha, A. (2015, April 19). Morgan Stanley, state talk $500 million pact. *Wall Street Journal*. Retrieved May 25, 2016 from http://www.wsj.com/articles/morgan-stanley-new-york-talk-500-million-mortgage-bond-pact-1429488157.

Barro, J. (2014, June 25). Why government pension funds become addicted to risk. *The New York Times*. Retrieved May 25, 2016 from http://www.nytimes.com/2014/06/26/upshot/why-government-pension-funds-became-addicted-to-risk.html?abt=0002&abg=0&_r=0.

Bidwell, A. (2013, July 3). One civil war veteran's pension remains on government's payroll. *U.S. News & World Report*. Retrieved May 25, 2016 from http://www.usnews.com/news/newsgram/articles/2013/07/03/one-civil-war-veterans-pension-remains-on-governments-payroll.

CalPERS (2014a). *CalPERS Economic Impacts in California*. Retrieved June 28, 2016 from https://www.calpers.ca.gov/docs/forms-publications/economic-impacts-ca-2014.pdf.

——— (2014b). CalPERS eliminates hedge fund program in effort to reduce complexity and costs in investment portfolio. Retrieved May 25, 2016 from https://www.calpers.ca.gov/page/newsroom/calpers-news/2014/eliminate-hedge-fund.

9 A few studies included in the meta-studies demonstrated neutral or negative impact of responsible investment practices on financial performance. This was the case primarily when only negative screening strategies were used when engaging in responsible investments (Caplan *et al.*, 2013; Dimson *et al.*, 2014).

Caplan, L., Griswold, J.S., & Jarvis W.F. (2013). *From SRI to ESG: The Changing World of Responsible Investing.* Retrieved May 18, 2016 from https://www.commonfund.org/wp-content/uploads/2016/01/Whitepaper_SRI-to-ESG-2013-0901.pdf.

Carleton Centre for Community Innovation (2015). *Canadian Responsible Investment Mutual Funds.* Retrieved June 28, 2016 from http://oceanrock.spiserver.com/doc_bin/3CI_RI_Fund_Risk_Return_Analysis_Final_052715.pdf.

Casey, M. (2015, March 24). Could a solar plane's journey make clean energy "sexy"? *CBS News.* Retrieved May 24, 2016 from http://www.cbsnews.com/news/solar-plane-impulse-2-make-clean-energy-sexy.

Clark, G., Feiner, A., & Viehs, M. (2014, October 20). *From the Stockholder to the Stakeholder: How Sustainability Can Drive Financial Outperformance.* doi:10.2139/ssrn.2508281.

Croce, R.D., Stewart, F., & Yermo, J. (2011). Promoting longer-term investment by institutional investors: selected issues and policies. *OECD Journal: Financial Market Trends,* 2011(1), 145-164. Retrieved May 25, 2016 from http://www.keepeek.com/Digital-Asset-Management/oecd/finance-and-investment/promoting-longer-term-investment-by-institutional-investors_fmt-2011-5kg55b0z1ktb#page1.

Croft, T.W., & Hebb, T. (2003). Collaboration between labor, academics and community activists to advance labor/capital strategies: the origins of the Heartland network. In I. Carmichael & J. Quarter (Eds.), *Money on the Line: Workers' Capital in Canada* (pp. 193-218). Ottawa, Canada: Canadian Centre for Policy Alternatives.

CWC (Committee on Workers' Capital) (2015). Global Unions Committee on Workers' Capital. Retrieved May 25, 2016 from http://www.workerscapital.org.

DB Climate Change Advisors (2012). *Sustainable Investing: Establishing Long-Term Value and Performance.* Retrieved June 2, 2016 from https://www.db.com/cr/en/docs/Sustainable_Investing_2012.pdf.

Dimson, E., Karakas, O., & Li, Xi. (2014). Active ownership. *Review of Financial Studies,* 28(12), 3225-3268. Retrieved May 25, 2016 from http://papers.ssrn.com/sol3/papers.cfm?abstract_id=2154724.

Eccles, R., Ioannou, I., & Serafeim, G. (2011). The impact of a corporate culture of sustainability on corporate behavior and performance. Retrieved May 25, 2016 from http://hbswk.hbs.edu/item/the-impact-of-corporate-sustainability-on-organizational-process-and-performance.

Financial Crisis Inquiry Commission (2011). *The Financial Crisis Inquiry Report.* New York: Cosimo Reports.

Finnish Environment Institute. (2014, February 5). Environmental impacts of the financial crisis evident. *ScienceDaily.* Retrieved May 25, 2016 from https://www.sciencedaily.com/releases/2014/02/140205075819.htm.

Freeman, R.B. (1985). Unions, pensions, and union pension funds. In D.A. Wise (Ed.), *Pensions, Labor, and Individual Choice* (pp. 89-122). Chicago, IL: University of Chicago Press. Retrieved May 25, 2016 from http://www.nber.org/chapters/c7131.pdf.

Galbraith, J.K. (2011). *The End of Normal: The Great Crisis and the Future of Growth.* New York: Simon & Schuster.

GIIN (Global Impact Investing Network) (2016). What is impact investing? Retrieved June 28, 2016 from https://thegiin.org/impact-investing/need-to-know/#s1.

Hawley, J.P., & Williams, A.T. (2000a). *The Rise of Fiduciary Capitalism: How Institutional Investors Can Make Corporate America More Democratic.* Philadelphia, PA: University of Pennsylvania Press.

——— (2000b). The emergence of universal owners: Some implications of institutional equity ownership. *Challenge,* 43, 43-61.

Hawley, J.P., Johnson, K., & Waitzer, E. (2011). Reclaiming fiduciary duty balance. *Rotman International Journal of Pension Management*, 4(2), 4-16. Retrieved May 25, 2016 from http://ssrn.com/abstract=1935068.

ITUC (2015). Sharan Burrow's speech to the Climate Change Conference – Oslo 13 March 2015. Retrieved June 29, 2016 from http://www.ituc-csi.org/sharan-burrow-s-speech-to-the?lang=en.

Johnson, K.L., & de Graaf, F.J. (2009). *Modernizing Pension Fund Legal Standards for the 21st Century*. Retrieved June 1, 2016 from http://www.sustainablefinancialmarkets.net/wp-content/uploads/2009/02/nsfm_modernizing1.pdf.

Junkin, A., & Toth, T. (2009). *The CalPERS Effect on Targeted Company Share Prices*. Pittsburgh, PA: Wilshire Associates.

Leitner, C., Mansour, A., & Naylor, S. (2007). *Alternative Investments in Perspective*. Retrieved May 25, 2016 from http://realestate.deutscheam.com/content/_media/Research_Alternative_Investments_in_Perspective_September_2007.pdf.

Kerber, R. (2014, November 20). U.S. managed assets with socially responsible criteria rise: report. *Reuters*. Retrieved May 25, 2016 from http://www.reuters.com/article/2014/11/20/us-funds-sustainability-idUSKCN0J41IS20141120.

Kusnet, D. (2002). *The Challenge and Promise of Cross-Border Capital Stewardship: Report on an International Trustee Roundtable*. Washington, DC: AFL-CIO Center for Working Capital.

Molko, D., & McKirdy, E. (2016, April 24). Solar Impulse 2 lands in California after Pacific flight. *CNN*. Retrieved June 28, 2016 from http://www.cnn.com/2016/04/24/travel/solar-impulse-2-plane-california/.

Oakley, D. (2014, November 17). Pension funds flock to riskier investments. *The Financial Times*. Retrieved May 25, 2016 from http://www.ft.com/intl/cms/s/0/03fea5c6-6e60-11e4-bffb-00144feabdc0.html#axzz3LYnWYDan.

O'Donohoe, N., Leijonhufvud, C., Saltuk, Y., Bugg-Levine, A., & Brandenburg, M. (2010). *Impact Investments: An Emerging Asset Class*. Retrieved June 28, 2016 from https://thegiin.org/assets/documents/Impact%20Investments%20an%20Emerging%20Asset%20Class2.pdf.

OECD (Organisation for Economic Co-operation and Development) (2013). *G20/OECD High-Level Principles of Long-Term Investment Financing by Institutional Investors*. Retrieved June 2, 2016 from http://www.oecd.org/finance/private-pensions/G20-OECD-Principles-LTI-Financing.pdf.

——— (2014). *Institutional Investors and Long-Term Investment: Project Report*. Retrieved May 25, 2016 from http://www.oecd.org/daf/fin/private-pensions/OECD-LTI-project.pdf.

Phillips, M.M. (2014, May 9). Still paying for the civil war. *Wall Street Journal*. Retrieved June 28, 2016 from http://www.wsj.com/news/articles/SB10001424052702303603904579493830954152394?mod=e2tw.

PRI (Principles for Responsible Investment) (2013). *PRI in Person 2013: Conference Highlights*. Retrieved June 28, 2016 from https://www.unpri.org/download_report/4001.

——— (2015). United Nations Principles for Responsible Investment. Retrieved May 25, 2016 from http://www.unpri.org.

Rhee, N. (2014). Pensionomics 2014: measuring the economic impact of DB pension expenditures. Retrieved June 28, 2016 from http://www.nirsonline.org/index.php?option=content&task=view&id=861.

Sandberg, J., Juravle, C., Hedesstrom, T.M., & Hamilton, I. (2009). The heterogeneity of socially responsible investment. *Journal of Business Ethics*, 87(4), 519-533.

SEC (Securities & Exchange Commission) (2010). Commission Guidance Regarding Disclosure Related to Climate Change. Securities and Exchange Commission: 17 CFR PARTS 211, 231 and 241. Retrieved June 18, 2016 from https://www.sec.gov/rules/interp/2010/33-9106.pdf.

SocialFunds (2015). Introduction to Socially Responsible Investing. Retrieved June 28, 2016 from http://www.socialfunds.com/page.cgi/article1.html.

Stewart, F., & Yermo, J. (2008). Pension fund governance: challenges and potential solutions. *OECD Working Papers on Insurance and Private Pensions*, 18. Retrieved June 5, 2016 from http://www.oecd.org/finance/private-pensions/41013956.pdf.

Tonello, M., & Rabinov, S. (2010). *The 2010 Institutional Investment Report: Trends in Asset Allocation and Portfolio Composition*. New York: Conference Board.

Towers Watson (2015). *Global Pensions Asset Study: 2015*. Retrieved May 26, 2016 from https://www.towerswatson.com/en-US/Insights/IC-Types/Survey-Research-Results/2015/02/Global-Pensions-Asset-Study-2015.

UN (2015, December 11). Adoption of the Paris Agreement. Retrieved June 30, 2016 from http://unfccc.int/2860.php.

U.S. Department of Energy (2015). *The History of Solar*. Retrieved May 25, 2016 from http://www1.eere.energy.gov/solar/pdfs/solar_timeline.pdf.

U.S. DOL (U.S. Department of Labor) (2015). DOL Interpretive Bulletin 15-01. *Employee Benefits Security Administration, Labor*. Retrieved June 28, 2016 from https://s3.amazonaws.com/public-inspection.federalregister.gov/2015-27146.pdf.

Vashishti, S. (2008, August 19). World's oldest pensioner Habib Miyan dies. *CNN-IBN UBN*. Retrieved June 28, 2016 from http://www.news18.com/videos/india/habib-miyan-295282.html.

Vitols, S. (2015). Introduction: a stakeholder perspective on the long-term investment debate. In S. Vitols (Ed.), *Long-Term Investment and the Sustainable Company: A Stakeholder Perspective. Vol. III* (pp. 9-18). Brussels: European Trade Union Institute.

Watson Wyatt Worldwide (2007). *2007 Global Pension Asset Study*. Retrieved June 28, 2016 from http://www.newunionism.net/library/working%20life/Watson%20Wyatt%20-%20Global%20Pension%20Assets%20Study%20-%202007.pdf.

Williamson, J. (2015, July 28). Andy Haldane: shareholder primacy is bad for economic growth. *TouchStone*. Retrieved May 25, 2016 from http://touchstoneblog.org.uk/2015/07/andy-haldane-shareholder-primacy-is-bad-for-economic-growth/.

Wood, D., & Hoff, B. (2008). *Handbook on Responsible Investment Across Asset Classes*. Retrieved June 2, 2016 from http://ccc.bc.edu/index.cfm?fuseaction=document.showDocumentByID&nodeID=1&DocumentID=1170.

Woods, C., & Urwin, R. (2010). Putting sustainable investing into practice: a governance framework for pension funds. *Journal of Business Ethics*, 92(1), 1-19.

Zanglein, J., & Clark, D. (2001). *Capital Stewardship Certificate Program*. Silver Spring, MD: National Labor College.

Section I:
The momentum toward responsible investments

1
Responsible investments in the U.S.A.

> What does labor want? We want more schoolhouses and less jails; more books and less arsenals; more learning and less vice; more leisure and less greed; more justice and less revenge.
>
> Samuel Gompers, Ex-President, AFL

There is a long and rich history of intentional responsible investments in the U.S.A. It is important that working people know about the role of labor unions in that history, as union members not only fought to win eight-hour workdays, work-free weekends, and paid vacations, and bargained for retirement benefits, but also pioneered many elements of the current global responsible investment movement.

For instance, the early textile and garment unions, comprised of women and immigrant workers, secured great improvements in the workplace and in the provision of health and welfare benefits for their members. Further, under labor leader Sydney Hillman, these unions built co-operative housing, a labor bank—the Amalgamated Bank, established in 1923—and worker-friendly insurance programs (Britannica, 2014). In 1927, Samuel Gompers, the first president of the AFL, founded the Union Labor Life Insurance Company (ULLICO), after the refusal of employers to insure industrial, mining, and construction workers (ULLICO, 2014). In the 1930s, the labor giant and founder of the CIO, United Mine Workers (UMW) President John L. Lewis, built eight hospitals and numerous health clinics across the Appalachia and also founded the National Bank of Washington (UMWA, 2014). Thousands of these investments are still standing as a testament to labor's stewardship in our nation.

> For most of this century, organized labor was at the forefront of the progressive housing movement. As early as 1914, at the AFL's annual convention, unions called for government action to provide workers with low-cost housing loans ... Truman's victory, and the Democrats' recapture of both houses of Congress that year, set the stage for the landmark 1949 Housing Act, which established a national goal of "a decent home and suitable living environment for every American family." (Dreier, 2000)

In the latter part of the 20th century, the AFL-CIO Committee for the Investment of Union Pension Funds helped drive new pension capital strategies to reinvest in the U.S. economy, later undertaking shareholder activism to combat corporate raiders who hurt companies and terminated pension plans. Jacob Sheinkman of the Amalgamated Clothing and Textile Workers (ACTWU) and Ed Durkin of the Carpenters' Union, among others, designed new strategies to effectively protect the jobs and wages of their members. In so doing, labor's advocates established effective capital stewardship offices and were among the most prolific sponsors of corporate governance proposals (van der Zwan, 2011). Recently, the AFL-CIO has urged wider adoption of responsible investment practices by pension plans (see the AFL-CIO's Resolution 11 at the end of this chapter).

Labor's investors have been the fiercest proponents for the "S" (social) in the ESG framework for responsible investment, fighting for union representation, worker participation, good wages, and workers' health and safety. Labor visionaries have, for decades, worked to promote strategic investments to make the "boss" accountable and grow the real economy. Indeed, many of the most successful investment initiatives to build affordable and workforce housing, revitalize the manufacturing sector, and grow the clean economy were started by workers' representatives, as shown in this chapter.

For example, we will show how, in the 1960s, working with the civil rights movement, the AFL-CIO formed new housing investment institutions as a new thrust in the movement for social and economic justice. With the leadership of the construction trades pension funds, these new institutions created affordable and livable workforce housing in dozens of cities. Since the 1980s, industrial labor leaders have designed shrewd capital strategies, deploying worker-friendly investment banks and new capital vehicles that turned around or expanded critical industries. And, in the new millennium, teachers, public, and service employees have invested their pension funds in energy, transportation, and infrastructure innovations to grow the clean economy.

These capital stewards have invested in the "real economy"—the part of the economy that is concerned with actually producing goods and services, as opposed to the part of the economy that is concerned with buying and selling on the financial markets (Financial Times, 2015). They have done so in ways that advance the interests of beneficiaries more broadly and that "do no harm." Since 1994, as described in this chapter, they have generally utilized the legal framework of economically targeted investments (ETIs), under the Employee Retirement Income Security Act (ERISA) and the U.S. Department of Labor (DOL) guidelines. ETIs are "investments selected for the economic benefits they create apart from their investment return to the employee benefit plan" (U.S. DOL, 2015). ETIs can include investments in real estate, private equity and venture capital, fixed income, infrastructure, and credit enhancement strategies. Such investments allow pension and other institutional funds to promote positive economic development, good employment and labor relations, and sustainable environmental practices among portfolio investments.

This chapter elaborates on labor's role as a forerunner in the pursuit of ETIs in the U.S.A. We describe the ETI and ESG investment frameworks, both of which encourage pension investments that:

- Increase the availability of sustainably built affordable and workforce housing
- Invest in retrofitting and modernizing the residential, commercial, and industrial built environment
- Provide capital to stabilize and turn around domestic manufacturing industries and other economically vital sectors of the industrial commons
- Provide growth capital to small and medium-size enterprises (SMEs)
- Increase the availability of worker-friendly, community-scale, sustainable infrastructure investments
- Support new market-driven innovations such as renewable energy, efficient transportation, transit-oriented developments, downtown revitalization, and smart growth in the clean economy

In the next chapter, we discuss the contribution of labor in other countries in promoting responsible investments, and recount the significant role of U.S. and international labor in the founding of the PRI.

1.1 A history of labor's responsible investment strategies

1.1.1 Rebuilding the built environment

The modern shift toward targeted investments as a responsible investment mechanism started during the 1960s when civil rights and trade union leaders encouraged multiemployer pension funds to invest in affordable housing and community development. In 1960, Dr. Martin Luther King, Jr. and AFL-CIO President George Meany began a yearlong mission to align the goals of the U.S.A.'s two most powerful progressive groups, the AFL-CIO and the civil rights movement, in the great crusade for social and economic justice. Dr. King proposed that the AFL-CIO invest pension assets in housing at the grass-roots level as a way to ease economic inequality in the U.S. economy. Together, they believed that one day these assets would be the major source of capital in our economy and had a vision of how pension capital could create an expansive movement for economic and social justice.

In response to Dr. King's proposal, Meany established the Investment Department within the AFL-CIO in August 1960. The department's mission was to guide individual union pension funds to invest in socially responsible projects. In 1964, President Meany sent a letter to AFL-CIO affiliated unions that outlined his vision for a new investment vehicle that would directly support housing creation and home ownership.

The cooperation was the impetus for the creation of the Mortgage Investment Trust fund, predecessor to the AFL-CIO's Housing Investment Trust (HIT) fund, now valued at $5 billion in net assets. The federation, under the leadership of Meany and Lane Kirkland, argued that workers had to take control of their capital to avoid manipulation by banks and the financial system. The purpose of the new fund was to help unions invest their retirement assets at a competitive rate of return and with a high degree of security, while emphasizing the construction of much-needed affordable housing. Since the mid-1960s, Taft–Hartley pension plans (particularly construction trades plans), as well as public plans, have capitalized fixed income and alternative investments, including HIT, the Building Investment Trust (BIT), the Multi-Employer Trust (MEPT), and ULLICO, to provide affordable and workforce housing and other responsible property investments. With these projects being built with unionized labor, the investments also increased good jobs for construction union members, while maintaining financial returns that matched or beat standard indices (Hunter and Costello, 2014).

These investments have also spawned local construction jobs and apprenticeship opportunities, furthering community development.

1.1.2 Revitalizing the industrial commons

Labor union and political leaders also sought to encourage pension plans to reinvest in industries and regions that had suffered deindustrialization (Rifkin and Barber, 1978). For example, while running for president in the early 1980s, Jerry Brown, building on his efforts around responsible investments as governor of California, advocated for a progressive pension capital program with a focus on the so-called "sunrise" industries, bringing these issues to national attention (California Governor's Office, 1982; Rothenberg, 1983). Similarly, in the late 1980s, New York Governor Mario Cuomo's Commission on Trade and Competitiveness sought to revitalize industries critical to the economic and defense security of the U.S.A. Shortly after, Cuomo's State Pension Investment Task Force sought to implement an economically targeted investment strategy that would utilize workers' capital to invest in manufacturing, housing, and economic revitalization (Kaden and Smith, 1988; Millstein, 1989).

Faced with a severe recession and restructurings in steel mill production and ownership in North America in the 1980s, Lynn Williams, President of the United Steelworkers of America (USW), began engaging with labor-friendly investment bankers, such as Felix Rohatyn at Lazard Frères. In the 1970s, Rohatyn had led the Municipal Assistance Corporation's (MAC) effort to turn around New York City's bankruptcy. The USW deployed an investment bank set up by Gene Keilin and Ron Bloom, formerly at Lazard, to intervene in the steel industry through defensive buyouts and other strategies, such as employee stock ownership plans (ESOPs), saving jobs and parts of the industry. Other unions, such as the machinists and pilots, followed suit in addressing the economic crises in their own industries (Vitello, 2014).

By the late 1990s, the AFL-CIO and USW's Secretary-Treasurer, Leo Gerard, assembled the Heartland Labor/Capital Network and commissioned the book *Working Capital* (Fung *et al.*, 2001), which asked how the labor movement might harness the power of pension funds to rebuild America. Multiemployer pension plans, and later public pension plans, began to invest in private capital funds, such as KPS, Yucaipa, Pegasus, and Blue Wolf, that respected workers' rights and that sought to provide a voice for workers as stakeholders in the company. This initiative gained ground slowly through the decade of the 2000s and was similar to efforts around worker-capitalized vehicles in Quebec (The Solidarity Fund) and Australia, where the Superannuated Funds established specific investment managers to invest in infrastructure, renewable energy, and other responsible alternatives.

1.1.3 Growing the clean economy

Since the 1970s, labor unions and pension funds have been joined with the broader global efforts to address environmental pollution and risk, and have subsequently urged investments in environmental technologies and other transformative strategies. The Oil, Chemical and Atomic Workers Union (OCAW) and other unions were influential in the passage of the 1970 Clean Air Act, and OCAW President Tony Mazzocchi famously led the fight for the passage of the Occupational Safety and Health Administration (OSHA) Act (Leopold, 2007). AFL-CIO President John Sweeney also promoted a labor–environmental dialogue in the 1990s, after the Kyoto Accords on global warming (Werback, 2004). Other labor–environmental business coalitions followed, including the Apollo and Blue-Green alliances, both of which called for hundreds of billions of dollars of investment in the clean economy frontier.

After the *Exxon Valdez* oil spill disaster in 1989, a small group of investors, including responsible investor Joan Bavaria, founded Ceres (formerly known as the Coalition for Environmentally Responsible Economies). The idea was to bring environmentalists and capitalists together to forge a new sustainable business model. Ceres created the Valdez Principles (now known as the Ceres Principles), a 10-point code of environmental conduct that Ceres' founding investor members encouraged companies to publicly endorse. Since that time, communities in the U.S.A. and around the world have suffered a series of disruptive weather events due to global warming, with profound implications for the economy. As a result, Ceres began working with the UN and pension leaders in 2003 to launch the UN Investor Network on Climate Risk (INCR). By 2014, INCR signatories had grown to more than 100 members, including some of North America's largest pension and institutional investors and asset managers, managing over $11 trillion in total assets (Ceres, 2014).

As a response to climate change, public pension plan giants such as CalPERS, CalSTRS and NYC Pension Funds, spurred on by teachers and public service trustees, also began to explore investment opportunities in green construction, clean technology, efficient transportation, infrastructure, and renewable energy. New investment vehicles funded by pensions have emerged since the mid-2000s in particular. As Kirsten Snow Spalding, the California Director of Ceres, notes, institutional investors and capital stewards have become more focused on developing strategies that will mitigate risks associated with climate change and related issues. These investors are simultaneously looking for opportunities to invest in sustainable solutions that will create green jobs and build durable value for their funds (Croft, 2011).

1.1.4 Engaging in active ownership

Active ownership involves engaging with companies in the "execution of ownership rights [that] can influence performance and risk over time" (Woods and Urwin, 2010, p. 12). Unions have a long history of pursuing active ownership strategies as shareholders of their employers. In 1949, the Association of Independent Telephone Unions used their share ownership in AT&T to bring fellow shareholders' attention to the unilateral decision by management to cut pension benefits (Eisenhofer and Barry, 2013). In the 1970s, the Amalgamated Clothing and Textile Workers Union (ACTWU) brought the unsavory employment practices of the southern textile firm J.P. Stevens to light at the company's shareholder meetings. As a result of its efforts, the union won representation for more than 3,000 of Stevens' workers. The campaign was also portrayed in a 1979 hit movie called *Norma Rae*.

Over the years, labors' capital stewards broadened the range of issues addressed through their shareholder activism to include fair employment practices, excessive executive compensation, and the independence of corporate boards of directors, improving the corporate governance of companies. In the 1980s and 1990s, with the rise of institutional investors as major stockholders, pension plans became increasingly vocal participants in the corporate governance of their portfolio companies. This new corporate accountability movement was symbolized by the creation of the Council of Institutional Investors (CII) in 1985. The CII is a non-profit association of pension funds, other employee benefit funds, endowments, and foundations with combined assets that exceed $3 trillion, and has become a leading voice for effective corporate governance and strong shareowner rights. Labor has generally filled a co-chair position on the CII Board.

By using their voice as shareholders, the labor movement's associated pension plans began to encourage their portfolio companies to adopt responsible business practices. These include:

- Responsible workplace practices and working conditions, including human rights and the mistreatment of workers, adequate training, health and safety, and fair employment
- Proxy fights to support business strategies that create long-term sustainable performance instead of short-term corporate transactions put forward by corporate raiders
- Reforming excessive executive compensation and perks, such as the provision of golden parachutes even after cases of gross mismanagement
- Championing the independence of boards of directors, board chairs, compensation committees, and auditors
- Democratizing shareholder meetings through annual director elections, eliminating dual-class stock with unequal voting rights, and enabling equal access to the proxy

In 1997, under the leadership of then Secretary-Treasurer Richard Trumka, the AFL-CIO launched the Capital Stewardship Program. Bill Patterson, having worked for ACTWU and set up the Amalgamated Bank's Long View Fund, initially directed the Office of Investment at the AFL-CIO and then later at Change to Win (CtW). These offices, under Patterson and various successors, issued proxy voting guidelines, coordinated shareholder and proxy voting initiatives, supported active ownership and corporate governance reform strategies, advocated for legislative and regulatory reform of the capital markets, launched trustee education programs (Voices for Corporate Responsibility, 2010), and created an executive compensation watchdog website (AFL-CIO, 2016), among other activities. These offices have influenced pension investment and corporate governance decisions on a wide range of issues over the years.

The AFL-CIO Office of Investment, currently led by Heather Slavkin Coro, Director, and Brandon Rees, Deputy Director, has, since 1997, published regular reports on the voting behavior of investment managers. The office has long advised votes against excessive management pay and short-term profit maximization, advocating that over 50% of total management remuneration should depend on long-term incentives. Further:

- The board of directors is supposed to control the management (and be) independent of the management

- At least two-thirds of the directors should be independent of the management. An independent director—and not the CEO—should be chair of the board of directors
- Proposals on better representation of women, employees, or certain minorities are supported
- Measures for decent jobs, such as further training, security of employment, and a supportive work environment, should in general be demanded because this contributes to productivity and long-term financial performance (Klec and Mum, 2015)

Global unions have called for capital stewards to adopt a greater active ownership role with respect to their members' pension funds. They also demand more respect for worker stakeholders in global companies and supply chains. In Chapter 6, we highlight share-ownership strategies meant to lever better corporate governance and board and management accountability.

1.2 Historical U.S. legal framework for alternative investments—economically targeted investments (ETIs)

Even in times when the capital markets are flooded with liquidity, market failures can result in capital gaps—a systemic lack of access to capital in isolated regions, inner cities, and labor-intensive sectors. In particular, there have been large capital gaps in affordable housing, advanced manufacturing, infrastructure, and the clean economy, and within the supply chains that feed these sectors. Smart capital stewards are aware that these market failures can yield significant investment opportunities. Competitive risk-adjusted financial returns and the provision of collateral benefits are not mutually exclusive, and ETIs are uniquely positioned to find and fill these gaps.

Pension funds invariably turn to alternative investments to diversify their asset allocation, which would otherwise be heavily represented by stocks and bonds. Alternative investments include private equity, venture capital, real estate, and hedge funds. ETIs in alternative investments can be used to generate specific collateral benefits, along with competitive financial returns. While we review ERISA and the fiduciary duties of pension trustees and capital stewards much more intensively in Chapter 5, we mention a few aspects of those rules here as they relate to ETIs.[1]

ERISA allows pension trustees to invest in ETIs as long as they do not sacrifice risk-adjusted market-rate financial returns (Hebb and Zanglein, 2014). ETIs provide a legal safe harbor, generally, for targeted investing of pension assets.

The U.S. Department of Labor (DOL) enforces ERISA's requirements that pension investments pass muster with the law. In the 1980s, Robert Monks, a longtime corporate governance expert, became the head of the Office of Pension and Welfare Benefit Programs in the DOL. Appointed by President Reagan, Monks understood the role of pension funds as institutional investors and encouraged fiduciaries to make prudent investments that also achieved social objectives. During this time, the Lanoff Letter was issued to encourage targeted investing.

Box 1.1: The Lanoff Letter

In 1980, DOL's first ERISA Administrator, Ian Lanoff, stated in the letter that, while ERISA "does not exclude the provision of incidental benefits to others, the protection of retirement income is, and should continue to be, the overriding social objective governing the investment of plan assets" (Lanoff, 1980, p. 389).

In 1994, under President Bill Clinton, DOL Secretary Robert Reich issued Interpretive Bulletin 94-1 regarding ETIs, which explained that a pension plan may choose an investment that provides "collateral benefits" if the investment has a risk-adjusted market rate of return which is equal or superior to alternative investments. The DOL's 94-1 bulletin stated that a fiduciary may invest plan assets in an ETI:

> if the ETI has an expected rate of return that is commensurate to rates of return of alternative investments with similar risk characteristics that are available to the plan, and if the ETI is otherwise an appropriate investment for the plan in terms of such factors as diversification and the investment policy of the plan. (U.S. DOL, 1994)

Touting a "new ethic of stewardship," Reich stated that "ETIs provide pension funds with competitive, risk-adjusted rates of return plus ancillary

1 Most of this section has been adapted from the works of Jayne Zanglein as highlighted in Croft (2011) and originally published in Croft (2009), with contributions by Dr. Teresa Ghilarducci (unless otherwise noted).

benefits, such as affordable housing, infrastructure improvements and jobs ... Significant successes, among them the housing construction program of CalPERS, prove that ETIs are, overall, successful" (Reich, 1994b, p. 9).

According to another DOL report, prudent investments exist in an inefficient market and remain unfunded due to information gaps and high administrative costs of consummating and monitoring deals: "To the extent that capital markets are judged to be tradition-bound, rigid or incapable of funding all 'worthy' investments, making funds available from the pension investment pool is seen as addressing capital gaps that would otherwise impede local economic development" (U.S. GAO, 1995, p. 6).

Collateral benefits obtained through ETIs can be applied broadly and can:

> create new jobs, provide capital to replace loan funds no longer rolling through the bank pipelines, provide startup businesses with access to capital, finance low-cost housing and improve the infrastructure of the nation, all without sacrificing a return on investments or otherwise jeopardizing the pensions of future retirees.
>
> (Lurie, 1996, quoted by Zanglein, 2001, p. 183)

Organized labor has long encouraged pension trustees and other capital stewards to consider ETIs (particularly those that utilize union labor) (Hebb and Zanglein, 2014). As Reich claimed as well, ETIs can benefit not only retirees but the economy as a whole and thus, indirectly, the wellbeing of pensioners. He also said that ETI investments would reward companies with high-performance workplaces, which in turn are associated with above-average returns. Funds adhering to such guidelines would do well by doing good (Reich, 1994a).

When the owners of workers' capital began investing in ETIs, they generally followed a strategy of investing in "worker-friendly" companies and projects. Also known as "high-performance" workplaces, such companies and projects are said to generate stable profits through increased labor and management productivity and higher levels of employee participation, including worker ownership. For example, in the construction industry, such companies choose to require the use of responsible contractors that respect workers' rights to collectively bargain and employ highly skilled tradespersons.

Such strategies better allow investors to reduce the potential risks and liabilities which arise from bad outcomes, such as shabby construction, delayed project completion, or even dangerous work sites.

Thus, responsible investors can seek portfolio investments that:

- Provide job security

- Adhere to responsible contractor policies and adopt "high-road" workplace practices
- Follow responsible health, safety, and environmental standards
- Treat workers with respect and provide for neutrality in labor relations

Unfortunately, there were political attacks against ETIs from the moment the DOL Interpretive Bulletin 94-1 was issued. Representative Jim Saxton (Republican, New Jersey), then the vice chairman of the Joint Economic Committee, attacked the bulletin and killed a proposed ETI Clearinghouse claiming that these would open the door for political misuses of pension funds, sacrificing returns. Contrary to Saxton's claim, the ETI Clearinghouse would have been a simple public information program, providing a voluntary market-matching service (Chrones Moore, 1995).

In October 2008, the DOL, in the last weeks of the outgoing Bush Administration and under prodding by the U.S. Chamber of Commerce, published Interpretive Bulletin 08-1 that modified and superseded the DOL's prior guidance regarding ETIs. The revised bulletin stated that before a fiduciary selects an ETI (over another investment), it must first conclude that the investment alternatives under consideration are "economically indistinguishable," that is, "truly equal, taking into account a quantitative and qualitative analysis of the economic impact on the plan" (U.S. DOL, 2008, p. 61735). This analysis must include consideration of an investment opportunity's level of diversification, degree of liquidity, and potential risk and return as compared to other investments that would fill a similar role in the plan's portfolio.

The DOL 08-1 Bulletin cautioned that any fiduciary who considers factors outside the economic interests of the plan should maintain a contemporaneous written account of the economic analysis concluding that the investment opportunities considered were of equal economic value. Further, the DOL noted that fiduciaries "will rarely be able to demonstrate compliance with ERISA" in the absence of such a written record (U.S. DOL, 2008, p. 61735). In the bulletin, the DOL also provided several examples of various investments that were not of equal economic value to the plan and therefore not permitted under ERISA.

It was generally held that while the DOL 08-1 Bulletin contained cautionary language about ETIs, it did not reflect a substantive change in the law on this issue. James Beall, a partner at Willig, Williams & Davidson (a labor and employment law firm), suggested that pension trustees should "treat the law as your friend, not your enemy" in considering what constitutes an investment that satisfies ESG principles. "That starts with the duties prescribed under ERISA," Beall reported. "It's very important, therefore, to have a stack of due diligence with which to defend your investment" (Trbovich, 2012).

On October 22, 2015, the U.S. DOL issued Interpretive Bulletin 15-01, a new guidance that confirmed the legality and importance of ETIs by pension funds under ERISA. In addition to reversing the unfortunate Bush Administration rule that clouded ETIs (in other words, they pressed "delete"), the new rule has adopted an ESG approach, aligning the U.S. fiduciary investment process with the modern global standard set by the PRI. The U.S. DOL is, thankfully, both reconfirming Interpretive Bulletin 94-1, and adapting a global responsible investment framework, moving from ETIs to ESG.[2]

Box 1.2: ESG and prudence

A 2016 report issued by the PRI presents two legal perspectives on integrating ESG factors within the new ETI guidelines (PRI, 2016). Per the report, while historical notions of ETIs view nonfinancial factors as "incidental" or "tie-breakers" between two otherwise equivalent investments in terms of risk and return expectations, the concept of responsible investments supported by the PRI views ESG factors as:

> material considerations in determining the prospects of a company and its ability to create long-term value. The focus is on the prudent evaluation of certain risks that, if disregarded, could adversely affect long-term investment returns ... As such, the argument in favor of incorporating ESG factors into the investment process is based on prudence considerations, not the objective of serving non-economic social goals.

As the report notes, DOL's Interpretive Bulletin 15-01 affirms this distinction and supports the use of ESG factors "solely to evaluate the economic benefits of investments and identify economically superior investments." Therefore, the new guidance views the inclusion of ESG factors as "'proper components' of a fiduciary's economic analysis," and not just as "collateral considerations or tie-breakers," as with ETIs. This historic ruling also makes it easier for pension funds to offer ESG options to plan participants within 401(k) plans.

Secretary of Labor Thomas Perez gave a remarkable speech on the new rule announcement, surrounded by and joined by labor, socially responsible

2 It was essentially annulling the Bush-era DOL 2008-01. An explanation is available at https://www.dol.gov/ebsa/newsroom/fsetis.html.

and mainstream bankers and investors who have been pushing hard for this change.[3]

Perez said, in part:

> A lot has changed in the years that followed [the Interpretive Bulletin 94-1]. Around the world, the ETI market has taken off remarkably as more and more investors recognized the promise of these opportunities. In 2005, the UN doubled down on this idea, putting ETI front and center on a global scale, with the development of new principles for responsible investing. Philanthropy got on board. Big asset managers across the country and around the world made the determination that this was a growth market they could embrace. For many investors and conventional investment firms, ETI investing has become mainstream. Decision-makers acquired new tools leaving them better equipped to evaluate this question of whether a given investment could both benefit plan participants *and* advance social goals …
>
> With that growth has come improved metrics, which were unavailable seven years ago, allowing us to more precisely evaluate the performance of a given investment. Some of the biggest fund managers out there are employing these tools and making decisions about their entire portfolio accordingly.
>
> And what those analytics often tell us, in fact, is that these so-called "collateral" benefits aren't necessarily collateral at all. In fact, the social impact can be intrinsic to the marketplace value of an investment. In other words, ETIs can be the place where doing well also means doing good …
>
> Today, we return to the sound principles, and reinstate the language, of 1994. We remove the thumb from the scale, restoring balance and leaving decisions to the marketplace. We assert that there should not be an automatic presumption against an investment that also promotes the public good.
>
> Today, the Labor Department is issuing this new guidance regarding Economically Targeted Investments made by retirement plans covered by ERISA. This guidance confirms the department's longstanding view, as laid out in the 1994 interpretation, that fiduciaries may take social impact into account as "tie-breakers" when investments are otherwise equal. (Perez, 2015)

As with any investment, pension plan trustees should consult with their legal and financial advisors when considering targeted responsible

3 Among the labor supporters of this change, in addition to the leadership of AFL-CIO and Change to Win, was Sean McGarvey, President of North America's Building Trades, who said, "This is a big win for union members. It gives investors more leeway to choose plans that also have a beneficial social impact" (ULLICO, 2015).

Box 1.3: AFL-CIO Resolution 11: Retirement Security for All

Submitted by the Committee on Shared Prosperity in the Global Economy and the Executive Council

Responsible Investment Section

Union members have a big stake in the success and integrity of our retirement system. They have chosen, through collective bargaining or other means, to defer a substantial portion of their wages into pensions and other retirement plans. Retirement savings are the primary way union members invest in the capital markets, and their retirement money is their biggest financial asset.

To aid in the creation of a sound economy, an essential condition for a secure retirement, we should invest the more than $9 trillion in government, corporate and multiemployer pension funds in economically productive ways. Pension funds need sustainable, long-term returns, and our economy needs patient, responsibly invested capital for broad-based prosperity. Meeting these objectives requires consideration of environmental, social and corporate governance ("ESG") standards.

The labor movement's long and successful track record of promoting responsible investing includes labor-invested real estate funds that have created good union construction jobs and affordable housing; worker-friendly private equity funds that have saved jobs from bankruptcies; and activist public equity funds that have encouraged greater corporate accountability. Through our participation in the governance of multiemployer and public pension funds, we will continue to promote new private and public infrastructure investment products designed to produce competitive returns while creating jobs, but we reject the notion that the investment necessary for a competitive economy requires the privatization of public infrastructure. The experience of the last 10 years is that privatization enriches Wall Street, while leading to losses for investors, higher fees for the public and, ultimately, inadequate investment in infrastructure.

While acknowledging our successes, we must scale up for the challenge of creating an economy that works for all. We strongly believe pension funds must be invested for the exclusive goal of providing workers with a secure retirement. Consistent with that, we encourage pension funds covering our members and retirees to update their investment policies and practices to address ESG standards and put at least some of their portfolio in responsible investments; use their voice as investors to promote sustainable business practices; encourage the disclosure of sustainable performance indicators; and promote the investment industry's acceptance of ESG standards. To support these goals, the AFL-CIO will develop model policy language on responsible investing and collaborate with other capital market participants to promote ESG standards.

Ensuring that workers' retirement assets are invested in their best interests also means rooting out the conflicts of interest of many financial advisers and other professionals. We call on the federal government to use its clear authority to expand prohibitions against conflicts of interest whenever financial professionals are providing advice on the investment of retirement money.

investments. Like any category of investments, there are examples of such investments that provided superior risk-adjusted returns, and others that performed poorly. Deep and unbiased due diligence, that is properly documented, is always warranted.

1.3 Takeaways

Labor's capital stewards have historically been at the front of the long march to build retirement security and responsibly invest in the real economy. Working families and their business and community allies have worked for over a century to make smart investments in our communities, helping those in need and spurring the growth of the middle class. And today, workers' capital leaders remain at the forefront of national campaigns to reinvest in our jobs, communities, and infrastructure.

In 2011, the American labor movement made a pledge, as part of the Clinton Global Initiative (CGI), to mobilize $10 billion in pension assets to invest in the nation's crumbling infrastructure, and to help facilitate $20 million in investment in energy-efficient retrofits, meant to also boost the sagging job market. The pledge was fulfilled two years ahead of schedule. Announcing this accomplishment at the 2014 CGI conference in Denver, President Clinton applauded the labor movement for its demonstration of "tremendous leadership in thinking about how to get America back to work and ... a commitment to doing that" (Proctor, 2014).

Working people and local unions, together with business and community partners, can have a dramatic impact on our society and on the health of our planet. As Dr. King said, "The arc of the moral universe is long, but it bends towards justice."

1.4 References

AFL-CIO (The American Federation of Labor and Congress of Industrial Organizations) (2016). Executive Paywatch 2016. Retrieved May 25, 2016 from http://www.aflcio.org/Corporate-Watch/Paywatch-2016.

Britannica (2014). Sidney Hillman: American labour leader. In *Encyclopedia Britannica*. Retrieved May 25, 2016 from http://www.britannica.com/biography/Sidney-Hillman.

California Governor's Office (1982). *Winning Technologies: A New Industrial Strategy for California and the Nation. Executive Summary*. Sacramento, CA: California Governor's Office.

Carmichael, I., & Quarter, J. (Eds). (2003). *Money on the Line: Workers' Capital in Canada*. Ottawa, Canada: Canadian Centre for Policy Alternatives.

Ceres (2014). Ceres homepage. Retrieved May 25, 2016 from http://www.ceres.org.

Chrones Moore, C. (1995, September 1). Whose pension is it anyway? Economically targeted investments and the pension funds. *Cato Policy Analysis*, 236. Retrieved May 25, 2016 from http://www.cato.org/pubs/pas/pa-236.html.

Croft, T. (2009). *Up from Wall Street: The Responsible Investment Alternative*. New York, NY: Cosimo Books.

——— (2011). Targeted responsible investing. In T. Hebb (Ed.), *The Next Generation of Responsible Investing* (pp. 199-218). Dordrecht, Germany: Springer Publishing.

Dreier, P. (2000). Renewing bonds. *NHI Shelterforce Online*, 111 (May/June). Retrieved June 28, 2016 from http://www.shelterforce.com/online/issues/111/dreier.html.

Eisenhofer, J.W., & Barry, M.J. (2013). *Shareholder Activism Handbook*. New York, NY: Aspen Publishers.

Financial Times (2015). Definition of Real Economy. *Financial Times Lexicon*. Retrieved May 25, 2016 from http://lexicon.ft.com/Term?term=real-economy.

Fung, A., Hebb, T., & Rogers, J. (Eds.). (2001). *Working Capital: The Power of Labor's Pensions*. Ithaca, NY: Cornell University Press.

Hebb, T., & Zanglein, J. (2014). Economically-targeted investing: changing of the guard. In J.P. Hawley, A.G.F. Hoepner, K.L. Johnson, J. Sandberg, & E.J. Waitzer (Eds.), *Cambridge Handbook of Institutional Investment and Fiduciary Duty* (pp. 112-126). Cambridge, UK: Cambridge University Press.

Hunter, E., & Costello, F. (2014, January 17). Dr. Martin Luther King and AFL-CIO President George Meany: creating a common agenda for economic and social justice. Retrieved June 28, 2016 from http://www.aflcio-hit.com/wmspage.cfm?parm1=3055.

Kaden, L., & Smith, L. (1988). *The Cuomo Commission Report: A New American Formula for a Strong Economy*. New York, NY: Simon and Schuster.

Klec, G., & Mum, D. (2015). Trade union influence on companies via pension fund investment. In S. Vitols (Ed.), *Long-Term Investment and the Sustainable Company: A Stakeholder Perspective. Vol. III* (pp. 119-146). Brussels: European Trade Union Institute.

Lanoff, I. (1980). The social investment of private pension plan assets: may it be done lawfully under ERISA? *Labor Law Journal*, 31(7), 387-389.

Leopold, L. (2007). *The Man Who Hated Work and Loved Labor: The Life and Times of Tony Mazzocchi*. White River Junction, VT: Chelsea Green Publishing Company.

Lurie, A. (1996). ETIs: a scheme for the rescue of city and county with pension funds. *Journal of Pension Planning & Compliance*, I (1996), 4.

Millstein, I.M. (1989). *Our Money's Worth: The Report of the Governor's Task Force on Pension Fund Investment*. Albany, NY: New York State Industrial Cooperation Council.

Perez, T. (2015, October 22). Remarks by U.S. Secretary of Labor Tom Perez: press conference announcing new ERISA guidance on economically targeted investments. Retrieved May 25, 2016 from https://www.dol.gov/_sec/media/speeches/20151022_Perez.htm.

PRI (Principles for Responsible Investment) (2016). PRI presents legal perspectives on addressing ESG factors under ERISA. Retrieved May 25, 2016 from https://www.unpri.org/news/pri-presents-legal-perspectives-on-addressing-esg-factors-under-erisa.

Proctor, C. (2014). Pension funds pledge $10.2B to spur construction, Bill Clinton announces at Denver forum. *Denver Business Journal*. Retrieved June 15, 2016 from http://www.bizjournals.com/denver/blog/earth_to_power/2014/06/clinton-global-initiative-america-big-pension-fund.html#i1.

Reich, R.B. (1994a, September 11). A moral workout for big money. *New York Times*, sec. 3, p. 9.

——— (1994b, October 26). Pension fund "raid" just ain't so. [Letter to the editor]. *Wall Street Journal*, A21.

Rifkin, J., & Barber, R. (1978). *The North Will Rise Again: Pensions, Politics and Power in the 1980s*. Boston, MA: Beacon Press.

Rothenberg, R. (1983, January 1). An RFC for today: a capital idea. *INC Magazine*. Retrieved May 25, 2016 from http://www.inc.com/magazine/19830101/4511.html.

Trbovich, M. (2012, April 13). AFL CIO's Housing Investment Trust (HIT) creating competitive returns and thousands of jobs. *Heartland Blog*. Retrieved May 25, 2016 from http://steelvalley.pairserver.com/heartlandnetwork.org/blog/35-afl-cios-housing-investment-trust-hit-creating-competitive-returns-and-thousands-of-jobs.

ULLICO (2014). The need for life insurance gave birth to ULLICO Inc. Retrieved May 25, 2016 from http://www.ullico.com/news-item/need-life-insurance-gave-birth-ullico.

——— (2015). *Ullico Bulletin*, 3(3). Retrieved June 20, 2016 from http://www.ullico.com/newsroom/bulletin-2015-3-1.

UMWA (United Mine Workers of America) (2014). UWMA History: John L. Lewis. Retrieved May 25, 2016 from http://www.umwa.org/?q=content/john-l-lewis.

U.S. DOL (U.S. Department of Labor) (1994). DOL Interpretive Bulletin 94-1. *Employee Benefits Security Administration, Labor*. Retrieved June 15, 2016 from http://webapps.dol.gov/FederalRegister/HtmlDisplay.aspx?DocId=21631&AgencyId=8&DocumentType=2.

——— (2008). Interpretive Bulletin 2008-1 Relating to Investing in Economically Targeted Investments. *Federal Register*, 73(202), 61734-61736. Retrieved July 1, 2016 from http://webapps.dol.gov/FederalRegister/PdfDisplay.aspx?DocId=21631.

——— (2015). DOL Interpretive Bulletin 2015-1 Relating to the Fiduciary Standard Under ERISA in Considering Economically Targeted Investments. *Federal Register*, 80(206), 65135-65137. Retrieved July 1, 2016 from http://webapps.dol.gov/federalregister/HtmlDisplay.aspx?DocId=28547&AgencyId=8.

U.S. GAO (U.S. Government Accountability Office) (1995). *Public Pension Plans: Evaluation of Economically Targeted Investment Programs*. GAO/PEMD-95-13. Retrieved June 28, 2016 from http://www.gao.gov/assets/230/221097.pdf.

van der Zwan, N. (2011). *Contentious Capital: The Politics of Pension Investment in the United States and Germany, 1974-2003* (Unpublished doctoral dissertation). New School for Social Research, New School University, New York, NY.

Vitello, P. (2014, May 11). Lynn Williams, 89, who led steelworkers union, is dead. *New York Times*. Retrieved May 26, 2016 from http://www.nytimes.com/2014/05/12/business/economy/lynn-williams-89-led-steelworkers-union-is-dead.html?_r=0.

Voices for Corporate Responsibility (2010). Advisory Board. Previously retrieved from http://www.voicesforcorporateresponsibility.com/advisoryboard.html (site now defunct).

Werback, A. (2004, January 20). Bridging the labor-environment gap. *In These Times*. Retrieved May 26, 2016 from http://inthesetimes.com/article/683/bridging_the_labor_environment_gap.

Woods, C., & Urwin, R. (2010). Putting sustainable investing into practice: a governance framework for pension funds. *Journal of Business Ethics*, 92(1), 1-19.

Zanglein, J. (2001). Overcoming institutional barriers on the economically-targeted investment highway. In A. Fung, T. Hebb, & J. Rogers (Eds.), *Working Capital: The Power of Labor's Pensions* (pp. 181-202). Ithaca, NY: Cornell University Press.

2
The global responsible investment movement and the launch of the UN PRI

> Importantly, pension funds have a social purpose, that of financing workers' rights to retirement ... Given their social purpose, it would make sense for pension funds to embrace ... long-term investment—shifting away from short-term to long-term, mainstreaming responsible investment practices, greater portfolio exposure to infrastructure and job creation projects.
>
> Sharan Burrow, President, International Trade Union Confederation (ITUC)

The approaches and legal frameworks to responsible investment in other countries were markedly different than those in the U.S.A. Labor parties historically have represented the interests of working people, unions, and the broader citizenry in many of the Western governments outside the U.S.A. Social democratic governments in European nations generally mandated employee consultation, stronger labor rights, and labor-friendly laws, though this varies within the community. The most progressive pension and institutional funds and banks claim to adhere to international conventions on human rights, labor, the environment, bribery, corruption, and the use of certain weapons.

The historical role of international labor in demanding and investing in social housing and jobs has been similar to labor in the U.S.A. And, parallel to the U.S.A., capital stewards in many of these countries follow the standards set by the UN PRI (see Box 2.4). But, along the way, there have been many divergences.

Box 2.1: Labor relations and engagement in the U.S.A. and Europe

According to Klec and Mum (2015, pp. 130-131):

> In Europe, in general the labour relations culture differs markedly from that of North America, which also manifests itself in the context of pension fund activism. In the United States, there is systematic and institutionalised dialogue between the company management and the trade unions only to a very limited extent. The trade unions, which own considerable portfolios of shares via their pension funds, thus have a major interest in exercising their shareholder's rights in order to insist on dialogue or to enforce their standpoint on voting in general meetings (or the related publicity).
>
> In contrast, the European social and company model is far more than a dialogue between employers and employees' representatives. Company codetermination is partly institutionalised, in particular in countries with the dualistic model of corporate structure, such as Germany, Austria and the Netherlands, but not Switzerland or the United Kingdom. The dialogue between the employees' side and companies thus takes place along a different track in Europe ... thus the approach to the exercise of shareholders' rights is mainly consensus-oriented and many investors tend to be passive.

While the U.S. employment model is based on the primacy of market forces, the EU:

> bases its conception of employment on the principle that unregulated markets create an imbalance between the employer and employee; therefore, governmental regulation and institutionalized unions are necessary to create countervailing power in the labor market that protects employees. Thus, the EU countries are seen as traditionally placing a higher value than in the United States on worker protection.
>
> (Block *et al.*, 2003, p. 7)

The EU includes collective bargaining in the Charter of Fundamental Rights, and requires labor consultation as a social partner with regards social policy legislation. EU directives require that firms must provide information to employees on financial and business matters, employment levels, and structural changes to the business (such as buyouts and closures). Individual nations within the EU also legislate these issues.

In Europe, the concept of corporate social responsibility (CSR), a variant of responsible corporate governance:

> differs a great deal from the American understanding because many social issues that are part of the original CSR social approach, such as employee participation, education and healthcare, are regulated by law in European countries. Many elements of the CSR concept,

> formulated and theoretically developed in the United States, were already implicitly part of European attitudes and laws long before the idea of explicitly formulated CSR strategies was brought to Europe.
> (Schreckenbach and Thannisch, 2012)

A number of European countries also follow the model of German works councils and codetermination in their industrial relations, models set by national laws. In the codetermination framework, workers and unions are viewed as company stakeholders, and workers' representatives on the councils and company supervisory boards have a legal voice in company policies. This "stakeholder" view of companies and their employee relations is a counterpoint to views in the U.S.A. and U.K., where the "shareholder" model is more prevalent. In stakeholder companies, workers balance their roles as both stakeholders (part of the operations, human capital, and knowledge foundation of the firm) and shareholders (in their role as pension fund investors in companies at large) (Vitols, 2015; Gollan *et al.*, 2010).

In terms of corporations:

> Trade union influence over pension funds in North American is more strongly anchored than in Europe. This is also due to the fact that the model of company financing in the United States is based much more on the issue of equity via the stock exchange, resulting in a higher volume of shares. In (continental) Europe, company financing takes place much more through external capital (banks) and even in the case of equity issues it is often the banks that hold company securities.
> (Klec and Mum, 2015, p. 125)

While the recent change in the DOL ETI (Interpretive Bulletin 15-01) in the U.S.A. has, for the first time, provided stronger guidance for U.S. pension funds to consider ESG as part of their fiduciary duties in making investments, other nations have been relying on the ESG framework for a longer period of time. As we mention in Chapter 5 on fiduciary duty, "outside the U.S., many countries already have in place legislation that requires consideration of ESG issues in the management of pension assets or by investment funds" (Caplan *et al.*, 2013, p. 5).

In Europe, member countries of the European Union (EU) will be required to adopt the Non-Financial Report Directive (NFR) by October 2016. This directive mandates that large companies will have to report nonfinancial information to their shareholders, including, at minimum, environmental, social, and employee matters, respect for human rights, anticorruption, and bribery issues (Levick, 2015).

Since U.S. unions have not had consultation rights outside of collective bargaining, capital stewards have promoted a stronger, earlier push toward shareholder rights. As mentioned in Chapter 1, union and public pension funds have generally been aggressive in proxy campaigns and shareholder engagements with companies.

Over the years, global labor leaders and capital stewards have increasingly recognized the importance of coordinated activist engagements and investment collaboration. This has led to the establishment of global labor networks that coordinate shareholder and political actions and provide mutual support. At the request of the Global Trade Unions and the AFL-CIO, the Dutch Federation of Trade Unions (FNV) organized a conference in 1998 at which the FNV presented the union policy on responsible investment and laid the foundation for the establishment of the Committee on Workers' Capital (CWC).

The final plans for the CWC were designed in a meeting at the Capitol Hill Restaurant in Washington, D.C. between AFL-CIO President John Sweeney and Bertil Jonsson, Executive President of the Swedish Trade Union Confederation. "American workers had a voice in over $6 billion in pension funds at the time," explained Ron Blackwell, former Chief Economist of the AFL-CIO.[1] "Globally, the labor movement had a voice in over $13 billion. We needed to organize Workers' Capital to demand a strategy for responsible shareholder action and real investment, in ways that were in the interests of working people." The CWC was launched by the Executive Board of the then International Confederation of Free Trade Unions (ICFTU), following a November 1999 conference in Stockholm of trade union leaders from ICFTU affiliates, national union federations, and the TUAC.

As an arm of the International Trade Union Confederation (ITUC), the CWC brings together representatives of the international labor movement to share information and develop strategies for joint actions. These national and international labor centers have advanced some of the most ambitious and aggressive corporate responsibility campaigns to date, including shareholder actions against companies working in Burma, which sanctioned slave labor, and against the multinational mining company Rio Tinto for massive labor abuses in the global South.

Creative capital stewards across countries have pushed the envelope by voting their shares in hundreds of companies, targeting a multitude of corporate issues and increasing the integration of ESG into their pension and institutional investments. They have invested in common pools of capital

1 Personal communication/interview, December 8, 2015.

across borders and globally with a focus on areas such as housing and infrastructure, clean energy, and climate change.

This chapter provides a review of responsible investment trends in the U.K., Sweden, the Netherlands, and Australia. Like the previous chapter, it briefly describes the evolution of retirement and institutional assets, and underlines the importance of trade unions in that development and the evolution toward responsible investment. While the review is not complete, the aim is to demonstrate not only divergences, but also commonalities across borders in relation to responsible investments.

2.1 Labor's responsible investment strategies internationally

2.1.1 The Netherlands

Dutch workers have been supporting the creation of social housing since the mid-1800s. As in many other European countries, labor unions launched co-operative (co-op) associations and housing societies; by the late 1800s, they targeted slum sections of Amsterdam for rebuilding. After the Second World War, Dutch labor unions of various denominations and hundreds of housing associations joined with the federal and municipal governments to replace or repair many of the 300,000 homes lost or damaged.

During the 1950s, the General Dutch Building Trades Union (NVV-ICFTY) pushed for the modernization of the industry, promoting labor–management cooperation, worker training, and new efficiencies that would also help bring down the cost of housing. The Dutch Federation of Trade Unions (NVV) worked with the Minister for Reconstruction and Housing and the National Housing Council to speed up housing construction and reduce costs (Umrath, 1952).

The Dutch pension funds, among the largest in the world and early PRI signatories, were among the earliest and most aggressive funds pursuing responsible investment and corporate governance mandates. The Dutch system has been widely praised for its adequacy and sustainability, as the occupational system is basically mandatory and covers 90% of the workforce. The system generally enjoys a fully funded status.[2]

2 Dutch pension systems are often ranked in the world's top ranking pension systems by the Melbourne Mercer Global Pension Index (Mercer, 2015). "This

> As in many other European countries, the Dutch pension system consists of three pillars: the state pension (AOW), the supplementary collective pensions and the private individual pension products that each person can arrange for him/herself. Together these three pillars determine the amount of pension that a person will receive when he/she retires at the end of his/her working life. Risk sharing, efficiency and collective schemes are key characteristics of the 2nd pillar system.
> (VB and OPF, 2008, p. 7)

ABP, the second-largest union-sponsored pension fund in the world, serves Dutch civil servants and has €350 billion in assets. The fund claims that while its first responsibility is to achieve the highest possible return on investment, it is also aware of its social responsibility, managing various ethical and sustainable investment policies and practices.[3]

Xander den Uyl, who stepped down as vice president of ABP in 2013, is a longtime labor leader who served as the General Secretary of Abvakabo FNV, a national union for employees in state and local governments. As one of the leading capital stewards of the Netherlands, he participated in the development of the responsible investment policy of ABP, adopted in 2007, and has worked to integrate ESG into the investment process of the fund. Since April of this year, he has returned to ABP as a trustee, and also serves on other trust boards. He has been an active member of the ITUC CWC and he was recently elected to serve on the Board of the PRI (den Uyl, 2016).

The ABP funds (and some smaller construction trusts) are primarily managed by APG, the Dutch pension fund manager. ABP manages the assets of over 4.5 million participants and is a founding member of the PRI. As such, ABP reports that it integrates ESG information factors across its portfolio. ABP also actively manages billions of euros in specialist strategies of what it calls "highly sustainable investments" that anticipate future ESG trends. ABP invests 20% in real estate and alternative investments, including renewable energy, infrastructure, and private equity. In its real estate investments, ABP was one of the instigators of the Global Real Estate Sustainability Benchmark (GRESB).

high ranking is thanks to the diversity of the Dutch pension system's funding sources, its accuracy in measuring costs and contributions to ensure fair distribution, and its strong regulation by the Dutch Central Bank and the Dutch Authority for the Financial Markets ... It incorporates different models of pension funding with a policy of solidarity and risk-sharing" (IamExpat, 2016).

3 This and other passages about Dutch pension funds are drawn from a special report: *The Netherlands: Dutch Institutions Engage for Change* (RI Insight, 2014).

The PFZW is the second-largest pension fund in the Netherlands, with over €140 billion in assets, and it supports healthcare workers. The PGGM, the fund's captive asset manager, was also a founding signatory of PRI, and also applies ESG criteria to its investments. It built, in 2013, an ESG index for €40 billion of passive investments and, instead of using a best-in-class approach, deployed a worst-in-class approach and elected not to invest in firms in the bottom 10% in terms of their rating in the index. The fund similarly invests in real estate and alternatives, and allocates 4% of its assets in themed approaches that include renewables, forestry, and cleantech.

PGGM helped start the Ampere renewables fund by Triodos Bank, and also took a stake in the world's largest private-sector carbon fund, Climate Change Capital's (CCC) Carbon II fund. The fund invests in developing countries aiming to reduce greenhouse gas emissions.

The largest Dutch trade union alliance, FNV, does not have a specific initiative concerning the exercise of voting rights, and so does not provide recommendations on voting rights for the voting behavior of pension funds, unlike, for example, the British Trades Union Congress (TUC) and the AFL-CIO. However, FNV does conduct training courses that introduce trustees to the basics of company pensions and also responsible investment. The FNV was the first union alliance in the Netherlands to have a responsible investment policy for union trustees, working together with such former union-affiliated companies as Reaal (insurer), the Hollandse Koopmansbank (former union investment bank), and the ASN bank (a former union savings bank) (Klec and Mum, 2015; Vitols, 2015).

Both of the Dutch pension funds have been aggressive in engagement and shareholder actions. ABP's process involves intense dialogue, asking key questions, and site visits. The fund has recently focused on poor working conditions for textile workers, for instance in Bangladesh and Burma, according to a 2015 presentation at the CWC. Along with the Dutch government, ABP has demanded safe working conditions in companies and production supply chains. After all else has failed, and usually after years of corporate engagement proved unsuccessful, one or both of the funds have divested shares from firms, including those that produce weapons that cause human suffering after military action (such as cluster bombs). They have also divested from Walmart, for labor rights violations in the U.S.A.; from Tepco, the Japanese nuclear company, after the Fukushima Daiichi nuclear power station melted down; and from the Chinese oil firm Petro-China.

The Dutch have built one of the most vibrant responsible investment markets on the planet (RI Insight, 2014). The Netherlands houses a number of progressive responsible investment actors, including:

- **Sustainalytics**, a leading global sustainable and responsible investment analysis firm, which partners with institutional investors who integrate ESG information and assessments into their investment decisions.
- **Triodos Bank, N.V.**, mentioned earlier, is a global pioneer in sustainable banking, and manages numerous funds that invest in sustainable businesses and energy projects. In 1980, Triodos launched the first "green fund," a fund for environmentally friendly projects, on the Amsterdam Stock Exchange. The bank's mission is to "make money work for positive social, environmental and cultural change." The bank has branches in several other countries (Triodos, 2016).
- The **Rabobank Group** of banks operates on cooperative principles whose origins lie in the Dutch local loan co-ops founded nearly 110 years ago. Overall, Rabobank Group is among the world's 30 largest financial institutions, and has approximately 55,000 employees serving about 10 million customers in 40 countries. The banks are members and shareholders of the supra-local co-op organization, Rabobank Nederland, which advises the banks and supports their local services (Rabobank, 2016).

2.1.2 Sweden

Historically, Sweden has had both strong labor unions and a robust co-op movement. At the beginning of the 20th century, Swedish co-op societies formed companies to compete against cartels and to lower the price of essential goods (Umrath, 1952). In 1916, the Central Union of Social Labour and the Stockholm County Council founded the Stockholm Co-operative Housing Society (KSB). Various co-op housing societies and tenants' savings funds were created during this century, including the most advanced and sophisticated investment and construction entities in the country, and Swedish labor invested in these vehicles to modernize the country's housing stock.

In later years, the Swedish Trade Union Confederation (LO), the national labor federation, and the national construction trades invested in these vehicles, and also partnered with municipalities and the Swedish government in this regard. Labor's partnerships have built hundreds of thousands of housing units through the decades.

In 1908, the LO and the Swedish Cooperative Union (KF) founded the Folksam insurance company, one of the largest insurers in Sweden. Folksam reports that it contributes to long-term sustainable social development and, as one of Sweden's biggest asset managers, works to influence the companies in which it invests. Folksam encourages firms to take a greater responsibility for the environment and human rights (Swedish Trade Union Confederation, 2013).

In 1913, Sweden was the first country in the world to pass a law on universal old-age pension insurance, guaranteeing coverage for all elderly citizens. The Swedish National Pension AP Funds Family, the primary public pension funds in Sweden, was started in 1960 after a public referendum and vote of parliament (Första AP-fonden, 2012). The AP funds have a combined $146 billion (1.2 trillion Swedish kroner) in assets. All persons that work, receive salaries, and pay taxes in Sweden receive a public pension, which consists of income pension and premium pension.

The leaders of the LO have had board seats on the AP funds, and labor has been active in the latter's development. The AP funds have different roles within the pension system, and include several buffer funds tasked with seeking greater returns during favorable economic and demographic conditions. The funds aim to build a buffer to protect the Swedish pension system during times when there are large cohorts of retiring workers (Riley, 2011).

In the 1960s, when the:

> Swedish government sought to marshal credit on favorable terms to housing as part of a massive social program of housing expansion … the labor movement … believed that "social investment" could best be accomplished through the state, rather than itself, and independent of the system of retirement finance. (Simon, 1993, p. 269)

But the AP Funds have, in recent decades, invested aggressively in housing and real estate, continuing the long-term efforts of labor unions to prudently invest to meet social housing needs.

As an early signatory of the PRI, the AP Funds have been very active in responsible investment and, in 2007, established a joint socially responsible investment (SRI) council to systematically screen non-Swedish investment portfolios to ensure compliance with international norms and conventions related to environment, human rights, and labor rights (Bandel, 2007).

The funds have also invested in CCC's Carbon II fund. More recently, the Swedish AP Funds have agreed to coordinate the way carbon footprints are reported (AP-Fonderna, 2015), and agreed to increase investments in alternative assets and infrastructure. Based on a major climate report from Mercer, AP recently increased its share of real assets in the portfolio, investing in real estate, agricultural land, and timberland.

2.1.3 Great Britain

The Industrial Revolution first took root in Great Britain. As such, the British people suffered the effects of slums and overcrowding brought about by the societal impacts of industrialization. From the 1830s onward, the government empowered, through a series of Housing Acts, local authorities to improve the worst conditions. However, Britain did not have the preponderance of housing societies as seen on the Continent and, unfortunately, building activities were not very fruitful. With the support of the trade unions, Local Government Boards were expanded in the early 1900s to build more workforce housing.

During the years before the First World War, the country built the first experimental "New Towns," such as the garden city of Letchworth. After the war, the British labour movement joined a nonpartisan push for a national housing policy.[4] During the depression, the labor movement strongly pushed for new housing and local authorities dramatically stepped their progress in this regard. After the war, the Labour government was active in local authority efforts to replace housing destroyed or damaged, as well as the broader problem of reconstructing industry.

In the late 1800s, occupational pension schemes were started for nurses, civil servants, teachers, and the police. Labor unions fought for the establishment of funds in railway companies, the first industrial plans, followed by other companies (Hunter, 2015). Trade unions continued to push for occupational retirement schemes through the 20th century.

4 John Wheatley, the Minister of Health of the first Labour government (1924), created a new program that attacked both the paucity of decent housing and also a lack of skilled workers. Interestingly, local authorities designed building contracts that guaranteed a set number of years of employment and also required that one apprentice had to be employed for every five building operatives. This approach increased the building of critically needed social housing by the public sector.

At the beginning of the 20th century, British governments passed laws providing for "old age pensions," around the same time it adopted workers' insurance programs, which emulated the German national insurance programs passed in the 1870s. This began the demise of the Elizabethan-era Poor Acts. Provision for the basic state pension, then known as the Old Age Pension Act, had passed in the U.K. in 1908. After the passage of the National Insurance Act of 1946, providing social security coverage, the British retirement system developed similarly to other European systems (Pensions Archive, n.d.).

Starting in the 1990s, the Trades Union Congress (TUC) rallied unions around the Campaign for Pension Fund Democracy, which demanded equal representation for labor trustees and pension trusts, up from the one-third ratio passed in legislation. Through the decade, union activists in particular continued their push with various Labour governments.[5] The U.K. Pensions Act of 2000, passed by the Labour government, required ESG disclosure in pension investments, and the Financial Reporting Council's Stewardship Code of 2010, updated two years later, spelled out stewardship activities for trusts, such as disclosing how they will carry out stewardship responsibilities and explaining their policies for voting and monitoring investee companies.

The TUC Member Trustee Network was established in the 1990s to provide information and resources to trade union pension trustees to enable them to carry out their duties professionally and effectively. It accomplishes this through networking, a regular newsletter, access to training and conferences, and the opportunity to meet and talk with fellow member trustees at other funds. The network currently links up around a thousand trade union trustees. Since 2003, the TUC has produced an annual report on the voting behavior of investment managers and, in October 2004, it published directives on voting behavior and engagement.

In 2013, the TUC and its two largest affiliated unions, Unite and UNISON, launched Trade Union Share Owners, a new group aiming to put union values at the heart of the world of corporate governance, with a new approach to the way in which their investments are voted on at company AGMs. Utilizing a new set of policy guidelines drawn up by the TUC, the group has been working through a shareholder advisory group to ensure that its funds, with over £1 billion of assets, take a common voting position in FTSE350

5 Tom Powdrill, Responsible Investment Coordinator at the International Transport Workers Federation, personal communication/interview, December 4, 2015.

companies where either the TUC staff pension fund or these unions hold shares:

> The new voting and engagement guidelines have been drawn up to ensure that corporate governance policies that unions have long been critical of—all-male boards, excessive director pay and bonus packages, and the non-advertisement of new director positions—will be challenged by union voting at company AGMs. (TUC, 2013)

Over the last decade, the TUC has tracked the importance to its members of issues such as these through its Fund Manager Voting Survey.[6]

There are other notable union initiatives and workers' capital institutions in the U.K. UNISON has had an active capital stewardship program since 2007 and Colin Meech, a UNISON national officer and director of its Capital Stewardship Programme, has been a forceful advocate in the U.K. in promoting labor's shareowner initiatives, responsible corporate governance, and universal ownership of pension funds.

The Environment Agency Pension Fund (EAP), representing the staff of the agency in England and Wales, applies an environmental overlay to its entire investment portfolio of £2.9 billion. Its property and private equity investments search for environmental opportunities in the renewable energy and technology field, and the fund will become the first to manage its assets in accordance with the UN-agreed principles of preventing global temperatures from rising by more than 2°C (Newlands, 2015).

Climate Change Capital (CCC) was founded in 2003 to develop solutions to climate change and resource depletion. Capitalized by institutional funds across the continent, CCC's carbon finance fund invests in an array of projects to mitigate climate change, including direct emission reduction projects. CCC's property fund was the first green fund in the U.K., focused on buying commercial green buildings or retrofitting existing properties in the U.K. Other funds invest in environmental technology and service firms (Croft, 2009b).

The British Telecom Pension Scheme (BTPS), with 340,000 members, is the U.K.'s largest corporate pension scheme. Hermes was created in 1995 to manage the assets of its initial sponsors, BT and the Post Office, before becoming wholly owned by the BTPS. As a fund manager with £29.5 billion of assets under management, while advising on another £146.6 billion, Hermes invests on behalf of BTPS and other union-sponsored pension funds, insurance companies, government entities, and financial institutions,

6 Janet Williamson, Senior Policy Officer, Economics and Social Affairs Department, TUC, personal communication/interview, January 7, 2016.

Box 2.2: King's Cross development, London

In 2000, a British Telecom Pension Scheme (BTPS)-capitalized real estate group began planning one of the largest city renewal projects in Europe. An immense multi-dimensional urban renewal strategy in London, the King's Cross Central Regeneration Project aimed to revitalize 27 ha of brownfield land in one of the most derelict parts of London, along the Regent's Canal:

> King's Cross is a mixed-use, urban regeneration project in central London that is also a major transport hub for the city. Located on the site of former rail and industrial facilities, the 67-acre (27 ha) redevelopment is ongoing and involves restoration of historic buildings as well as new construction, with the entire plan organised around internal streets and 26 acres (10.5 ha) of open space to form a new public realm for the area. Principal uses include 3.4 million square feet (316,000 sq m) of office space, close to 2,000 residential units, 500,000 square feet (46,400 sq m) of retail and leisure space, a hotel, and educational facilities. The site is served directly by six London Underground lines, two national mainline train stations, and an international high-speed rail connecting to Paris.
>
> Spanning a … site of disused railway lands in central London, King's Cross is being transformed from an area once known for lost industry into a vibrant mixed-use city quarter. Thousands of workers, residents, and students now inhabit King's Cross, the largest area of city-centre redevelopment in Europe. When it is completed in 2020, 45,000 people a day will benefit from the 3.4 million square feet (316,000 sq m) of office space, 500,000 square feet (46,400 sq m) of retail and leisure space, and close to 2,000 homes. (ULI, 2014)

King's Cross will have 500 homes classed as affordable housing, 250 homes dedicated to shared equity, home-buy purchase, and key worker rent, and another 650 units for student accommodation. The project will create 30,000 jobs. The project has been enhanced by open space, new parklands along the canal, cultural and arts amenities, and a huge commitment to sustainable development, including alternative energy sources and carbon-reducing technologies on-site.

as well as charities and endowments. Its ownership is supposed to ensure a close alignment to the needs of other long-term investors, especially pension funds.[7] In 2002, Hermes launched the landmark "Hermes Principles" document, which sets out what a shareowner should expect of a publicly listed company, and what these companies should expect from their owners (Hermes, 2015).[8]

Donald MacDonald, a long-serving trustee director of BTPS, previously served as Chair of the Board of the PRI. He was the Telecom Organizing Officer for the Communication Workers Union in the U.K. from 1999 to 2004.

7 This section on U.K. pension funds borrowed from Croft (2009a).

8 It has been pointed out, however, that while Hermes has been a leader in responsible investing, it too often votes against other union shareholder actions.

Mr. MacDonald serves as the chairman of the Institutional Investors Group on Climate Change (IIGCC), an investor forum for collaboration on climate change, representing around €7.5trillion of funds under management (BT Pension Scheme, 2015). Its purpose is to encourage public policies, investment practices, and corporate behavior that address long-term risks and opportunities associated with climate change. In his role as IIGCC Chair, he asserts that pension funds and asset managers ignoring climate science is akin to not heeding expert legal advice and represents a breach of fiduciary duty to beneficiaries and clients (Brooksbank, 2015).

Mr. MacDonald is particularly proud of the King's Cross development, an immense urban reshaping project in London financed by BTPS's real estate initiative, that is revitalizing a large section of the city that was in long-term decay (Croft, 2009b).

2.1.4 Australia

In the late 1800s and early 1900s, unions and friendly societies were involved in workers' welfare and housing needs in Australia, similar to many European countries. Starting in the late 1930s, housing societies and co-op housing societies became active in providing financing and mortgages for affordable rental and owned housing, partnering with provincial governments and becoming dominant home lenders in the 1950s in some provinces. The Chifley Labour government after the Second World War made federal funds available for housing to provincial housing authorities, which until that point had provided most of the public housing as part of an overall postwar reconstruction campaign. The maritime unions had helped build social housing in one of the earliest suburbs in Sydney for their members, especially elderly seamen, and the New South Wales Builders' Labourers' Federation famously led campaigns in the early 1970s against efforts to privatize, destroy, or gentrify hundreds of houses and apartments in the Rocks (National Museum Australia, 2015).

The first pensions were established in the mid-1800s for some public servants and corporate managers. Social security schemes were introduced in some provinces in the early 1900s, and a national "Age Pension" system replaced these schemes in 1909. By the 1980s, only 40% of the country's citizens were covered by so-called "annuation," or private pension schemes.

Led by the Australian Council of Trade Unions (ACTU), national campaigns were launched in the mid-to-late 1980s to create Industry Super Funds. The Keating Labour government won, in 1993, a compulsory superannuation guarantee. The new program began requiring all employers to make mandatory contributions for their employees (starting at just under 10% of pay) as part of a tripartite agreement among unions, government, and employers. "This new scheme allowed millions of working Australians to now enjoy superannuation benefits of their own, and this helped relieve the growing burden on the taxpayer-funded government pension scheme" (Industry Super Funds, 2015).

Today, the not-for-profit superannuation sector manages total assets of A$650 billion, out of about A$2 trillion in total national pension savings (ASFA, 2015). ACTU is active in workers' capital issues, and collaborates with Industry Super Holdings, an amalgamation of fund management services. ACTU also worked with recent Labour governments on affordable housing and other jobs programs.[9] In concert, ACTU and the supers are active in corporate governance campaigns in the country and globally, and ACTU was a coalition member with other national and international bodies, and the International Trade Union Confederation (ITUC), in the decades-long campaign to end Burma's use of forced labor and its suppression of workers' rights.

It is difficult to discuss the success of the Australian Superannuation Funds without mentioning Mavis Robertson, one of its greatest pioneers, who passed away in early 2015. A left and labor activist since the Great Depression, Ms. Robertson served in the Federation of Engine Drivers and Firemen's Association, the precursor to the Construction, Forestry, Mining and Energy Union, and ACTU.

Ms. Robertson was behind the creation of most of the industry super fund institutions that exist today: the Conference of Major Superannuation Funds, the Australian Institute of Superannuation Trustees, Industry Fund Services, the Australian Council of Super Investors, and Women in Super. She also led the 1984 merger of two super funds for construction workers to form Cbus, which today oversees more than A$27 billion in assets. She served on the board of the AFL-CIO Center for Working Capital and was Chair of the Membership Committee of the International Corporate Governance Network. Ms. Robertson was awarded membership in the Order of Australia in 1994 (Stephens, 2015).

Industry Super Holdings Pty Ltd (ISH) is owned by 30 superannuation funds. All told, ISH offers retail and business banking, wholesale and retail funds management, financial planning, and other superannuation-related services. There are several institutions under the ISH umbrella:

9 This section on the Super Fund institutions and case study from Croft, 2009a.

Box 2.3: Pacific Hydro

Pacific Hydro (PH), owned by IFM, is one of the world's largest independent renewable energy companies, with hydro and wind assets in Australia and Latin America. PH defines itself as a global clean energy solutions provider.

With hydro and wind power projects at varying stages of development, construction, and operation in Australia, Brazil, and Chile, PH's vision is to create economic, social, and environmental value. In addition to prioritizing profit growth and rewarding investors and financial partners, PH claims it is committed to innovative renewable energy projects that respect the environment and benefit communities.

The Portland Wind Project, in Victoria, nearing completion after a decade, is expected to generate enough clean energy to power the equivalent needs of more than 31,000 homes, abating around 180,000 tons of carbon pollution annually. PH claims it consulted widely to gain community support for this A$50 million project, which injected A$20 million into the local economy and supported a building and maintenance crew of 60 people at its peak. When construction of the farm commenced, it also marked the opening of a nearby blade factory by Danish wind turbine-maker Vestas, which has also created many new jobs in the region (Croft, 2009, p. 216). After running into headwinds in the solar industry in 2015, IFM sold Pacific Hydro. "IFM Investors finished 2015 on a high with the reported but unconfirmed sale price marking a fourfold return on the purchase price of Pacific Hydro" (White, 2015).

- **The Industry Fund Services (IFS).** A subsidiary of ISH, IFS provides a range of services and products to industry superannuation funds and unions and their members. Its objective is to provide cost-effective, market-leading services that the funds are not able to provide directly themselves due to regulatory and/or cost considerations. Shared ownership of core fund managers yields lower fees and commissions.
- **Members Equity Bank (ME Bank).** Initially founded to offer access home loan products, ME Bank today focuses on providing a range of low cost banking products including home loans, term deposits, and transaction accounts for individuals and businesses.
- **Industry Funds Management (IFM).** IFM manages A$62.7 billion, and claims that it is committed to making significant long-term investments in renewable energy and infrastructure internationally. IFM is known to be a pioneer in infrastructure investing on behalf of institutional investors globally, managing A$30 billion in infrastructure on behalf of more than 150 institutional investors. It is a signatory to the UN PRI and claims to adhere to the UN Global Compact. The firm owns Pacific Hydro, the largest renewable energy company in Australia (IFM Investors, 2015).

2.2 The emergence of the UN PRI

The Principles for Responsible Investment (PRI), launched in 2006 by the UN Environment Programme Finance Initiative (UNEP FI) and investment leaders, inspired investors globally to think long-term and strategically about ESG risks and opportunities. Among the PRI's founding board members were labor pension investment leaders who pushed the PRI to align ESG with labor's values, a testimony of labor's historic leadership in the responsible investment field.

These leaders in the first few years included:

- Michael Musuraca, former trustee of the New York City Pension Funds and former staff member of the New York City AFSCME Local 37
- Daniel Simard, CEO of Bâtirente Retirement System and a member of Bâtirente's Board since 1988, who worked within the CSN union in areas of collective bargaining, benefit plans, and labor court representation

Box 2.4: The Principles for Responsible Investment

As institutional investors, we have a duty to act in the best long-term interests of our beneficiaries. In this fiduciary role, we believe that environmental, social, and corporate governance (ESG) issues can affect the performance of investment portfolios (to varying degrees across companies, sectors, regions, asset classes and time). We also recognize that applying these Principles may better align investors with broader objectives of society. Therefore, where consistent with our fiduciary responsibilities, we commit to the following:

- We will incorporate ESG issues into investment analysis and decision-making processes
- We will be active owners and incorporate ESG issues into our ownership policies and practices
- We will seek appropriate disclosure on ESG issues by the entities in which we invest
- We will promote acceptance and implementation of the Principles within the investment industry
- We will work together to enhance our effectiveness in implementing the Principles
- We will each report on our activities and progress towards implementing the Principles

Source: PRI, 2016b.

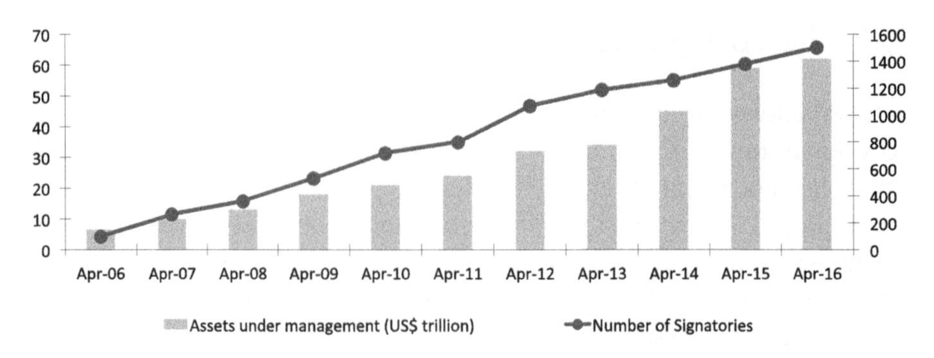

FIGURE 2.1 Growth of the PRI initiative

Source: PRI, 2016a.

Box 2.5: Key achievements of the PRI

Since its launch in 2006, the PRI has been instrumental in raising awareness about responsible investment among the global investment community and fostering collaboration between signatories, including:

- **Growth of responsible investment (RI).** Assets under management by PRI signatories now stand at more than $60 trillion, up from $4 trillion at the PRI's launch in 2006
- **RI policy.** Ninety-four percent of signatories now have a responsible investment policy in place, covering an increasing range of asset classes; many signatories publish their policies online
- **ESG incorporation.** Over half of the externally managed funds of its asset owner signatories are integrating ESG; 65% of these external assets are managed by investment manager signatories
- **Collaboration.** Ninety percent of signatories have collaborated with one or more other investors on RI-related topics
- **Disclosure.** Seventy-one percent of signatories have asked companies to integrate ESG information into their financial reporting
- **Asset class guidance.** PRI signatories have participated in designing guidance reports for public and private equity companies, fixed income, real estate, and other subclasses on responsible investment
- **Clearinghouse.** Signatories engaged with more than 1,800 companies via the PRI Clearinghouse to encourage improvements in ESG disclosure and performance

(PRI, 2015)

- Donald MacDonald, chairman of the Institutional Investors Group on Climate Change (IIGCC) and a trustee of the BT Pension Scheme in the U.K., who has previously served as chair of the UN PRI Board and as an officer for the Communication Workers Union

Unlike the ETI framework which focuses on the provision of collateral benefits, the PRI reframes the investment decision to better ensure that investors account for the real risks of their investments.

There is an increasing recognition by trade unions around the world that the investment of workers' capital should reflect the intrinsic interests of workers, not only by earning competitive financial returns, but also by contributing to the long-term vitality of society and the environment. In December 2007, the Global Unions approved a statement on responsible capital stewardship that calls on investors to take into account the broader social and environmental consequences of their investment decisions, and which finishes with the following recommendation: "In particular, the Global Unions urge trustees and institutional investors to embrace this responsible approach to investment decision-making as promoted by initiatives such as the Principles for Responsible Investment (PRI)" (read the full statement at the end of this chapter). Since then, many trust institutions and unions, corporations, and banks alike have joined the PRI.[10]

10 Although there are related global initiatives, as highlighted in Appendix C, the PRI has fashioned the largest umbrella for responsible investment.

2.3 Takeaways

Labor unions have been active across continents in much of the last century in investing in and fighting for decent social housing and good jobs. Unions and their pension funds have, historically, invested directly in social housing and collaborated with municipalities and cooperative and social housing institutions, for instance. They invested in banks, credit unions, insurance companies, and cooperative and private businesses, similar to unions in the U.S.A. And they have been, in cooperation with other capital stewards, investing in the clean economy.[11]

Today, many institutional investors encourage responsible pension investments in the real economy, in local companies, and in affordable housing. There has been continual innovation in designing investment policies and strategies that promote the use of responsible investment approaches within pension funds, and other asset owners and union-sponsored funds have been among the leaders in good corporate governance campaigns. Some states and national governments have encouraged infrastructure partnership projects and other initiatives that promote the public good. Therefore, capital stewards need to know what they are and how to use them.

Of note is that, in crafting their funds' investment strategy, pension trustees must make workers' retirement security their first priority. They must never lose sight of the fact that their first duty is to oversee the investment of plan assets prudently and solely in the long-term interests of plan participants and beneficiaries. They must never jeopardize investment returns in order to promote nonfinancial goals.

11 In terms of labor's role in the European economy, it is also important to remember that the world wars not only destroyed national economies in Europe, but also devastated housing and shelter for most member countries. "In the years 1945 and 1946, 25 million people were without a roof over their head. Over 7 million dwellings had been totally destroyed, and, what is more, during the period 1939–1946 no building had taken place, which meant another loss of 5 million dwellings which would normally have been erected during this period" (Umrath, 1952). Thus, the rebuilding of housing and cities was a priority for the entire continent, and European labor was a strong participant in these efforts.

Box 2.6: Statement by the Global Unions on responsible approaches to the stewardship of workers' capital

December 2007

Worldwide, trillions of dollars' worth of investments are made on behalf of workers and their families. The money behind these investments is workers' capital. Those entrusted with the management of workers' capital have responsibilities under the laws of their countries. Generally, these responsibilities include the loyal and prudent management of workers' capital in these same workers' interests. Generally, the trustees and managers of workers' capital, which usually takes the form of retirement funds, have an obligation to take factors such as historical investment return, diversification, and investment management costs into account in selecting and monitoring investments.

The labour movement believes that as part of the prudent and loyal management of workers' capital, fund trustees and managers need to account for the broader social and environmental consequences of their investment decisions. The manner in which they should do so is a matter of national laws and regulations, but the economic rationale for doing so applies around the world.

Pension funds and other funds investing workers' capital tend to have long-term horizons and usually have highly diversified assets. To the extent that they are diversified across industries and countries, pension funds can be considered "universal owners", meaning that their financial performance is tied to the overall health of the economy and to ever-improving environmental, governance and social practices and standards. As long-term investors, pension funds are doubly exposed to the consequences of irresponsible corporate behavior. First, they suffer losses when corporate misconduct is revealed and stock prices decline in response to a loss of investor confidence. Second, they suffer when the costs of irresponsible corporate behavior is passed on to society rather than being paid for by the offending corporation. Thus, workers' capital is diminished when the violations of human rights and labour rights damage the brand owned by the companies they invest in, when environmental misconduct must be cleaned up, when communities at home or abroad are destabilized or destroyed, or when exploitive business strategies prove unsustainable.

The Global Unions call upon all involved in making decisions about the investment of workers' capital to be mindful of the international legal framework in which investment decisions are being made, which includes respect of internationally recognized human rights and labour standards. Moreover, investors should take steps to ensure that the behavior of the companies in which workers' capital is invested is consistent with the ILO Tripartite Declaration of Principles concerning Multinational Enterprises and Social Policy and the OECD Guidelines for Multinational Enterprises.

Consequently, the Global Unions urge pension funds, their trustees and fund managers to include in their investment decision-making process consideration of the impact, both positive and negative, of their investments on workers, communities and the environment. In particular, the Global Unions urge trustees and institutional investors to embrace this responsible approach to investment decision-making as promoted by initiatives such as the Principles for Responsible Investment (PRI).

Source: TUAC, 2007.

2.4 References

AP-Fonderna (2015, November 24). *AP-Fonderna: The Swedish National Pension (AP) Funds Coordinate the Way Carbon Footprints Are Reported for Investment Portfolios* [Press release]. Retrieved June 28, 2016 from http://www.apfond6.se/globalassets/pdf-som-lankas-till/2015-11-24_press-information_the-swedish-ap-funds-co-ordinate-the-way-carbon-footprints-are-reported.pdf.

ASFA (Association of Superannuation Funds of Australia) (2015). Superannuation Statistics. Retrieved May 26, 2016 from https://www.superannuation.asn.au/resources/superannuation-statistics.

Bandel, C. (2007, February 7). Sweden's AP funds launch joint SRI council to vet foreign equities. *Investment & Pensions Europe*. Retrieved May 26, 2016 from http://www.ipe.com/swedens-ap-funds-launch-joint-sri-council-to-vet-foreign-equities/21155.fullarticle.

Block, R., Berg, P., & Roberts, K. (2003). Comparing and quantifying labor standards in the United States and the European Union. Presented at the 13th World Congress of the International Industrial Relations Association, Berlin, September 8–12, 2003. Retrieved June 20, 2016 from http://www.ilo.org/public/english/iira/documents/congresses/world_13/track_3_block.pdf.

Brooksbank, D. (2015, April 23). Investor Climate Group Chief MacDonald says ignoring climate science a breach of fiduciary duty. *Responsible Investor*. Retrieved May 26, 2016 from https://www.responsible-investor.com/home/article/iigcc_fidduty_dm/.

BT Pension Scheme (2015). Your Trustee Directors. Retrieved May 26, 2016 from http://www.btpensions.net/34/255/your-trustee-directors.

Caplan, L., Griswold, J.S., & Jarvis W.F. (2013). *From SRI to ESG: The Changing World of Responsible Investing*. Retrieved May 18, 2016 from https://www.commonfund.org/wp-content/uploads/2016/01/Whitepaper_SRI-to-ESG-2013-0901.pdf.

Croft, T. (2009a). *Helping Workers' Capital Work Harder: A Report on Global Economically Targeted Investments (ETIs)*. Vancouver, Canada: Global Unions Committee on Workers' Capital. Retrieved June 6, 2016 from http://www.workerscapital.org/images/uploads/Helping%20Workers%20Cap%20Work%20Harder.pdf.

——— (2009b). *Up from Wall Street: The Responsible Investment Alternative*. New York, NY: Cosimo Books.

den Uyl, X. (2016). *Candidate Statement, Biography, Signatory and Comparative Information Form. PRI*. Retrieved June 16, 2016 from https://www.unpri.org/explore/?q=Uyl+candidate&hd=on&hg=on&he=on&sp=rel&sc=rel&se=rel&ptv=&tv=%2520for%25202016.

Första AP-fonden (2012, August 30). History of the AP Funds. Retrieved May 26, 2016 from http://www.ap1.se/en/About-AP1/History-of-the-AP-funds/.

Gollan, P., Lewin, D., Marchington, M., & Wilkinson, A. (2010). *The Oxford Handbook of Participation in Organizations*. Oxford, UK: Oxford University Press.

Hermes (2015, September 30). Responsibility. Retrieved May 26, 2016 from https://www.hermes-investment.com/responsibility/.

Hunter, T. (2015, April 9). A turbulent history of British pensions, since 1874. *The Telegraph*. Retrieved May 26, 2016 from http://www.telegraph.co.uk/finance/personalfinance/special-reports/11523196/A-turbulent-history-of-British-pensions-since-1874.html.

IamExpat (2016). Pensions and retirement age in the Netherlands. Retrieved May 26, 2016 from http://www.iamexpat.nl/expat-page/official-issues/pensions.

IFM Investors (2015). About us. Retrieved May 26, 2016 from http://www.ifminvestors.com/about-us.

Industry Super Funds (2015). History. Retrieved May 26, 2016 from http://www.industrysuper.com/about/history/.

Klec, G., & Mum, D. (2015). Trade union influence on companies via pension fund investment. In S. Vitols (Ed.), *Long-Term Investment and the Sustainable Company: A Stakeholder Perspective. Vol. III* (pp. 119-146). Brussels: European Trade Union Institute.

Levick, K. (2015). Non-financial report directive. *ESG Magazine*, 1, 31.

Mercer (2015). Mercer Melbourne Global Pension Index. Retrieved May 26, 2016 from http://www.mercer.com/our-thinking/mercer-melbourne-global-pension-index.html.

National Museum Australia (2015). Prime Ministers of Australia: Ben Chifley. Retrieved May 26, 2016 from http://www.nma.gov.au/primeministers/ben_chifley.

Newlands, C. (2015, October 18). Environment Agency makes landmark pension move. *Financial Times*. Retrieved May 26, 2016 from http://www.ft.com/cms/s/0/0a5c23a6-7348-11e5-bdb1-e6e4767162cc.html.

Pensions Archive (n.d.). *State Pension*. Retrieved June 20, 2016 from http://www.pensionsarchive.org.uk/107/text/174/files/State%20pension.pdf.

PRI (Principles for Responsible Investment) (2015). *Responsible Investment*. London: PRI.

——— (2016a). About the PRI. Retrieved June 16, 2016 from https://www.unpri.org/about.

——— (2016b). The six Principles. Retrieved June 16, 2016 from https://www.unpri.org/about/the-six-principles.

Rabobank (2016). The Netherlands. Retrieved May 26, 2016 from https://www.rabobank.com/en/locate-us/europe/netherlands.html.

RI Insight (2014). *The Netherlands: Dutch Institutions Engage for Change*. Retrieved May 26, 2016 from https://www.responsible-investor.com/reports/ri_insight_netherlands_2014/.

Riley, S. (2011, July 6). Swedish fund takes the long view. *Top1000Funds.com*. Retrieved May 26, 2016 from http://www.top1000funds.com/profile/2011/07/06/swedish-fund-takes-the-long-view/.

Schreckenbach, S., & Thannisch, R. (2012, April 2). Corporate social responsibility: the situation in Germany from the trade unions' point of view. *CWC Blog*. Retrieved May 26, 2016 from http://www.workerscapital.org/blog/post/corporate-social-responsibility-the-situation-in-germany-from-the-trade-unions-point-of-view/.

Simon, W. (1993, September). The prospects of pension fund socialism. *Berkeley Journal of Employment & Labor Law*, 14(2), 251-274. Retrieved June 18, 2016 from http://scholarship.law.berkeley.edu/cgi/viewcontent.cgi?article=1220&context=bjell.

Stephens, T. (2015, February 27). Mavis Robertson: fighter for the rights of many, has died. *The Sydney Morning Herald*. Retrieved May 26, 2016 from http://www.smh.com.au/comment/obituaries/mavis-robertson-fighter-for-the-rights-of-many-has-died-20150226-13qhd4.html.

Swedish Trade Union Confederation (2013, June 3). Trade union members' insurance schemes. Retrieved May 26, 2016 from https://lo.se/english/social_security/trade_union_members_insurance_schemes.

Triodos (2016). Triodos homepage. Retrieved May 26, 2016 from https://www.triodos.co.uk/en/personal/.

TUAC (Trade Union Advisory Committee) (2007). Statement by the Global Unions on responsible approaches to the stewardship of workers' capital. Retrieved June 16, 2016 from http://www.tuac.org/en/public/e-docs/00/00/05/E0/document_doc.phtml.

TUC (Trades Union Congress) (2013, March 25). New share owner group will ensure union values are reflected at company AGMs. Retrieved May 26, 2016 from https://www.tuc.org.uk/economic-issues/corporate-governance/pensions-and-retirement/member-trustees/new-share-owner-group.

ULI (Urban Land Institute) (2014). *ULI Case Studies: King's Cross*. Retrieved May 26, 2016 from http://uli.org/wp-content/uploads/ULI-Documents/kingscross_16pgs_v11.pdf.

Umrath, H. (1952). *European Labour Movement and Housing*. Copenhagen, Denmark: Standing Housing Committee of European Regional Organization.

VB (Dutch Association of Industry-wide Pension Funds) and OPF (Dutch Association of Company Pension Funds) (2008). *The Dutch Pension System: An Overview of the Key Aspects*. Retrieved June 15, 2016 from http://www.pensioenfederatie.nl/Document/Publicaties/English%20publications/Nederlandse_pensioensysteem_Engelstalige_versie.pdf.

Vitols, S. (2015). Introduction: a stakeholder perspective on the long-term investment debate. In S. Vitols (Ed.), *Long-Term Investment and the Sustainable Company: A Stakeholder Perspective. Vol. III* (pp. 9-18). Brussels: European Trade Union Institute.

White, A. (2015). IFM cashed-up after $3bn Pacific Hydro sale to Chinese. *The Australian*. Retrieved June 15, 2016 from http://www.theaustralian.com.au/business/financial-services/ifm-cashedup-after-3bn-pacific-hydro-sale-to-chinese/news-story/4d9279c7de89679ce947a88a8eb876c4.

Section II: Pension fund management, governance and fiduciary considerations

3
Pension fund management

> Trustees have the power to shape the market but they have little influence in the pension value chain. We need to train people to become the checks and balances in the pension community. Unions at the turn of the last century built housing, built health clinics—built the middle class. We can do it again.
>
> Randi Weingarten, President, American Federation of Teachers

The investment or asset management industry plays an important role in financial intermediation. In the context of this *Handbook*, asset management refers to the management of financial assets by asset management companies on behalf of investors. Investments can be through pooled funds that aggregate capital from a number of investors for investment in financial assets, and segregated accounts that manage the assets of a single large investor, such as an institutional investor or a high-net-worth individual.

Essentially, asset managers provide "professional investment services," acting as intermediaries who help move funds from those that have saved to those that have a shortage. By "directing the investment decisions for investors who have chosen to have their assets professionally managed ... asset management companies act as stewards of their clients' interests" (Vox, 2012).

However, this delegation of day-to-day investment management by investors to asset managers and other intermediaries introduces incentive issues, and therefore greater separation of interests, between the end asset owners (pension plan participants and beneficiaries in our discussion) and the intermediaries. In addition, financial market complexities resulting from a large volume of available investment products and complicated securities and regulatory guidance have exacerbated these issues, perpetuating a culture of investment short-termism that ignores the negative impacts of its action on society and our environment.

This chapter aims to help trustees put in to practice the power that Randi Weingarten of the American Federation of Teachers (AFT) references in the opening quotation. In so doing, we discuss the structure of pension fund management, help trustees better understand prevalent "agency separation" issues, and present some key determinants of pension fund management for greater consideration.

3.1 The investment value chain

The management of pension investments involves a number of players, ranging from the asset owners (workers, retirees, and their beneficiaries), the asset manager intermediaries, and various investment professionals that help invest pension plan assets, to the users of capital (investee companies/projects seeking investments and providing returns). Also included are regulatory authorities that pass the rules and regulations that govern pension plan management and investments. Together, these players can be referred to as the "investment value chain." Most players in this chain are regarded as fiduciaries of workers' capital. Ultimately, the value chain's role is to prudently govern, manage, and invest pension assets on behalf of the plan participants and beneficiaries.

As is evident from Box 3.1, a number of players participate in the investment value chain. However, the role of the players in the chain is mismatched. While consultants and investment managers tend to exert an oversized influence on the investment of plan assets, plan participants and beneficiaries—the ultimate owners of plan assets—have little say on the same. One reason for this is the intentional delegation of investment responsibilities to professional advisors and investment managers in order to relieve trustees of direct investment decision-making responsibilities.

As a result, rather than being engaged in a linear fashion—i.e., seamlessly moving capital from owners to users—the players in the chain are interconnected, with disparate motives and a potential for conflicting interests with those of the plan participants and beneficiaries (Zadek *et al.*, 2005). For example, many players in the chain are motivated by a short-term, narrow interpretation of investments, whereas plan participants and beneficiaries would judiciously prefer a long-term investment strategy matching their retirement security needs. The resulting "agency separation" (Stewart and Yermo, 2008) underscores potential conflicts of interest and suggests why the investment industry as a whole does not give full consideration to the

Box 3.1: Key players in the pension investment value chain

- **Plan participants and beneficiaries.** The owners or providers of capital whose investments are expected to provide retirement benefits.
- **Trustee.** A person who holds legal title to property in trust for the benefit of another person (beneficiary) and who must carry out specific duties with regard to the property. Thus, the trustee owes a fiduciary duty to the plan participants and beneficiaries.
- **Board of trustees or a single trustee.** The board of fiduciary trustees who govern the pension funds, including developing a strategic plan, overseeing internal management, consultants, and asset managers, establishing key policy goals (benefits levels, asset allocation, etc.) and monitoring investment performance.
- **Plan administrator.** Person designated by the trustees in order to perform daily administrative duties and act as custodian for the trust.
- **Investment consultants.** Individuals or firms that advise and assist trustees in establishing investment policies and objectives, evaluating investments, reviewing asset allocation, and selecting and monitoring the investment manager. For smaller pension funds, consultants and similar advisors may play the role of an outsourced Chief Investment Officer (CIO).
- **Research providers.** Sell-side analysts who uncover investment opportunities from a universe of listed investments.
- **Internal investment team.** Consisting of a CIO and investment staff team that combine strategy selection and/or execution of the investment plan.
- **External investment manager.** An individual or firm responsible for investing the assets of the plan, on proper authority from the trustees. External managers generally have expertise in certain asset and sub-asset classes, such as public equities, bonds, real estate, etc. Investment managers include Qualified Professional Asset Managers (QPAMs).
- **Universe of investee companies/projects.** The users of capital who are the ultimate recipients of the asset owners' investment, and provide commensurate returns.

Note: While accountants, attorneys, auditors, and bank custodians obviously play a role in this chain, we have limited the list to the above-mentioned key players.

Source: Zanglein and Clark, 2001; Zadek *et al.*, 2005.

impact of material ESG risks and opportunities in arriving at the intrinsic value of investments.[1]

> Pension fund trustees and their consultants ought to be fully educated on ESG factors because investment returns are just one factor in a pension fund's growth and viability. Investments that can generate man-hours and contribute to the economic activity and vitality of both the industry that the pension fund serves as well as the community(ies) in which the participants live and work will further enhance the long-term performance of the pension fund. To neglect ESG as a factor in investment decisions is tantamount to leaving money on the table.
>
> Sarah Stettinius, Senior Vice President,
> Bentall Kennedy (U.S.) LP/MEPT[2]

As noted in a 2005 World Economic Forum report, the disconnect between players in the investment value chain is not necessarily due to differences in their personal values, but rather due to a "blend of available information, participant competencies and, most of all, the institutionalized incentives that drive their behavior" (Zadek *et al.*, 2005, p. 27). These incentives are often driven by an obsession with quarterly financial results. As such, a majority of the players in the value chain perpetuate a herd mentality that prevents them from going against conventional market wisdom and adopting longer-term value-enhancing responsible investment strategies.

Thus, as the report asserts, any expansion in the application of responsible investment considerations will require "multiple, diverse reforms at different places in the investment value chain." Further, to minimize the agency separation issue within the chain, fundamental improvements need to be put into place regarding pension fund governance, the competences of the board of trustees and internal pension staff, and the incentive structures for players in the chain.

The 2012 *Kay Review of UK Equity Markets and Long-Term Decision Making*, an important report produced in the aftermath of the 2008 financial market crisis, noted a continued misalignment of interests between players in the investment value chain and the resulting investment short-termism that led up to the crisis. As the report asserts, there is a need to "restore relationships of trust and confidence in the investment chain, underpinned by the

1 Intrinsic value is defined as "the actual value of a company or an asset based on an underlying perception of its true value including all aspects of the business, in terms of both tangible and intangible factors. This value may or may not be same as the current market value" (http://www.investopedia.com/terms/i/intrinsicvalue.asp, retrieved June 21, 2016).

2 Personal communication/interview, January 2015.

application of fiduciary standards of care by all those who manage or advise on the investments of others" (Kay Review, 2012, p. 9). Among its recommendations, the report calls for a shorter investment value chain, such that "deeper" relationships may be pursued at each stage of the intermediation.

Similarly, the Canada Pension Plan Investment Board (CPPIB) and McKinsey & Co. are leading an initiative called "Focusing Capital on the Long Term" (FCLT), which has brought together investment professionals with a total of over $6 trillion in assets under management. The initiative's goal is to "develop practical ideas for how institutional investors might reorient their portfolio strategies and management practices to emphasize long-term value creation and, by doing so, be a powerful force in promoting a long-term mind-set throughout the investment value chain" (Focusing Capital on the Long Term, 2015, p. 4). To achieve this goal, the FCLT provides recommendations across five core areas:

1. Investment beliefs
2. Risk appetite statement
3. Benchmarking process
4. Evaluations and incentives
5. Investment mandates

3.2 Key determinants of pension management

Responsibilities of a pension trustee board may vary in scope but generally include the following:

- Establish investment objectives and create an investment policy statement (IPS) to include financial performance objectives and risk considerations, including those related to material ESG factors
- Develop a strategy to execute investment objectives through asset allocation, the setting of actuarial assumptions, and the selection of appropriate internal and external investment management staff
- Establish appropriate fund governance structures related to the fund's long-term strategy and investment objectives, including whether there is a need to appoint a chief investment officer (CIO) or create subcommittees

- Monitor the fund's investment success by reviewing the performance of the fund as well as that of the internal and external investment management staff
- Monitor the fund's governance success by reviewing the adequacy of the established governance structures in meeting investment objectives

In this section, we briefly discuss three key determinates from the above list, with insights on other areas in chapters to follow.

3.2.1 Developing an investment policy statement (IPS)

The IPS or statement of investment policy (SIP) is a written statement that provides trustee fiduciaries, as well as other key players in the investment value chain, with guidelines on the management of the fund's investment portfolio. The DOL states that "a statement of investment policy designed to further the purposes of the plan and its funding policy is consistent with the fiduciary obligations set forth in ERISA" (Code of Federal Regulations, 2008, p. 365).

A well-constructed IPS should include clear responsibilities for the players involved in the management of the fund's assets, including the trustee board, investment managers, advisors, and custodians. It should set forth the fund's financial and nonfinancial objectives based on the risk appetite of the trustee board and the fund's governing documents. It should also include the asset allocation mix, including acceptable ranges for the fund's investments, in line with the fund's long-term investment goals. The IPS should also establish rules for periodically monitoring and reviewing the management of the investment portfolio (Coffey, 2011).

The responsible mission and investment beliefs statements discussed in the next chapter should complement the IPS. In so doing, the IPS can serve as an important starting point for addressing any fund governance deficiencies, as well as enabling responsible investments.

Links to sample IPSs for trustees' reference are included in Appendix B.

3.2.2 Asset allocation

Trustee fiduciaries are required to oversee the prudent investment of plan assets in line with the long-term economic interests of plan participants and beneficiaries. Asset allocation is the starting point in conducting this duty. It refers to the selection of appropriate asset classes for the investment of the fund's assets in relation to its investment objectives, risk tolerance, and investment horizon. A well-diversified portfolio consists of a range of asset classes in order to appropriately spread investment risk.

Stocks, bonds, and cash are referred to as traditional asset classes. Private equity, real estate, hedge funds, infrastructure investments, derivatives, etc., are referred to as alternative asset classes. In recent years, alternative investments have seen increased allocations by pension funds in an effort to increase the overall expected investment returns generated by the funds' assets. The 2015 Towers Watson survey reported a significant increase in allocations to alternative investments by the seven largest global pension markets, from 5% in 1995 to 25% in 2014 (Towers Watson, 2015).

Each of the asset classes within an investment portfolio exhibits specific attributes, including risk–return expectations, investment horizons, and correlations with other asset classes. Trustees should clearly understand these attributes before making investments in order to ensure they are appropriate to the fund's long-term objectives. We discuss traditional and alternative asset classes in more detail in Chapters 7 and 8, respectively.

3.2.3 Setting actuarial assumptions

Actuarial assumptions refer to the assumptions used by a fund's actuary to calculate the present value of the fund's long-term assets and liabilities. Since pension benefits are paid out far into the future, their levels and timing can be uncertain (American Academy of Actuaries, 2004). Therefore, the fund's actuaries use certain assumptions to smooth the stream of future cash flows and better predict the timing of benefit payments (American Academy of Actuaries, 2013).

Actuarial assumptions are selected by trustees with guidance from the fund's actuary, and can be categorized into the following (American Academy of Actuaries, 2004):

- **Economic assumptions**, such as those related to the discount rate, salary inflation, price inflation, and expected long-term return on assets
- **Demographic assumptions**, such as those related to when the participants may terminate employment or retire, how long they are expected to live, as well as assumptions on any disability they may experience during their working years

Box 3.2: Understanding different discount rate methods

Below we use an example provided by the American Academy of Actuaries to illustrate the difference between the market-based and the expected return-based methods, and the resulting impact on pension fund obligations:

- Assume you promise to pay $1 million to another party in 10 years and that you are deemed certain to pay your debt. You could fund this debt with a 10-year zero coupon Treasury note. If the note had an effective return of 3%, an investment of $744,000 would be sufficient to fund the debt with 100% certainty. You might also fund the debt with a smaller amount invested in a diversified portfolio of assets. If you could reasonably expect the portfolio to return 6%, an investment of just $558,000 would be expected to fund the debt, but the ability to meet the obligation with the invested assets would be less certain. The portfolio might earn more or less than 6% over the 10 years.
- Your creditor would be willing to accept the $744,000 Treasury note in settlement of the debt now, since both your debt and the note are certain to pay $1 million in 10 years. But your creditor would not accept the $558,000 diversified portfolio in lieu of the debt because there is no longer certainty that $1 million will be available in 10 years and there is no compensation for the additional risk accepted.
- The higher $744,000 required using the Treasury investment can be considered the price of providing certainty and the $186,000 reduction using the diversified investment is the anticipated savings to the debtor that may result when the debtor accepts the additional investment risk.

Source: American Academy of Actuaries, 2013, pp. 2-3.

The discount rate to be used is perhaps the most important of all actuarial assumptions. Discount rate refers to the rate of return used by funds to calculate the present value of the fund's future pension obligations.

There are two methods for selecting the appropriate discount rate: the **market-based method**, which uses the rate of return on high-quality fixed-income securities at the measurement date, and the **expected return-based method**, which uses the average expected return for the total investment portfolio.

Since the actual investment portfolio is invested in a diverse range of asset classes, the returns generated are expected to be higher than just fixed-income returns. Therefore, the discount rate used under the expected return-based method is higher than the discount rate used under the market-based method, and the resulting present value of pension obligations will be lower or higher, respectively. As a result, the two methods "differ in the relative certainty (the confidence level or probability) that assets equal to the present value would grow as expected if invested as the method assumes" (American Academy of Actuaries, 2013, p. 2).

In the U.S.A., differences in pension fund regulations for public- and private-sector pension plans have impacted the choice of discount rates and consequently asset allocation decisions (Andonov *et al.*, 2013). U.S. public-sector pension plans are subject to the Government Accounting Standards Board (GASB) guidelines that allow the use of the expected returns-based method for discounting future pension obligations. As a result, these plans link their future obligations to expected returns on fund assets rather than the riskiness of these assets. Multiemployer pension plans also use an expected return discount rate. Single-employer pension plans, however, are subject to regulations requiring the use of the market-based method.

Because higher returns can be expected from investments that entail higher risks, the discount rate method used can have an impact on the asset allocation of the fund's assets. As such, it has been observed that public plans have had higher allocations to riskier investments than private plans due to the discount rate method used. Recent proposals to GASB have suggested doing away with linking liability discount rates with expected rates of returns, though the proposals are limited to public pension funds that are classified as being underfunded (Andonov *et al.*, 2013).

The OECD's Guidelines on Funding and Benefit Security state that liability discount rates "should be prudently chosen taking into account the plan liabilities' risk and maturity structure" (Antolin and Stewart, 2009, p. 10). Given the impact of discount rates on asset allocation decisions and on the ability of pension assets to meet future retirement liabilities, trustees should pay special attention when selecting a discount rate. They should also take care to ensure that the selected rate is based on the fund's long-term objectives for its participants and beneficiaries rather than short-term trends.

3.3 Takeaways

With a number of players engaged in the investment value chain, the potential for conflicts of interest is inevitable. What is important is that trustees are aware of this conflict and collectively work to create an incentive structure that rewards players in the chain for doing the right thing, i.e., acting in the ultimate, long-term interest of plan participants and beneficiaries.

A well-constructed IPS can greatly assist trustees in effectively conducting their fund management duties. In addition, trustees should select an asset allocation mix and liability discount rates that appropriately value the long-term, intergenerational nature of pension assets and that are better aligned with the pension fund's investment objectives and goals.

3.4 References

American Academy of Actuaries (2004). *Fundamentals of Current Pension Funding and Accounting for Private Sector Pension Plans: An Analysis by the Pension Committee of the American Academy of Actuaries.* Washington, D.C.: American Academy of Actuaries.

——— (2013). *Measuring Pension Obligations: Discount Rates Serve Various Purposes.* Washington, D.C.: American Academy of Actuaries.

Andonov, A., Bauer, R., & Cremers, M. (2013). Pension fund asset allocation and liability discount rates: Camouflage and reckless risk taking by U.S. public plans? *Social Science Research Network.* Retrieved May 26, 2016 from http://papers.ssrn.com/sol3/papers.cfm?abstract_id=2214890.

Antolin, P., & Stewart, F. (2009). Private pension and policy responses to the financial and economic crisis. *OECD Working Papers on Insurance and Private Pensions,* 36. doi:10.1787/224386871887.

Code of Federal Regulations (2008). *Interpretive Bulletin Relating to the Fiduciary Standard under ERISA in Considering Economically Targeted Investments (29 CFR 2509.94-2 (1)).* Washington, D.C.: Government Printing Office. Retrieved June 15, 2016 from https://www.gpo.gov/fdsys/pkg/CFR-2008-title29-vol9/pdf/CFR-2008-title29-vol9.pdf.

Coffey, G. (2011). Elements of a clearly defined investment policy statement for non-profits. Retrieved June 28, 2016 from http://non-profits.russell.com/outsourced-cio/research/elements-of-a-clearly-defined-investment-policy-statement-for-non-profits.page.

Focusing Capital on the Long Term (2015). *Long-Term Portfolio Guide: Reorienting Portfolio Strategies and Investment Management to Focus Capital on the Long Term.* Retrieved May 26, 2016 from http://www.top1000funds.com/wp-content/uploads/2015/03/FCLT_Long-Term-Portfolio-Guide.pdf.

Kay Review (2012). *The Kay Review of UK Equity Markets and Long-Term Decision Making.* Retrieved May 26, 2016 from https://www.gov.uk/government/uploads/system/uploads/attachment_data/file/253454/bis-12-917-kay-review-of-equity-markets-final-report.pdf.

Stewart, F., & Yermo, J. (2008). Pension fund governance: challenges and potential solutions. *OECD Working Papers on Insurance and Private Pensions,* 18. doi:10.1787/241402256531.

Towers Watson (2015). *Global Pension Assets Study 2015.* Retrieved June 15, 2016 from https://www.towerswatson.com/en-US/Insights/IC-Types/Survey-Research-Results/2015/02/Global-Pensions-Asset-Study-2015.

Vox, 2012. Key functions of asset management. Retrieved June 15, 2016 from http://www.voxeu.org/article/key-functions-asset-management.

Zadek, S., Merme, M., & Samans, R. (2005). *Mainstreaming Responsible Investment.* Geneva, Switzerland: World Economic Forum.

Zanglein, J., & Clark, D. (2001). *Capital Stewardship Certificate Program.* Silver Spring, MD: National Labor College.

4
Pension fund structures and governance

> Every pension fund should have a governing body vested with the power to administer the pension fund and who is ultimately responsible for ensuring the adherence to the terms of the arrangement and the protection of the best interest of plan members and beneficiaries. The responsibilities of the governing body should be consistent with the overriding objective of a pension fund which is to serve as a secure source of retirement income. The governing body should retain ultimate responsibility for the pension fund, even when delegating certain functions to external service providers.
>
> OECD, Guidelines for Pension Fund Governance 2009

As former teacher and union leader Isla Carmichael has pointed out, pension fund trustees are guardians of workers' assets. Strong governance of trustee boards is therefore important for securing the value of these assets for the benefit of workers and their beneficiaries. Unions have long struggled to win better benefits for their members, as well as to strengthen worker representation on trustee boards. Where workers have joint trusteeship, the fund's governance function is greatly enhanced, giving workers a direct opportunity to influence the fund's investment policy alongside workers' goals. As paraphrased from Isla Carmichael, joint trusteeship allows workers the freedom to collaborate with trustees in establishing a protocol that is beneficial to working families while continuing to be financially sound for the pension fund (Carmichael, 2003, p. 57).

Over the years, several trends and events have occurred that have both changed the nature of, and placed greater scrutiny on, the governance structures of pension funds. Among these are:

- A gradual shift in the structure of pension plans from defined benefit (DB) to defined contribution (DC) plans and/or hybrid plans which accelerated after the 2001 technology crisis (Broadbent *et al.*, 2006)
- An ever-increasing focus on short-term, riskier investments at the expense of long-term value creation
- The impacts of the financial crises of the last 15 years that have called into question the "suitability of their [pension funds'] investment strategy and the adequacy of their governance techniques" (Woods and Urwin, 2010, p. 1)

The fallouts of the above trends and events on workers' retirement security have placed much pressure on trustees. In addition, increasing capital market complexities and a multitude of regulations have increased the skill requirements and workload of trustees, many of whom have separate full-time jobs. Nonetheless, trustees owe fiduciary responsibilities to workers, retirees, and their beneficiaries and, as such, must ensure the best management of the assets under their oversight.

In this chapter, our focus is on providing trustees with guidance on good pension fund governance principles, including those required for the implementation of responsible investment strategies. We begin below with a short history of retirement security in the U.S.A.

4.1 The three-legged stool

During the Great Depression of the 1930s the U.S. president, Franklin D. Roosevelt, declared that one of the "Four Freedoms" that citizens ought to enjoy is the "freedom from want," or, in other words, economic and retirement security for those who are at the end of their work life or are incapacitated. As a result, the president signed the Social Security Act (SSA) in 1935 to prevent poverty and deprivation for the nation's seniors, and his assertion that retirement security is a human right has since been enshrined in international law. Prior to that point, many elderly people lived in poverty across the country, but the passage of the SSA began "retiring" this cruel and embarrassing reality (Blackburn, 2002).

Box 4.1: Brief chronology of milestones in the history of pension plans in the U.S.A.

1875 **The first private pension plan** in the U.S.A. is started by the American Express Company

1935 **Social security** is established, with the belief that most people will not live for too long after retirement at age 65

1947 **The Labor–Management Relations Act** (LMRA or "Taft–Hartley" Act) is enacted to provide legal collective bargaining frameworks for pension plans administered jointly by an employer and a union

1974 **The Employee Retirement Income Security Act** (ERISA) is passed by Congress to protect the benefits of private pension retirees

2006 **Pension Protection Act of 2006** is enacted

Source: Georgetown University Law Center, 2010

In another significant milestone, in 1974 the U.S. Congress passed the Employee Retirement Income Security Act (ERISA), which is applicable to both DB and DC plan structures, to better govern the conduct of pension trustees in the private sector. ERISA created the Pension Benefit Guaranty Corporation (PBGC), which collects premiums from private plan sponsors and pays benefits (subject to limitations) if the plan is terminated (Munnell *et al.*, 2007).

Public-sector plans are regulated under state and local laws, as well as certain rules of the federal Internal Revenue Code (IRC) that also apply to private-sector plans. For public plans, constitutional and statutory guarantees at the state level provide member employees similar protections available to ERISA-regulated private plans under federal law (Employee Benefit Research Institute, 2005). Although ERISA covers private pension plans, many aspects of the act are also followed by public-sector plans.

These private- and public-sector employment-based pension plans are seen as one leg of the three-legged stool metaphor of retirement security, with social security and personal savings constituting the other two legs (DeWitt, 1996).

After ERISA, the next major regulation was the enactment of the Pension Protection Act (PPA) of 2006. The PPA was intended to encourage a long-term approach to pension funding and to give trustees tools to reach financial stability. The act subjected public and private pension plans to greater scrutiny with regards to their funding gaps and actuarial accounting practices. In combination with the impacts of the financial crises of the last 15 years, however, some observers claim that the PPA has had the effect of pushing pension plans toward shorter-term investment horizons[1] and accelerating a shift from traditional DB plans to DC plans (Broadbent *et al.*, 2006).

As with the PPA, more recent pension funding legislation, meant to similarly bolster underfunded multiemployer pension plans, was passed at the end of 2014 (in this case, there were political divisions, even among labor leaders, about the extent of the law) (Fletcher, 2014).

4.2 Pension structures

Employment-based pension plans offered by public and private entities fall under the following main categories (Broadbent *et al.*, 2006):

- **Defined benefit (DB) plans.** DB plans are the traditional form of pension plan wherein employers are legally obligated to provide employees with a contractually defined level of benefits (once the benefits have been accrued and vested) based on a formula that takes into account the employees' wages/salary and years of service with the sponsoring employers. As such, benefits are fixed and employers bear the investment risk.
- **Defined contribution (DC) plans.** In DC plans, employees make contributions to their pension plans out of their own pay that are generally matched (to different degrees, once vested) by their employers based on a fixed percentage of earnings. As such, contributions are fixed and employees bear the investment risk (e.g., 401(k) plans, IRAs, etc.).

Within DB plans, some plans have converted to **hybrid plans** that combine features of both DB and DC plan structures. These plans are generally treated as DB plans for tax, accounting, and regulatory purposes but the benefits, accruing in the form of contributions, can be redeemed as a lump sum on retirement, plan termination, or if an employee changes jobs. In hybrid plans, contributions are fixed and both the employers and employees share in the investment risk (e.g., cash balance plans).

DB plans may be further classified as either:

1 Jack Marco, Chairman, Marco Consulting Group, personal communication/interview, December 8, 2014.

- **Single-employer-based private plans**, in which the sponsoring employer selects trust fiduciaries to fully manage the fund
- **Multiemployer-based private plans**, also called "Taft–Hartley" plans, in which a joint retirement pool is established between a union and multiple employers in similar fields of business
- **Public plans**, in which state constitutions and/or statutes often require the plan to be managed as trust funds and overseen by a single trustee or a board of trustees (Bovbjerg, 2008).

In the U.S.A., single-employer plans are not required to have employee representations on their board of trustees; however, in multiemployer plans, the participating employer(s) and the employee union(s) have equal representation on the board (Stewart and Yermo, 2008). Many public plans also have employee representatives who are either directly elected by participants and beneficiaries or are appointed to the board of trustees. The participation of employee representatives on boards of trustees gives plan participants a voice in how their pension plan assets are invested.

4.2.1 DB vs. DC plans

As mentioned, in a DB plan, employers bear the risks associated with investing future retirement income, whereas in a DC plan it is the employees who bear these risks (Broadbent *et al.*, 2006). Most public-sector plans still maintain a DB structure, while most private-sector plans have gradually moved to a DC structure. Where DB plans still exist in the private sector, employee participation in pension plans has been high (U.S. DOL and U.S. BLS, 2013).

In regards to returns for the two types of plan, a recent Towers Watson study reported that DB plans outperformed DC plans on both an asset-weighted and plan-weighted basis between 1995 and 2011 (McFarland, 2013).[2] Importantly, the study points out that in bear markets DB plans better protect retiree assets compared with DC plans; Table 4.1 provides more details:

Studies have also shown that DB plans can deliver the same retirement income at nearly half the cost than that of an individual DC plan account. DB plans are able to achieve higher returns at lower costs for various reasons, including being able to better access and retain professional managers,

2 An asset-weighted measure assigns greater weight to plans with more assets, while a plan-weighted measure weights all plans equally: see McFarland, 2013.

TABLE 4.1 Asset-weighted and plan-weighted median rates of return for DB and DC plans, 1995–2011

	Asset-weighted		Plan-weighted	
	DB	DC	DB	DC
1995 (n=3063)	20.99%	18.72%	19.35%	17.39%
2011 (n=2080)	2.74%	-0.22%	0.36%	−1.15%
Average	8.01%	7.25%	6.73%	6.61%
Average last 10 years	5.87%	5.01%	4.72%	4.65%
Average last 5 years	3.01%	2.62%	2.47%	2.36%
Bear market (00–02, 07–08, 11)	−4.38%	−6.56%	−4.90%	−7.54%
Bull market (95–99, 03–06, 09–10)	14.77%	14.78%	13.07%	14.33%

Source: McFarland, 2013

pool risks, maintain a more diversified portfolio, and negotiate down excess investment management fees (Almeida and Fornia, 2008).

Because DC plans shift the investment risk onto the employee—relying on the employees to adequately contribute toward their own retirement savings while making complex investment decisions—the growth of these plans has brought into question the adequacy of retirement security for millions of participating employees. This is particularly true for low-income employees.[3]

DB plans were once a bastion of the American retirement system; however, pension plans in the U.S.A. have gradually shifted away from DB plans

3 According to a recent survey (Wells Fargo, 2014), the average middle-class American may only have $20,000 in retirement savings. The survey questioned more than a thousand middle-class Americans about the state of their savings plans. Roughly two-thirds of respondents said saving for retirement was "harder" than they had anticipated. A full third of Americans said they won't have sufficient funds to "survive," a glum assessment that flared out among the older respondents with nearly half of Americans in their 50s sharing that concern. Only 40% of Americans 40–50 years old were even saving for retirement. Perhaps the most startling response came from the 22% of Americans who said they would prefer to suffer an "early death" than retire without enough funds to support a comfortable standard of living. Another recent article on the topic (Sputnik International, 2015) points out that many Americans over 55 years of age "have no savings at all or lack the expertise and time to determine whether their employers' retirement plan is a good one."

Box 4.2: From DB to DC plans

Various reasons have been linked to the shift from DB to DC plans, including large pension funding gaps in the aftermath of the 2008 financial crisis; regulatory and accounting reforms that increased DB plan administration costs (particularly the PPA of 2006); greater worker mobility; and the effects of increased longevity of workers on the plan's funding levels (Broadbent *et al.*, 2006).

Teresa Ghilarducci, one of the most respected pension scholars in America, notes that employers moved to DC plans primarily to shift costs and risks to employees. As she explains, when ERISA was passed, it was a time when companies provided pensions to retain skilled workers and reward loyalty. But when employers began shedding older workers, a change in the design of pension plans started to come about. Since the introduction of the 401(k) plans at the beginning of the 1980s, Ghilarducci notes that "the biggest trend we're picking up is that employers are not providing any way for Americans to save for their retirement. So on top of the shift away from traditional plans to 401(k) plans is actually a lesser probability that a firm will even have a retirement account at work" (Breslow, 2013).

In light of the shift from DB to DC plans, pension experts such as David Blitzstein and Ghilarducci have helped design innovative hybrid or variable plans (Blitzstein, 2014) claiming these to be a more sustainable alternative to DC structures. Blitzstein's variable DB plan model, which recently received an IRS determination letter, resembles the Dutch and northern European models that have remained well funded despite economic down cycles (Blitzstein *et al.*, 2006). Similarly, innovations such as the guaranteed retirement account (GRA) proposed by Ghilarducci would "borrow the best features of defined-benefit and defined-contribution plans, including guaranteed retirement benefits that last a lifetime, low administrative costs, and steady contributions" (Ghilarducci and Weller, 2007, p. 2; see also Labor and Employment Relations Association, 2007). In such plans, low-wage workers who otherwise would not have a pension plan "can watch their benefits grow each year as an account balance, but the assets that secure the benefits are held in a pooled trust" (Williams Walsh, 2012).

Though in their early stages of adoption, these models present a heartening alternative to the decline in workers' retirement security in recent years.

to DC plans (see Fig. 4.1). As of 2014, the U.S. DB/DC asset share split stood at 42% and 58%, respectively.

The shift in plan structures is much more pronounced for private plans than public plans; between 1975 and 2005, private-sector plans went from 73% to 36% in DB plans, respectively, whereas the public-sector plans went from 94% to 77% in DB plans during the same time (Pension Review Board, 2013).

DB plans demonstrably provide retirement income security more effectively than other vehicles, though workers may also seek additional sources of income to retire with dignity. Funding these plans and generating sustainable and risk-appropriate investment returns within volatile financial markets are ongoing challenges for trustees and individual investors.

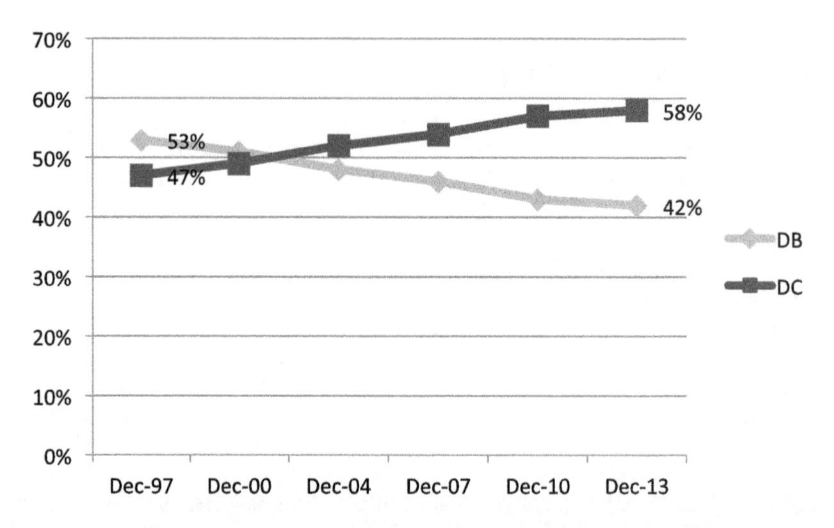

FIGURE 4.1 Shift in the percentage share of U.S. DB and DC pension plan assets, 1997–2003

Source: Towers Watson, 2015

4.3 Pension governance

An important component of a responsible investment strategy is ensuring transparent, inclusive, and sound corporate governance practices, represented by the "G" in ESG, which we discuss in more detail in Chapter 6. Closely related to—and just as important as—the sound governance of companies is the sound governance of pension funds themselves.

Pension fund governance is defined as "the oversight, accountability, transparency, and decision-making norms underpinning the operations and investments of a pension plan," according to governance expert, Ashby Monk (Monk, 2009, p. 3). The goal of good pension fund governance is to minimize potential conflicts of interest between the asset owners and the managers and users of assets (the key players of the investment value chain), with the dual aim to deliver better investment performance and lower the investment costs for all stakeholders.

Some of the benefits of good pension fund governance include:

- **Better returns.** Similar to the positive correlation between good corporate governance and good returns, good pension fund governance has been linked to good investment returns for the fund's asset owners.

- **Lower risk.** When governance controls are tight, pension trustees can better pursue sophisticated investment strategies that may otherwise be deemed riskier—be it investing in alternative asset classes and/or applying responsible investment considerations.
- **Better governance at investee companies.** Strong internal pension fund governance enables capital stewards to also push for higher standards of governance at investee companies, achieving better investment returns in the process. It supports the ability of pension funds to diligently vote proxies, where applicable, as well as engage in active shareholder actions of financial and nonfinancial importance that have the potential to impact the long-term economic value of the fund's assets.
- **Improved bargaining power.** Good fund governance allows trustees to have greater influence on the fund's own corporate sponsors so that retiree benefits may be better secured, particularly in instances of takeovers, mergers, and restructurings.
- **Higher trust among all stakeholders.** Good governance reduces, and is better able to manage, conflicts of interest, thereby increasing trust among all stakeholders.
- **Positive collateral effects on the economy.** As universal owners, pension funds, if governed well, are able to "strengthen the fund's role as effective shareholders" and that of other participants in the capital markets. Good governance may also reduce the need for "prescriptive regulation," benefiting all within the economy (Stewart and Yermo, 2008, p. 5).

4.3.1 Principles of good fund governance

Under numerous laws, particularly ERISA, pension fund trustees owe certain fiduciary duties, including transparency, competence, and accountability, to the beneficiaries of the funds that they manage. With increasing underfunding of pension obligations, high opacity around investment decision-making, and often short-term and riskier investment focus, however, pension plans, particularly DB plans, have come under much scrutiny for their governance structures. These factors are compounded for multinational corporate pension plans that may be subject to slimmer requirements depending on the pension governance laws of the countries in which they operate (Mercer Human Resource Consulting, 2006).

Box 4.3: DC plan governance challenges

Although details on the structure of DC plans are beyond the scope of this *Handbook*, the increasing number of such plans bears a need to shed some light on their governance structures and resulting challenges. DC plans have a "dual model of governance" in the form of participant self-governance and the plan sponsor governance. The lack of investment expertise of plan participants, combined with their "lack of capacity" to regulate plan sponsors who may have a lower stake, or no stake at all, in the structure and performance of the plan, adds additional complexity to DC plan governance (Clark and Urwin, 2010).

As a result of these challenges, few DC plans offer responsible investment options to plan participants. However, when a DC plan is managed by an activist plan sponsor, such as TIAA-CREF or Calvert Investments, participants get better access to responsible investment options and are also more likely to invest in such options. According to a recent survey by Calvert of 1,231 DC plan participants and 295 eligible nonparticipants, "if a plan offered responsible investment fund options in all asset classes, 32% of all respondents would direct all plan contributions into the responsible investment mutual funds, 53% would direct a portion and 15% are unsure" (Burr, 2015).

Many union-affiliated Taft–Hartley plan sponsors offer both DB and DC plans to their employee beneficiaries. Given that a large and growing percentage of retirement assets are in DC plans, it is important to find ways to better manage DC retirement assets—to close the performance gap with DB plan portfolios, to find ways for DC retirement investments to promote sustainable and worker-friendly goals and values, and to develop DC governance structures that empower workers and their representatives, ensuring that these goals and values guide investment managers. A number of experts are now working on new models for the management of DC retirement savings that can remedy many of traditional deficiencies of this type of plan and better promote workers' interests in the investment of their retirement savings.

It is important to note that pension funds and other large institutional investors have been instrumental in the increased adoption of good governance practices among the companies they invest in, particularly for public-sector companies (Clapman, 2007). However, according to a World Economic Forum report, pension funds themselves have failed to meet the "bedrock governance standards" they demand of their investee companies (Zadek *et al.*, 2005). If pension funds are to better secure retiree benefits alongside the inclusion of responsible investment practices, it is important that trustees work toward improving the fund's own governance models to stricter standards of risk management.

Table 4.2 summarizes common areas of shortfall in pension fund governance, and provides examples for good governance principles in each of those areas. These insights have been gleaned from numerous reports by practitioners, academics, and global organizations active in the promotion of good pension fund governance standards, as listed in Appendix B.

Box 4.4: Good governance and fiduciary duty

Good pension governance and fiduciary duty are strongly linked. The principles of good governance that we describe below go hand in hand with the fiduciary responsibilities of trustees as stewards of workers' capital. In fact, the Canadian Association of Pension Supervisory Authorities (CAPSA) in its governance guidelines defines good governance as "the structure and process for overseeing, managing and administering a plan to ensure that fiduciary and other obligations are met" (CAPSA, 2004).

As an example, without a clear delineation of the roles and responsibilities of the players involved in the management of a pension fund's assets, the fiduciary responsibility to the fund is compromised. But good governance practices that clarify the fiduciary duties of players in the value chain allow the fund to have better accountability of its investment decisions and improve its risk management processes—outcomes that are part of a fund's fiduciary obligations. Similarly, improving trustees' knowledge and understanding of the investment management process empowers both trustees and internal staff to take better control of pension investment decisions and thus better meet their fiduciary responsibilities.

Trustee fiduciary duties are discussed in more detail in the next chapter.

4.3.2 Good fund governance and responsible investments

The most important goal of good pension fund governance is the alignment of the fund's investment strategy with the provision of risk-adjusted and positive long-term returns on assets. A good pension fund governance strategy should therefore recognize and prepare for all material risks and opportunities that can be expected to have an impact on the long-term value of pension assets. These risks and opportunities may relate to financial factors such as future earnings, or nonfinancial factors such as environmental safety and workers' rights. As such, good fund governance is intricately aligned with responsible investment strategies that enhance the fund's long-term investment value while enabling trustees to effectively conduct their fiduciary responsibilities.

Unfortunately, lack of clarity on fiduciary responsibilities and weak governance structures have continued to "dissuade trustees from adopting investment strategies ... that break with convention" (Woods and Urwin, 2010, p. 13). In order to align fund governance with responsible investment strategies, we suggest the model advanced by pension fund governance experts Woods and Urwin, with its focus on achieving mission clarity and developing a strong set of investment beliefs (Woods and Urwin, 2010).

Well-articulated mission and investment beliefs statements will provide clarity on investment objectives not only to trustees, but also to the

TABLE 4.2 Common governance shortfalls and principles of good governance

Attributes	Shortfalls	Principles of good governance
Plan governance documents	Lack of risk-based metrics to governance. Plan documents that are weak and not clear on the mission, investment beliefs, aims, or the goals of trustees.	Start with setting risk-based governance principles for the board, "focusing on the main threats facing pension fund beneficiaries and the pension system as a whole" (Antolin and Stewart, 2009). Also, set up a comprehensive investment policy statement (IPS) along with clearly articulated responsible mission and investment beliefs statements that together outline the "goals of trustees and their agents in investing trust funds on behalf of beneficiaries" (Woods and Urwin, 2010, p. 6).
Investment value chain responsibilities	Lack of clear delineation of the roles and fiduciary responsibilities among players in the value chain, leading players to evade responsibility, particularly in the aftermath of economic down cycles.	Clarify the fiduciary duties of players in the value chain as part of the fund's governance set-up. This will help increase accountability with regards to investment decisions.
Fund management	Opaque, with little information to participants on how their funds are managed and invested.	Increase transparency and reporting of pension investments and management so that participants have greater confidence in plan governance.
Duration of strategy	Short-term focused.	Align investment strategy with the long-term horizon of plan liabilities and intergenerational pension equity.
Worker/employee representation	Currently restricted to multiemployer plans and some public employee plans, per regulations. Where not mandated by law, participants have limited voice in fund management and operations.	Include workers/employees on trustee boards, beyond where mandated by law, for increased alignment with workers' retirement goals. As mentioned, trustees are guardians of workers' capital, so workers' interests must be represented in trustee decisions.

Attributes	**Shortfalls**	**Principles of good governance**
Trustee and internal staff expertise	Lack of in-house knowledge of fiduciary responsibilities, governance requirements, and/or capital markets, leading to over-reliance on external advisors and managers, herding, and myopic benchmarking.	Empower trustees and internal staff to take better control of pension investment decisions. Increase trustee knowledge of fiduciary, management, and investment principles so that they may be "fit-for-purpose" (Clark and Urwin, 2010) and better able to carry out their fiduciary responsibilities. Invest in hiring internal staff talent—it can decrease investment costs and reduce agency separation.
Responsibility vs. expertise	Mismatched levels of trustee responsibilities vs. expertise, potentially leading to investments in riskier assets that are not well understood.	Before investing in an asset class or company, trustees should first exhibit understanding of those asset classes and determine whether they have the necessary skills to internally invest and/or select and monitor external managers in a particular strategy (Stewart and Yermo, 2008).
Manager/advisor selection and oversight	Lack of fit between the pension fund's mission and investment beliefs and those of the external service providers. Weak oversight of hired firms.	Perform a thorough upfront selection of managers and advisors to ensure alignment with plan mission and goals. Once a selection has been made, trustees still have responsibility to set appropriate oversight controls—outsourcing pension management duty doesn't mean trustees can wash their hands of oversight.
Conflicts of interest	Reactive approach to conflicts.	Establish a process for proactively addressing conflicts through a participatory process that brings trustees, internal staff, and other fiduciaries on the same page from the very beginning.
Self-evaluation/ review	Not engaged in self-evaluation of board effectiveness or lacking sufficient strength or influence to do so.	Trustees should establish self-evaluation processes so that they may be better able to identify and improve weaknesses in their monitoring and decision-making activities. They should promote a culture that questions conventional wisdom and learns from and adapts to changing conditions (Stewart and Yermo, 2008).

Box 4.5: How a multiemployer fund improved its internal governance structure

The **IAM National Pension Fund,** which represents the International Association of Machinists and Aerospace Workers, has $11 billion in assets, and is the fifth-largest multiemployer fund.

In 2011, the pension fund decided to first restructure its board of trustees in an effort to better align the fund's investment goals with responsible investment strategies. Prior to the restructuring, the employer representatives on the board of the IAM Fund were mostly from small companies and often these representatives were retirees. The resulting board composition created a more distant relationship between the employers represented by the IAM and the board itself. To correct this misalignment, IAM began to include on its trustee board current employee representatives from larger employers, such as General Dynamics and United Airlines. The restructuring is helping the board achieve both better buy-in from member employers and greater exposure to the corporate world (Sleigh, 2014).

Source: Steve Sleigh, Former Fund Director, IAM National Pension Fund, personal communication/interview, November 5, 2014.

fund's advisors, investment managers, and plan participants and beneficiaries. Such clarity can be expected to reduce conflicts of interest among key stakeholders in the investment value chain and to increase trustee confidence in their decision to pursue a responsible investment strategy. Please see Appendix B for sample responsible investment beliefs statements from investor practitioners.

Furthermore, trustees "should be able to demonstrate that their decisions were in the best interests of beneficiaries" (Woods and Urwin, 2010, p. 13) via appropriate and thorough documentation of these decisions. We further discuss the need for appropriate documentation of trustee actions in subsequent chapters.

In addition to developing strong mission and investment beliefs statements, other best-practice governance principles to achieve the alignment between good governance and responsible investments include (Clark and Urwin, 2008):

- Better trustee education and leadership around responsible investments
- Clear delineation of the roles and responsibilities of the players in the investment value chain
- A risk-based ESG integration framework for pension investments

Box 4.6: Investment mission and beliefs statements

An **investment mission statement** is explained as a document that articulates "the goals of trustees and their agents in investing trust funds on behalf of beneficiaries" (Woods and Urwin, 2010, p. 6). Whether these goals also include a desire to invest for the long term and/or via responsible investment practices, the mission statement should clearly articulate all such considerations. Similarly, an **investment beliefs statement** is seen as providing insights into the "assumptions underlying the pension funds' investment practices" (Woods and Urwin, 2010, p. 7).

Box 4.7: Aligning staff and trustee board interests

Allan Emkin, managing director and founder, Pension Consulting Alliance (PCA), notes that for:

> responsible, progressive investments, we need Boards to push in that direction. The staff is not always interested in the same values as those of some of the trustees. Large Canadian funds like the Ontario Municipal Employees Retirement System (OMERS) and the Ontario Teachers' Pension Plan (OTPP) have a decent connection between their boards and staff and so that leads to more aligned outcomes. (Personal communication/interview, July 16, 2014)

Similarly, Michael Garland, assistant comptroller for Corporate Governance and Responsible Investment at New York City Office of the Comptroller, points to mechanisms that are being put in place within the New York City Pension Funds' governance structure to give staff and other subcommittees more authority in relation to their roles while ensuring appropriate oversight by the trustee board (personal communication/interview, December 17, 2014).

4.4 Takeaways

Various trends are shaping the retirement security of everyday working people. In light of these trends, trustees need to pay special attention to the governance structures of the pension plans under their oversight and management. The provision of joint trusteeship on trustee boards in particular is an important step toward strengthening fund governance structures.

If held to the principles of good fund governance, pension funds can not only better manage and avoid the conflicts of interest discussed in the previous chapter, but also better integrate responsible investment strategies into their investment decision-making process.

4.5 References

Almeida, A., & Fornia, W.B. (2008). A better bang for the buck: the economic efficiencies of defined benefit pension plans. *National Institute for Retirement Security*. Retrieved June 28, 2016 from http://www.nirsonline.org/index.php?option=com_content&task=view&id=121&Itemid=48.

Antolin, P., & Stewart, F. (2009). Private pension and policy responses to the financial and economic crisis. *OECD Working Papers on Insurance and Private Pensions*, 36. doi:10.1787/224386871887.

Blackburn, R. (2002). *Banking on Death or Investing in Life: The History and Future of Pensions*. London: Verso.

Blitzstein, D.S. (2014). *United States Pension Benefit Plan Design Innovation: Labor Unions as Agents of Change*. Pension Research Council WP 2014-10. Retrieved June 1, 2016 from http://ssrn.com/abstract=2523167.

Blitzstein, D., Mitchell, O.S., & Utkus, S.P. (Eds). (2006). *Restructuring Retirement Risks*. New York, NY: Oxford University Press.

Bovbjerg, B.D. (2008). *State and Local Government Pension Plans: Current Structure and Funded Status*. Retrieved June 28, 2016 from http://www.gao.gov/new.items/d08983t.pdf.

Breslow, J.M. (2013, April 23). Teresa Ghilarducci: Why the 401(k) is a "failed experiment." *PBS Frontline*. Retrieved June 1, 2016 from http://www.pbs.org/wgbh/frontline/article/teresa-ghilarducci-why-the-401k-is-a-failed-experiment/.

Broadbent, J., Palumbo, M., & Woodman, E. (2006). *The Shift from Defined Benefit to Defined Contribution Pension Plans: Implications for Asset Allocation and Risk Management*. Retrieved June 28, 2016 from https://www.bis.org/publ/wgpapers/cgfs27broadbent3.pdf.

Burr, B.B. (2015, September 24). Despite confusion, responsible investing a draw for DC plan participants, survey finds. *Pensions & Investments*. Retrieved June 1, 2016 from http://www.pionline.com/article/20150924/ONLINE/150929923/despite-confusion-responsible-investing-a-draw-for-dc-plan-participants-survey-finds.

CAPSA (Canadian Association of Pension Supervisory Authorities) (2004). *CAPSA Guideline No. 4: Pension Plan Governance Guidelines and Self-assessment Questionnaire*. Toronto, Canada: CAPSA.

Carmichael, I. (2003). Fiduciary responsibility. In I. Carmichael & J. Quarter (Eds.), *Money on the Line: Workers' Capital in Canada* (pp. 53-69). Ottawa, Canada: Canadian Centre for Policy Alternatives.

Clapman, P. (2007). *Committee on Fund Governance: Best Practice Principles*. Retrieved June 1, 2016 from http://www.aztreasury.gov/wp-content/uploads/2012/12/Stanford-Institutional-Investors-Forum.pdf.

Clark, G.L., & Urwin, R. (2008). Best-practice pension fund governance. *Journal of Asset Management*, 9(1), 2-21.

——— (2010). DC pension fund best-practice design and governance. Retrieved June 1, 2016 from http://papers.ssrn.com/sol3/papers.cfm?abstract_id=1652680.

DeWitt, L. (1996). Research note #1: origins of the three-legged stool metaphor for social security. Retrieved June 1, 2016 from http://www.ssa.gov/history/stool.html.

Employee Benefit Research Institute (2005). 39: Regulation of Public-Sector Pension Plans. In *Fundamentals of Employee Benefit Plans*. Washington, D.C. Retrieved June 1, 2016 from http://www.ebri.org/pdf/publications/books/fundamentals/fund39.pdf.

Fletcher, M. (2014, December 9). Congressional leaders hammer out a deal to allow pension plans to cut retiree benefits. *The Washington Post.* Retrieved June 1, 2016 from https://www.washingtonpost.com/business/economy/congressional-leaders-hammer-out-deal-to-allow-pension-plans-to-cut-retiree-benefits/2014/12/09/4650d420-7ef6-11e4-9f38-95a187e4c1f7_story.html.

Georgetown University Law Center (2010). A timeline of the evolution of retirement in the United States. Retrieved June 1, 2016 from http://scholarship.law.georgetown.edu/legal/50.

Ghilarducci, T., & Weller, C.E. (2007). *Briefing Paper #204: Guaranteed Retirement Accounts: Toward Retirement Income Security.* Retrieved June 28, 2016 from http://www.epi.org/publication/bp204/.

Labor and Employment Relations Association (2007). *Employee Pensions: Policies, Problems and Possibilities.* Champaign, IL: Labor and Employment Relations Association.

McFarland, B. (2013). DB versus DC investment returns: the 2009–2011 update. Retrieved May 26, 2016 from http://www.towerswatson.com/en-US/Insights/Newsletters/Americas/insider/2013/DB-Versus-DC-Investment-Returns-the-2009-2011-Update.

Mercer Human Resource Consulting (2006). *Global Governance of Retirement Plans Survey 2006: Meeting the Challenge of Implementation: Europe.* New York, NY: Mercer Human Resource Consulting.

Monk, A.H. (2009). The geography of pension liabilities and fund governance in the United States. *Environment and Planning A,* 41(4), 859-878. Retrieved June 28, 2016 from https://www.researchgate.net/profile/Ashby_Monk/publication/46559773_The_geography_of_pension_liabilities_and_fund_governance_in_the_United_States/links/0deec53211eb5a7e33000000.pdf/download?version=vrp.

Munnell, A.H., Haverstick, K., & Soto, M. (2007). *Why have defined benefit plans survived in the public sector?* Retrieved June 1, 2016 from http://crr.bc.edu/wp-content/uploads/2007/12/slp_2.pdf.

Pension Review Board (2013). *Retirement Benefits in the Public and Private Sectors: A Comparison of Trends, Regulatory Environments, and Related Issues.* Austin, Texas: Pension Review Board.

Sputnik International (2015, June 8). Most Americans aren't ready for retirement, half over 55 have no funds. *Sputnik International.* Retrieved May 26, 2016 from http://sputniknews.com/us/20150608/1023067957.html.

Stewart, F., & Yermo, J. (2008). Pension fund governance: challenges and potential solutions. *OECD Working Papers on Insurance and Private Pensions,* 18. doi:10.1787/241402256531.

Towers Watson (2015). *Global Pensions Asset Study: 2015.* Retrieved May 26, 2016 from https://www.towerswatson.com/en-US/Insights/IC-Types/Survey-Research-Results/2015/02/Global-Pensions-Asset-Study-2015.

U.S. DOL (U.S. Department of Labor), & U.S. BLS (U.S. Bureau of Labor Statistics) (2013). *National Compensation Survey: Employee Benefits in the United States, March 2013.* Retrieved June 1, 2016 from http://www.bls.gov/ncs/ebs/benefits/2013/ebbl0052.pdf.

Wells Fargo (2014, October 22). Wells Fargo survey finds saving for retirement not happening for a third of middle class. Retrieved May 26, 2016 from https://www.wellsfargo.com/about/press/2014/middle-class-retirement-saving_1022/.

Williams Walsh, M. (2012, March 26). New ideas on pension: use states. *The New York Times.* Retrieved June 28, 2016 from http://www.nytimes.com/2012/03/27/business/ideas-on-company-pensions-include-turning-to-states.html.

Woods, C., & Urwin, R. (2010). Putting sustainable investing into practice: A governance framework for pension funds. *Journal for Business Ethics,* 92(1), 1-19.

Zadek, S., Merme, M., & Samans, R. (2005). *Mainstreaming Responsible Investment.* Geneva, Switzerland: World Economic Forum.

5
Reclaiming fiduciary duty

> The primary thing that workers need for their retirement [is] money, but don't [workers] also need a safe, clean, decent world in which to spend it? These ends are not economically exclusive, institutional shareholders hold not only the proxy power but also the legal obligation to help deliver both.
>
> Robert Monks, corporate governance guru

Fiduciary duty is an old concept, embedded in common law, that provides a framework for how trustees govern pension assets. In titling this chapter, we are purposefully borrowing from a modernized approach to fiduciary duty put forward by progressive pension scholars (Hawley *et al.*, 2011).

Outside the U.S.A., as we mentioned earlier, modernized laws drive the consideration of ESG and other nonfinancial issues in the management of pension assets or by investment funds:

> For example, the U.K. Pensions Act (2000) requires pension funds to disclose how they account for sustainability factors in constructing their investment portfolios. Germany requires the use of sustainability criteria as part of the fiduciary's duty, and France requires public pension funds to [disclose] how their investment policy guidelines address social and environmental issues. Australia's Financial Service Reform Act requires superannuation (i.e., retirement) and mutual funds to disclose the extent to which ESG considerations are taken into account. South Africa mandates that institutional investors, including pension funds, "before making an investment into and while invested in an asset, consider any factor which may materially affect the sustainable long-term performance of the investment, including those of an environmental, social and governance character."
>
> (Caplan *et al.*, 2013, p. 5; their quotation from Hawley *et al.*, 2011)

The PRI's publication, *Fiduciary Duty in the 21st Century* (PRI, 2015), settles the argument and notes that fiduciary duty can no longer be used as a barrier to implementing ESG principles. The global report, drawn from extensive outreach and interviews, finds that ESG issues are in fact integral to financial performance. "We've found that failing to consider longer term drivers like ESG in investment practices is actually a failure of fiduciary duty," argues Fiona Reynolds, managing director, PRI (Rundell, 2015).

And in the U.S.A., though focused on ETIs, the recent U.S. DOL Interpretive Bulletin 15-01 (U.S. DOL, 2015), the new guidance on such targeted investments, is potentially a game-changer. ERISA states that the first duty of pension trustees is to oversee the investment of plan assets prudently and solely in the interests of plan participants and beneficiaries (U.S. DOL, 2014). In crafting their funds' investment strategy, pension trustees must make workers' retirement security their first priority and can never sacrifice returns for extra-financial goals (Croft, 2009). But this new DOL rule, and other guiding laws and court rulings, have long held that trustees can take nonfinancial goals into account in their investment decisions. We cite this and other decisions in this chapter, which primarily focuses on the U.S.A. but references common law.

Pension trustees often fear the personal liability associated with their responsibilities as fiduciaries; however, the duty is a relatively simple and straightforward concept. If trustees do their homework, follow the basic standards, and, most importantly, document their processes in carrying out their fiduciary duty—the most basic of trust principles—they can protect themselves and ensure that they do the best by the plan's participants and beneficiaries.

In this chapter, we use the framework provided by ERISA to discuss the following fiduciary duty standards:

- Exclusive benefit rule
- Prudence duty
- Plan document rule
- Diversification rule
- Fair costs rule

Fiduciary duty has at times been defined erroneously as the maxim of solely maximizing profit. Since there is conflicting legal reasoning for this interpretation error, we begin with some history on the evolution of the fiduciary duty standard to help clarify it.

5.1 A brief history of fiduciary duty

The idea of fiduciary duty is ancient, emerging in Europe during feudalism. The word "prudence" derives from the Latin term for "foresight" and means acting with or showing care and thought for the future. The concept of fiduciary trusts came about as a way for families to pass on their wealth to their children. Trusts were established to ensure that, according to the law of primogeniture, a "prudent" man overseeing a family's assets would act only in the interests of the male heirs of the family, and not on his own behalf.

But we begin with U.S. trust law, which originated with an 1830 case in Massachusetts, Harvard College v. Amory. The ruling stated that the trustee's duty is to:

> Conduct himself faithfully and exercise a sound discretion, observe how men of prudence, discretion and intelligence manage their own affairs, not in regard to speculation, but in regard to the permanent disposition of their funds, considering the probable income as well as the probable safety of the capital to be invested.

The above decision overturned the rules of the English courts of equity that had restricted investments to government debt and well-secured mortgages and had explicitly banned certain other investments. These rules,

Box 5.1: DOL and prudence rules

Prudence focuses on the process for making fiduciary decisions. Therefore, it is wise to document decisions and the basis for those decisions. For instance, in hiring a plan service provider, a fiduciary may want to survey a number of potential providers, asking for the same information and enforcing the same requirements. By doing so, a fiduciary can document the process and make a meaningful comparison and selection. Here are, from pension legal expert Jayne Zanglein, steps to ensure procedural prudence:

1. Review your plan documents
2. Delegate investment duties, where appropriate
3. Prudently select and monitor advisors and service providers
4. Hire experts to evaluate and structure proposed transactions
5. Do your "due diligence"
6. Avoid conflicts of interest and prohibited transactions
7. Carefully evaluate proposed transactions with board, staff, and appropriate advisors

Source: Zanglein and Clark, 2001, p. 56.

called the "legal list" approach, were adopted generally after the South Sea bubble of the early 1700s. The changing complexities of the financial and economic markets made the legal list rule impractical, however (Hawley *et al.*, 2011). As such, the Harvard case articulated an objective, behavioral standard for trustee investment practice, focusing on conduct and imposing duties of care and loyalty rather than following the legal list approach. While subsequent decisions reversed or confused the 1830 case, modern law now stands behind it.

The passage of ERISA by Congress in 1974 codified the prudent person rule as the crux of fiduciary duty into permanent law in the U.S.A. As Jayne Zanglein pointed out, ERISA was enacted to protect the interests of pension plan participants and beneficiaries, and to ensure that plan assets would be properly managed and available at retirement (Zenglein and Clark, 2001). We take a closer look into the ERISA mandate that underlies fiduciary responsibility in the following sections.[1]

5.2 ERISA rules for fiduciary duty

The DOL, which oversees ERISA, notes that fiduciaries have important duties and responsibilities and are subject to standards of conduct because they act on behalf of the ultimate asset owners. For pension fund trustees subject to ERISA, these responsibilities include a requirement to manage the fund:

> with the care, skill, prudence and diligence under the circumstances then prevailing that a prudent [person] acting in a like capacity and familiar with such matters would use in the conduct of an enterprise of a like character and with like aims.
>
> (Legal Information Institute, 2015)

Many of the actions involved in operating a plan make the person or entity performing them a fiduciary. As such, fiduciary status is based on the functions performed for the plan, not just on a person's title. A plan must have at least one fiduciary (a person or entity) named in the written plan—or through a process described in the plan—as having control over the plan's

1 A new rule anticipated by the U.S. Labor Department would raise investment advice standards for retirement accounts. The new regulation will require investment advisors and brokers alike to adopt the fiduciary investment standard, hopefully reducing conflicts of interest and high-fee investment products.

operations. The named fiduciary can be identified by office or by name and can be an administrative committee or a company's board of directors. Plan fiduciaries will ordinarily include the trustee, investment advisers, all individuals exercising discretion in the administration of the plan, all members of a plan's administrative committee (if it has such a committee), and those who select committee officials. Furthermore, the fiduciary rules *do not just affect trustees*. As noted in the PRI paper, *Responsible Investment and Fiduciary Duty*:

> In the United States, ERISA explicitly states that fiduciary liability attaches not only to trustees but also to anyone exercising discretion over investment plan assets. That is, under ERISA, asset managers have direct fiduciary obligations, and the appointment of asset managers is itself a fiduciary function. (PRI, 2014, p. 1)

Box 5.2: The ERISA Prudent Person Standard of Care

1. Subject to sections 1103(c) and (d), 1342, and 1344 of this title, a fiduciary shall discharge his duties with respect to a plan solely in the interest of the participants and beneficiaries and–
   A. for the exclusive purpose of:
      i. providing benefits to participants and their beneficiaries; and
      ii. defraying reasonable expenses of administering the plan;
   B. with the care, skill, prudence, and diligence under the circumstances then prevailing that a prudent [person] acting in a like capacity and familiar with such matters would use in the conduct of an enterprise of a like character and with like aims;
   C. by diversifying the investments of the plan so as to minimize the risk of large losses, unless under the circumstances it is clearly prudent not to do so; and
   D. in accordance with the documents and instruments governing the plan insofar as such documents and instruments are consistent with the provisions of this subchapter and subchapter III.
2. In the case of an eligible individual account plan (as defined in section 1107(d)(3) of this title), the diversification requirement of paragraph (1)(C) and the prudence requirement (only to the extent that it requires diversification) of paragraph (1)(B) is not violated by acquisition or holding of qualifying employer real property or qualifying employer securities (as defined in section 1107(d)(4) and (5) of this title).

Source: Legal Information Institute, 2015.

5.3 A short summary of ERISA fiduciary responsibilities

5.3.1 Exclusive benefit rule: acting solely in the interest of plan participants and their beneficiaries and with the exclusive purpose of providing benefits to them

The exclusive benefit rule represents the duty of loyalty, which is perhaps the cardinal rule of fiduciary duty. Trustees must ensure that any decisions related to pension fund management primarily benefit the plan's participants and beneficiaries. There may be an incidental benefit to other individuals as long as this cardinal rule is not violated. The duty of impartiality, an element of the duty of loyalty, "requires that trustees balance short-term and long-term considerations" and refers to the intergenerational nature of pension equity (Hawley *et al.*, 2011). Impartiality also requires that trustees' conduct cannot be influenced by their personal favoritism. This duty also requires attention to long-term issues, especially where myopic investment practices might have the effect of destroying long-term value.

As legal scholar Keith Johnson has noted, little attention has been paid to the introductory phrase in the ERISA Prudent Person standard which, it bears repeating:

> sets forth a separate, overarching requirement that fiduciaries "*shall*" discharge their duties "*in the interest of the participants and beneficiaries*," imposing an obligation that is independent from the following phrase, "*and* for the exclusive purpose of providing benefits" [their emphasis]. It appears that excessive investment herding behaviors, obsession with short-term performance and inattention to systemic risks, raises concerns about compliance with the first prong of the ERISA fiduciary duty clause cited above, because such practices may not be in the long-term interest of participants.
>
> (Johnson and de Graaf, 2009, p. 5 n. 14)

5.3.2 Prudence duty: carrying out duties with care and forethought

During Congressional hearings held before the passage of ERISA, evidence was presented that exposed gross misuse and theft by certain employers and others of workers' pension assets. In response, Congress adopted the prudence rule as a core tenet of ERISA. The duty to act prudently is one of the central responsibilities of fiduciaries under ERISA, according to which prudent investors must consider diversification and returns whether relative, projected or expected (U.S. DOL, 2014).

Prudence is not judged by the success of the investment viewed in hindsight, but is determined by the procedural process by which the investment decision was made (Marshall v. Glass/Metal Association). In addition, trustees are protected by the safe harbor rule, which states that if a fiduciary complies with the prudence regulation, the investment is deemed prudent. However, if the fiduciary does not comply with that regulation, the investment is not imprudent *per se* (Snow Spalding and Kramer, 1997).

Exercising fiduciary duties requires expertise in a variety of areas, such as investments and financial planning. A fiduciary lacking experience in a particular area will want to hire someone with the professional knowledge to carry out these responsibilities for plan assets.

Pension scholars point out that pension fiduciary standards are stricter than standards for corporate directors:

> Though often compared to corporate directors in terms of statutory duties, pension fiduciaries are held to a higher standard of conduct that has different legal roots ... Also, the duty of loyalty owed by pension fiduciaries is to the actual human beneficiaries, not to the legal entity. There is not the same ambiguity as may be inherent in corporate law, which imposes a duty to act in the best interests of "the corporation." (Hawley *et al.*, 2011, p. 7)

5.3.3 Plan document rule: following the plan (unless inconsistent with ERISA)

The plan document rule is a mainstay of fiduciary duty. Plan documents serve as the foundation for plan operations, and ERISA requires trustees to act in accordance with the documents and instruments governing the plan. As DOL notes, plan documents include the plan description, summary plan description, collective bargaining agreement, trust agreement, investment management agreement, investment guidelines, and other instruments under which the plan was established or is operated (Snow Spalding and Kramer, 1997).

Trustees will want to be familiar with their plan documents, especially when drawn up by a third-party service provider, and periodically review the documents to make sure these remain current. For example, if a plan official named in the document changes, the plan document must be updated to reflect that change.

5.3.4 Diversification rule: diversifying plan investments

Ensuring appropriate diversification is another key fiduciary duty of trustees. The diversification of investments is the practice whereby investments are made in different asset classes, geographies, or industries with different risk–return characteristics. The basic rationale is that by allocating funds to a variety of investments (rather than putting all your eggs in one basket), any losses that may occur in one area due to a particular event may be offset by gains in another area. In addition, each class of investments should be considered in light of its impact on the pension fund's total investment portfolio.

Once again, trustees will want to document their evaluation and investment decisions with regards to the plan's asset allocation. Trustees should also note that while diversification can help minimize the risk of loss to the plan's total investments, it does not, in itself, guarantee protection from losses.

The popularity of the diversification of pension investments has its roots in Modern Portfolio Theory (MPT) developed by Nobel laureate Harry M. Markovitz in the late 1950s. MPT attempts to maximize a portfolio's expected return for a given amount of risk by selecting various uncorrelated investments. The idea is that investments should not be selected based on their own merits, but rather based on their impact on the entire portfolio. However, as demonstrated during the 2008 Wall Street financial crisis in particular, previously uncorrelated asset classes can converge just as the benefits of diversification are most needed (Hawley *et al.*, 2011). In a survey of pension trustees after the financial crash, two Harvard researchers noted:

> For instance, conventional notions of risk and return do not seem to match up to fund's recent experience, as diversification could not protect portfolios against the crisis, and many trustees have found the crisis leading them to revisit the role that Modern Portfolio Theory (MPT), among other theories, plays in guiding their investment strategy. (Wood and Youngdahl, 2011, p. 4)

As noted in a report by Ceres:

> the interpretation of fiduciary duty has evolved significantly over time and must continue to evolve to adjust to changing social and economic realities. For example, rigid rules specifying prohibited and permitted investments gave way to MPT and diversification across multiple asset classes. It is again time to re-examine current concepts of "prudent" institutional investing in light of basic fiduciary duty principles and new factors affecting investment risk and opportunity.
> (Ellsworth and Snow Spalding, 2013, p. 11)

5.3.5 Fair costs rule: paying only reasonable plan expenses

As DOL explains, fees are just one of several factors fiduciaries need to consider when selecting service providers and plan investments. While the law does not specify a permissible level of fees, it does require that fees charged to a plan be "reasonable." When fees for services are paid out of plan assets, fiduciaries will want to understand the fees and expenses charged and the services provided. They will want to monitor the plan's fees and expenses to ensure that they continue to be reasonable.

In comparing estimates from prospective service providers, trustees should ask which services are covered for the estimated fees and which are not. Some providers offer a number of services for one fee, referred to as a "bundled" service arrangement. Others charge separately for individual services. Trustees should compare all services to be provided with the total cost for each provider. They should consider whether the estimate includes services not specified or needed. Remember, all services have costs.

In recent years, pension funds have become much more diligent in enforcing the fair costs rule. There have been a number of highly publicized decisions by pension funds that strongly questioned the reasonableness of service provider fees, especially those charged by hedge funds and private capital funds.

5.4 The faulty theory of solely maximizing profits

Pension funds, as fiduciary institutions, have large and diverse investment portfolios and long-term time-horizons. It makes little logical or financial sense for pension funds to focus solely on maximizing the short-term price of a company's shares. A small shareholder might benefit from encouraging a company to pursue risky strategies that put the company at risk and/or harm bondholders; pension funds, as universal owners, do not benefit from such approaches.

Indeed, pension funds, and other large institutional funds who, "own the economy as a whole" (Bernstein and Hawley, 2014, p. 172), may actually harm their overall portfolio's returns by focusing solely on maximizing share value on a firm-by-firm basis. For example, a fund's equity portfolio may decline in aggregate value when the companies it holds increase their profits by imposing external costs on, and withholding external benefits from, each other. Such short-term strategies hurt a universal owner that holds equity in thousands of firms, owns bonds and real estate, and whose beneficiaries have interests not only as stockholders, but also as "stakeholders"—employees, consumers, and citizens:

> ULLICO's responsible investment philosophy is based on designing products to deliver attractive and competitive returns to institutional investors. As an ERISA fiduciary, we prudently invest assets with the goal of optimizing investment performance. That said, our corporate mission it to serve America's workers and it is our belief that a project with serious ESG concerns would generally not meet our investment goals. We do not believe there is a trade-off between ESG benefits and financial returns.[2]

Investment professionals often utilize sophisticated financial techniques. To do so, they depend on complex networks of people and institutions and elaborate layers of information. Processing all this information requires a great deal of judgment, knowledge of history, and technical prowess; however, since one cannot foresee the future, there is always a risk of being wrong. If they have to be wrong, investment professionals want to be wrong for the same reasons as everyone else. As they do not want to be seen as "outliers," their behavior exhibits a number of specific biases.

For example, in selecting investments, larger enterprises are generally preferred to smaller ones; high-growth geographical areas are preferred to areas where growth is slow; and information coming from mainstream sources is trusted over information from other lesser-known sources. Though profits can be competitively high in small enterprises in stable communities, the reputational price of being wrong about such "atypical" investments is higher than the price of being wrong in more conventionally pursued investments (Croft, 2009).

As the editors of the *Cambridge Handbook of Institutional Investment and Fiduciary Duty* state:

> It is increasingly argued that prevailing finance theories give an impoverished and deeply skewed view of financial value that is focused too much on short-term gains at the expense of sustainable growth over the longer term. Financial industry participants have also focused too much on the individual company, forgetting how companies are interdependent and exert influence on each other throughout the economy ... This increased emphasis on achieving a balance between short- and long-termism is supported by the fiduciary principle of

2 Edward Smith, President and CEO, ULLICO, personal communication/interview, November 24, 2014.

> impartiality: when there are both current income and future interest beneficiaries, fiduciaries should act impartially and not arbitrarily favor the interests of one over the other. (Hawley *et al.*, 2014, pp. 2-3)

5.5 Integrating ESG factors into fiduciary responsibility

In light of their fiduciary responsibilities under ERISA, how can trustees and other fiduciaries justify making responsible investments? As the PRI paper on fiduciary duty (PRI, 2015) states, the importance and materiality of ESG factors has often been ignored in the pursuit of the status quo while carrying out investment responsibilities. This is changing, however, largely as a result of four factors:

1. **Breach of duty.** The ground-breaking 2005 Freshfields Report on Fiduciary Duty stated: "in our opinion, it may be a breach of fiduciary duties to fail to take account of ESG considerations that are relevant and to give them appropriate weight" (UNEP FI, 2005, p. 100)

2. **Changing laws and regulations.** As noted below, the U.S. Congress and the Securities and Exchange Commission (SEC) are beginning to require companies to disclose certain material ESG issues, and the DOL's new Interpretive Bulletin 15-01 (U.S. DOL, 2015) views the inclusion of ESG considerations as part of a fiduciary's prudent analysis of investment opportunities

3. **Changing expectations.** Investor expectations are changing: as more and more investment organizations make commitments to responsible investments, it is likely that the duties that investors owe their clients will also evolve to reflect these changes

4. **Faulty financial assumptions.** Assumptions in relation to the efficiency of markets underlying the prevailing finance theories used in the last half of the 20th century have come under great scrutiny, particularly as a result of the financial crisis: in making their investment decisions, investors are now expected to take into account systemic risk and low probability events, as well as insights from areas such as behavioral finance

Further, some analysts believe that we are on the cusp of another fiduciary evolution due to the globalization of financial markets, asset concentration, increasing economic shocks, and the related computerization of the investment industry, resource limitations, etc.:

> Both academics and practitioners increasingly stress the importance of looking beyond what are today's financial concerns (indeed, often too narrowly conceived) to consider wider environmental, social and governance (ESG) matters. What are sometimes called "extra financial" are often "not yet financial." ... Arguments for an emphasis on ESG factors have been mounted from the fiduciary principle of impartiality, but also from an appeal to beneficiaries' broader interests in a healthy society and planet, as well as from general ethical and precautionary principles. Views of a particular issue can and often have become transformed into a broad social norm and as such can become "material" factors that affect asset prices.
>
> (Hawley *et al.*, 2014, p. 3)

This framework was articulated years ago in legal commentary by Professor A.W. Scott, a leading American scholar on trust law, who said, presciently:

> Trustees, in deciding whether to invest in, or retain, the securities of a corporation, may properly consider the social performance of a corporation. They may decline to invest in, or retain, the securities of corporations whose activities or some of them are contrary to fundamental and generally accepted ethical principles. They may consider such matters as pollution, race discrimination, fair employment, and consumer responsibility ... a trustee of funds for others, is entitled to consider the welfare of community and refrain from allowing the use of funds in a manner detrimental to society (Scott, 1987, p. 277).

The future of integrating ESG considerations into fiduciary duty has arrived. A 2015 report published by the PRI (in collaboration with UNEP FI, UNEP Inquiry and the UN Global Compact) emphasizes that fiduciary duty is not an obstacle to asset owner action on ESG issues (PRI, 2015). In another report published in 2016 (as referenced in Chapter 1), the PRI notes that the DOL's Interpretive Bulletin 15-01 views the inclusion of ESG factors as "'proper components' of the fiduciary's economic analysis" and not just as "collateral considerations or tie-breakers," as with previous interpretations of such investments, such as through ETIs (PRI, 2016, p. 3). In addition, the SEC now recognizes climate change risk as a material issue that needs to be disclosed by companies: "information is material if there is a substantial likelihood that a reasonable investor would consider it important in deciding how to vote or make an investment decision, or, put another way, if the information would alter the total mix of available information" (SEC, 2010, p. 11). Further, under the Dodd–Frank Act, Congress has required the SEC to adopt certain disclosure requirements of U.S. companies related to the

CEO/employee pay ratio, the sourcing of conflict minerals, resource extraction payments, and mine safety, among others. Underpinning this shift toward greater disclosure of ESG-related issues is the launch of the Sustainability Accounting Standards Board (SASB), an independent non-profit organization that is developing robust accounting standards to help public corporations disclose "material, decision-useful" information to investors (SASB, 2015). The SASB believes that these broader extra-financial disclosures may be material under existing securities law disclosure requirements (Goelzer, 2014).

There are more concrete and comprehensive disclosure rules being established in the European Union (EU) that are expected to ultimately affect many U.S. companies as well. For example, in September 2014, the EU Council formally adopted Directive 2014/95/EU on disclosure of non-financial and diversity information by certain large undertakings and groups (EU, 2014), introducing measures that will strengthen the transparency and accountability of approximately 6,000 companies (firms with more than 500 employees) in the EU. Affected firms will be:

- Required to report on environmental, social, and employee-related human rights, anticorruption and bribery matters
- Required to describe their business model, the outcomes and risks of the policies on the above-mentioned areas, and the diversity policy applied for management and supervisory bodies
- Encouraged to rely on recognized responsible frameworks such as the Global Reporting Initiative's (GRI) Sustainability Reporting Guidelines, the UN Global Compact (UNGC), the UN Guiding Principles on Business and Human Rights, OECD Guidelines, International Organization for Standardization (ISO) 26000 and the International Labour Organization (ILO) Tripartite Declaration (GRI, 2014)

In relation to environmental issues, a 2011 mega-analysis of 25 pension funds (Hoepner *et al.*, 2011) showed that there are no negative effects on financial performance resulting from incorporating these issues. The authors of the report developed a test of the prudent integration of ESG criteria in realistic and synthetic pension fund investment processes, analyzing more than 1,500 firms from 26 developed countries over a 77-month period using aggregated and disaggregated corporate environmental responsibility ratings. They concluded that there are "zero indications that the integration of aggregated or disaggregated corporate environmental responsibility ratings into pension fund investment processes has detrimental financial performance effect" for pension funds concerned about the environment" (p. 1). In fact, they found that the downside volatility (of incorporating ESG) is substantially lower.

What is left is for trustees and capital stewards to begin integrating ESG issues into the fiduciary duty process? As noted in the Ceres report:

> Today, new investment risks and opportunities based on emerging trends like climate change and resource scarcity require consideration by prudent fiduciaries. This approach, which we have termed sustainable investing, adopts a longer term focus, is less tied to short term benchmarks as the sole measure of success, and incorporates ESG factors into investment analysis and strategy.
>
> (Ellsworth and Snow Spalding, 2013, p. 11)

There are various approaches for integrating ESG considerations into fiduciary processes, from adopting ESG language into investment policy statements to incorporating such language in investment contracts. In their seminal work, "Reclaiming fiduciary duty balance," Hawley *et al.* (2011) include among these approaches a commitment to:

1. Allocate resources and time to understand challenges
2. Adopt an enterprise risk management approach
3. Ensure sustainable plan design

Thus, as part of their fiduciary oversight responsibilities, trustees need to ensure that there is both expertise to address ongoing challenges, as well as to research long-term issues. This includes the ability to manage ESG risks and opportunities for sustainability and impartiality (UNEP, 2009).

5.6 Takeaways

Trustees and capital stewards have an incredibly difficult task—especially when the work of managing trust funds is a part-time job, separate from a full-time occupation. While there have been considerable shifts or reinterpretations over the years as to what constitutes fiduciary duty, trustees are on solid ground when they consider the retirement security and the long-term interests of the participants and beneficiaries as their primary duty, and appropriately document their investment policies and procedures. As

Mercer Investment Consulting notes, there is "an increasing body of evidence ... to show that ESG factors can impact investment performance. Therefore, fiduciaries concerned with long-term preservation and growth of capital should have some understanding of how ESG factors may affect their portfolios" (UNEP, 2009, p. 74).

5.7 References

Bernstein, A., & Hawley, J.P. (2014) Is the Search for Excessive Alpha a Breach of Fiduciary Duty. In J.P. Hawley, A.G.F. Hoepner, K.L. Johnson, J. Sandberg, & E.J. Waitzer (Eds.), *Cambridge Handbook of Institutional Investment and Fiduciary Duty* (pp. 171-180). Cambridge, UK: Cambridge University Press.

Caplan, L., Griswold, J.S., & Jarvis W.F. (2013, September). *From SRI to ESG: The Changing World of Responsible Investing*. Retrieved May 18, 2016 from https://www.commonfund.org/wp-content/uploads/2016/01/Whitepaper_SRI-to-ESG-2013-0901.pdf.

Croft, T. (2009). *Up from Wall Street: The Responsible Investment Alternative*. New York, NY: Cosimo Books.

Ellsworth, P., & Snow Spalding, K. (2013, June). *The 21st Century Investor: Ceres Blueprint for Sustainable Investing*. Retrieved June 1, 2016 from http://www.ceres.org/resources/reports/the-21st-century-investor-ceres-blueprint-for-sustainable-investing/view.

EU (2014). Directive 2014/95/EU on disclosure of non-financial and diversity information by certain large undertakings and groups. Retrieved June 1, 2016 from http://eur-lex.europa.eu/legal-content/EN/TXT/?uri=CELEX:32014L0095.

Federal Register (1979). Preamble to Rules and Regulations for Fiduciary Responsibility; Investment of Plan Assets under the "Prudence" Rule (1979, June 26). 44 Fed. Reg. 37,221.

Goelzer, D. (2014). Corporate environmental sustainability programs: U.S. sustainability reporting requirements and risks. Washington, D.C.: Presentation at 2014 International Environmental Law Conference.

GRI (Global Reporting Initiative) (2014, October 1). *GRI Welcomes the Adoption of NFR Directive*. Retrieved June 1, 2016 from https://www.globalreporting.org/information/news-and-press-center/Pages/GRI-WELCOMES-THE-ADOPTION-OF-NFR-DIRECTIVE.aspx.

Harvard College v. Amory, 26 Mass (9 Pick.) 446 (1830).

Hawley, J.P., Johnson, K., & Waitzer, E.J. (2011). Reclaiming fiduciary duty balance. *Rotman International Journal of Pension Management*, 4(2), 4-16. Retrieved May 25, 2016 from http://ssrn.com/abstract=1935068.

Hawley, J.P., Hoepner, A.G.F., Johnson, K.L., Sandberg, J., & Waitzer, E.J. (2014). Introduction. In J.P. Hawley, A.G.F. Hoepner, K.L. Johnson, J. Sandberg, & E.J. Waitzer (Eds.), *Cambridge Handbook of Institutional Investment and Fiduciary Duty* (pp. 1-6). Cambridge, UK: Cambridge University Press.

Hoepner, A.G.F., Rezec, M., & Siegl, S. (2011, September 19). *Does Pension Funds' Fiduciary Duty Prohibit the Integration of Environmental Responsibility Criteria in Investment Processes? A Realistic Prudent Investment Test*. Retrieved June 1, 2016 from http://www.st-andrews.ac.uk/business/rbf/workingpapers/RBF13_010.pdf.

Johnson, K.L., & de Graaf, F.J. (2009). *Modernizing Pension Fund Legal Standards for the 21st Century*. Retrieved June 1, 2016 from http://www.sustainablefinancialmarkets.net/wp-content/uploads/2009/02/nsfm_modernizing1.pdf.

Legal Information Institute (2015). ERISA, 29 U.S. Code § 1104: Fiduciary Duties. Retrieved June 1, 2016 from http://www.law.cornell.edu/uscode/text/29/1104.

Marshall v. Glass/Metal Association, 507 F. Supp. 378 (D. Haw. 1980).

PRI (Principles for Responsible Investment) (2014). *Responsible Investment and Fiduciary Duty*. Retrieved June 1, 2016 from https://www.unpri.org/download_report/4082.

——— (2015). *Fiduciary Duty in the 21st Century*. Retrieved June 1, 2016 from http://www.unepfi.org/fileadmin/documents/fiduciary_duty_21st_century.pdf.

——— (2016). *Addressing ESG Factors Under ERISA*. Retrieved June 18, 2016 from http://2xjmlj8428u1a2k5o34l1m71.wpengine.netdna-cdn.com/wp-content/uploads/Addessing-ESG-factors-under-ERISA.pdf.

Rundell, S. (2015, September 11). Debate around fiduciary duty moves on. *Top1000Funds.com*. Retrieved June 16, 2016 from http://www.top1000funds.com/pri-in-person/2015/09/11/debate-around-fiduciary-duty-moves-on/.

SASB (Sustainability Accounting Standards Board) (2015). SASB homepage. Retrieved June 1, 2016 from http://www.sasb.org.

Scott, A.W. (1987). *The Law of Trusts* (4th ed.). Boston, MA: Little, Brown & Co.

SEC (Securities & Exchange Commission) (2010). Commission Guidance Regarding Disclosure Related to Climate Change. Securities and Exchange Commission: 17 CFR PARTS 211, 231 and 241. Retrieved June 18, 2016 from https://www.sec.gov/rules/interp/2010/33-9106.pdf.

Snow Spalding, K., & Kramer, M. (1997). *What Trustees Can Do Under ERISA (the Employee Retirement Income Security Act): A Study of Permissible Trustee Activism*. Retrieved June 1, 2016 from http://laborcenter.berkeley.edu/pdf/1997/erisa.pdf.

UNEP FI (UN Environment Programme Finance Initiative) (2005). *A Legal Framework for the Integration of Environmental, Social and Governance Issues Into Institutional Investment*. Retrieved June 18, 2016 from http://www.unepfi.org/fileadmin/documents/freshfields_legal_resp_20051123.pdf.

U.S. DOL (U.S. Department of Labor) (2014). Fiduciary responsibilities. Retrieved June 1, 2016 from http://www.dol.gov/dol/topic/health-plans/fiduciaryresp.htm.

——— (2015). DOL Interpretive Bulletin 15-01. *Employee Benefits Security Administration, Labor*. Retrieved June 28, 2016 from https://s3.amazonaws.com/public-inspection.federalregister.gov/2015-27146.pdf.

Wood, D., & Youngdahl, J. (2011). *Public Pension Fund Trustees and Fund Culture: Responsible Investment and the Trustee Leadership Forum*. Retrieved June 1, 2016 from http://hausercenter.org/iri/wp-content/uploads/2012/05/UNPRI-Youngdahl-Wood-Working-Paper.pdf.

Zanglein, J., & Clark, D. (2001). *Capital Stewardship Certificate Program*. Silver Spring, MD: National Labor College.

Section III: Responsible investment approaches and asset allocation

6
Responsible corporate governance and active ownership

> There is a growing base of evidence to highlight that companies which bring sustainability into the heart of their business strategy, outperform their counterparts over the long-term, both in terms of stock market and accounting performance.
>
> PRI

As the ownership and management of corporate America began to change hands in the mid-1900s, from founder-owners to institutional investors and professional managers, a separation between owners and managers resulted (Hawley and Williams, 2000a; Zanglein and Clark, 2001). This separation became evident in the 1970s, as company directors and executives struggled to maintain control over sprawling corporate empires. During this time, dozens of U.S. public companies were "busted" due to widespread corruption practices, prompting concerns about managerial accountability. In the 1980s and 1990s, concerns grew that weak corporate governance and managerial shortcomings had contributed to the U.S.A.'s economic decline relative to Germany and Japan. Further fracturing occurred in the next 15 years:

> Executives in U.S. public companies stood accused of forsaking the production of dependable, worthwhile products in favour of pursuing hasty growth by acquisition and ... counterproductive diversification to (offset) business setbacks. By the early 2000s, with one of the proposed remedies for America's purported corporate malaise—incentivizing allegedly overly bureaucratic senior executives with potentially lucrative performance-oriented managerial compensation—the cure arguably became worse than the disease as chief executive officer (CEO) pay sky-rocketed to unprecedented and highly controversial levels. (Cheffins, 2013)

Simultaneously, by the mid-1980s, institutional investors such as pension funds began in earnest to exercise their rights as owners, holding management accountable (Hawley and Williams, 2000b) on a variety of issues impacting their investments (from board governance and financial management issues to broader ESG matters). One important result of these efforts was the formation of the Council of Institutional Investors (CII) in 1985, during:

> a time of corporate takeovers, imperial CEOs and insulated boards of directors. Shareowners had little say in most corporate decisions and did not appreciate the potential power of their proxy votes. The founders were a group of 21 visionaries, most public pension fund officials, who believed that the companies in which they were investing their members' retirement assets needed more oversight by shareholders.
>
> (CII, 2013)

Despite advancements, there continues to be a division among the interests of shareholders, managers, and employees of corporations. According to van der Velden and van Buul (2012, p. 50), this increasing separation means that "the balance of power at public companies has been gradually shifting away from shareholders to management, the day-to-day agents at these companies," and that:

> labor unions have been in steady decline as mobility of production and employment has decreased their bargaining position ... This shift in power balance is leading to what Lord Myners calls "ownerless corporations" ... This situation leads to short-term thinking dominated by a trading mentality, manifesting itself in short-term business strategies that can imperil long-term corporate success and organizational stability.

In the aftermath of the financial crises of the last 15 years, corporate governance practices have again been placed front and center in the minds of investors. As the OECD's 2015 report on principles of corporate governance states, "The degree to which corporations observe basic principles of good corporate governance is an increasingly important factor for investment decisions" (OECD, 2015b, p. 13). Supported by investors' concerns, the Sarbanes–Oxley Act of 2002 and the Dodd–Frank Act of 2010 (passed as a result of the 2001 accounting scandals and the 2008 financial market crisis, respectively), were enacted to increase corporate board involvement and objectivity and improve accountability to shareholders.

As discussed, pension funds as universal owners cannot simply exclude investments in whole sectors through negative screening practices. Nor can they, in general, effectively engage in divestment strategies without risking a potential negative impact on the performance of their portfolios. They can, however, wield their collective clout as representatives of thousands of shareholders (Zanglein and Clark, 2001)—the workers and retirees on whose behalf the investments are made—and can have a say in affecting corporate change as active shareholders. By doing so, pension funds can choose to engage in "Wall Street Talk" over "Wall Street Walk" (see Box 6.5). In addition, pension funds can seek to integrate material ESG considerations alongside financial strength indicators into the investment decision-making process for their investments.

As such, in this chapter, we highlight good corporate governance practices that trustees should seek from their plan investments, and discuss available responsible investment strategies, particularly those related to active ownership, that can enable trustees to positively influence corporate behavior.

6.1 What is good corporate governance?

Corporate governance is about how companies are directed and controlled. It involves many different actors who have a stake in the ownership and control of companies, including shareholders, management, corporate boards, workers and their unions, and other stakeholders. The question of governance influences everything about how a company is run. The U.S. Department of Labor (U.S. DOL, 2008) has identified the following as examples of issues that are appropriate subjects for shareholder activism by pension plans under ERISA:

- Independence and expertise of candidates for the corporation's board of directors
- Assuring that the board has sufficient information to carry out its responsibility to monitor management
- Appropriateness of executive compensation
- Corporation's policy regarding mergers and acquisitions
- Extent of debt financing and capitalization
- Nature of long-term business plans
- Corporation's investment in training to develop its workforce

- Other workplace practices and financial and nonfinancial measures of corporate performance that are reasonably likely to affect the economic value of the plan

Good corporate governance, as CalPERS has noted, is about making "the boss" accountable.[1] It involves establishing a healthy relationship among a company's stakeholders. Good corporate governance should provide:

- The structure through which the objectives of the company are set, the means for attaining those objectives, and the tools to measure performance
- Proper incentives for the board and management to pursue objectives that are in the interests of the company, its shareholders, and other stakeholders
- Confidence in the proper functioning of a market economy

By advocating for good corporate governance, pension plans can use their collective voice as shareholders to encourage greater management accountability, giving workers a voice in the governance of their companies and the capital markets as a whole.

In addition to the active participation of pension plans in corporate governance, there are also many complementary workplace practices that protect workers' rights, engage and empower workers, and facilitate productivity and higher bottom-line results:

- **Responsible employment relations.** Companies should adopt provisions such as responsible contractor policies, card check neutrality,[2] best-value contracting, prevailing wages, and other

1 The front page of the CalPERS governance principles document (CalPERS, 2006) carries this quotation from "Corporate governance: watching the boss" (*The Economist*, January 29, 1994): "Everywhere shareholders are re-examining their relationships with company bosses—what is known as their system of 'corporate governance.' Every country has its own, distinct brand of corporate governance, reflecting its legal, regulatory and tax regimes ... The problem of how to make bosses accountable has been around ever since the public limited company was invented in the 19th century, for the first time separating the owners of firms from the managers who run them."

2 Growing numbers of workers and their employers are forming collective bargaining relationships by using "card count neutrality" or "card check neutrality" agreements. Through card count, the employer agrees to recognize the union as the official bargaining agent of the employees once a third party verifies that a

practices, and should provide a safe harbor for good labor relations for their worker stakeholders. This outcome gives workers a voice on the job, leads to better labor–management cooperation, and allows for improved wages, benefits, education, and working conditions (often a proxy for improved productivity).

- **Workforce participation and ownership.** Companies should support "high-road," high-performance business practices, which include positive labor–management relationships and other workforce participation approaches. Some corporations have achieved this by adding employee representatives to their board of directors. Companies can also share profits with their workers by utilizing mainstream employee ownership programs, such as employee stock ownership plans (ESOPs) and worker co-operatives. Good governance approaches engage workers and labor representatives from the shop floor to the boardroom. So-called "participatory firms" have long exhibited improved productivity and higher performance (Appelbaum *et al.*, 2014).
- **Workforce training and knowledge sharing.** Companies should think of their employees as "knowledge workers," not as production costs. Well-governed firms provide extensive training on team approaches, operations, and overall corporate affairs. Smart companies share more financial information with—and provide financial literacy training for—their workers. These boost worker understanding of businesses and the economy, improve labor–management co-operation, and increase job security.
- **Empowerment and diversity strategies.** Companies should provide greater employment opportunities to women and minority populations. This approach benefits organizational decision-making by including diverse points of view, fosters goodwill in the community by signaling that companies are partners with their community neighbors, and creates new economic ladders that reinforce workforce diversity.

majority of the entire group of employees has signed union membership cards. The employer then agrees to begin negotiating for a first contract as soon as it recognizes the union, avoiding prolonged legal delays. Neutrality means that the employer agrees not to interfere in the employees' decisions about whether to join the union, and the employees and the union agree not to disrupt the workplace through strikes, picketing or boycotts. In most card count neutrality agreements, binding arbitration is included to quickly resolve conflicts (Unite Here!, n.d.).

Box 6.1: TUAC's governance principles for corporations[3]

Workers' voice

- Recognizing workers' right to information, consultation, representation, and negotiation based on the OECD Guidelines for MNEs and the UN Guiding Principles on Business and Human Rights
- Protecting workers' creditor claims[4]
- Promoting sustainability and tax reporting

Investment chain

- Ensuring transparency and accountability of asset managers and other intermediaries to asset owners and addressing conflicts of interest
- Reducing the reliance on performance-related pay

Shareholder rights

- Securing shareholders' right to hold boards accountable
- Promoting responsible use of shareholder rights to help curb short-termist market behavior
- Recommending merger and takeover rules to be subject to the long-term interests of the company

Board organization and duties

- Setting principles for board diversity (gender, minority, and employee representation)
- Enhancing the duties of directors and risk management to account for the growing complexity of businesses and their responsibility *vis-à-vis* all stakeholders
- Adopting the separation of CEO and board chair functions as a principle

3 In its efforts to strengthen the 2014 revisions of the 2004 OECD Principles of Corporate Governance, TUAC presented its corporate governance priorities as part of the OECD's review process (TUAC, 2014a). In 2015, the OECD released a new set of *Principles of Corporate Governance*, updating its earlier version from 2004. TUAC raised renewed concerns about the contents of the document, and reiterated its earlier positions to strengthen responsible corporate governance (TUAC, 2014b).

4 TUAC notes that best practice in the case of a bankruptcy includes setting workers' creditor claims over the firm—unpaid wages, severance, unemployment, pension, and other benefits—to have senior status and precedence over other creditors.

Executive pay

- Reining in executive pay to rebuild confidence and trust in executive management by reducing the reliance on performance-related pay and designing remuneration packages that are in line with the long-term interests of the company; and
- Ensuring disclosure of individual pay and CEO/worker pay ratio, and approval by shareholders and independent directors.

Source: TUAC, 2014a, p. 3.

The Trade Union Advisory Committee (TUAC)[5] to the OECD asserts that corporate governance principles should not accept the status quo standards that contributed to the 2008 crisis but should instead aim for aspirational governance standards to achieve the long-term interests of a company. As TUAC notes:

> various mechanisms exist across OECD and G20 economies to ensure workers' voices in the governance of the firm. These rights are recognised and upheld by several ILO conventions, and by the OECD Guidelines for Multinational Enterprises (MNE). The most fundamental form of contractual governance consists of collective bargaining between senior management and worker representatives ... But other important mechanisms to participate in company decision-making also exist such as works councils and board-level employee representation. (TUAC, 2014a, pp. 3-4)

TUAC's proposals to strengthen corporate governance principles and practices include the fundamental principles listed in Box 6.1.

5 As the official voice of the labor movement at the OECD, TUAC is a key partner of the organization, representing more than 60 million workers in 30 countries in the work of the OECD. The OECD represents the governments of its 30 member countries, but it does not work for them in a vacuum. The major stakeholders of democratic societies—business, trade unions, and other members of civil society—also have an important role in OECD work (TUAC, 2008).

6.2 Why is participation in corporate governance important?

Pension trustees should promote good corporate governance because:

6.2.1 There is a strong business case for good corporate governance

The investment performance studies discussed in the Introduction have shown that responsible governance can lower the cost of capital and encourage more efficient use of resources (OECD, 2015b). In addition, being a good corporate citizen and responsible business—that is, taking into account the firm's impact on society and the environment as well as the economy—can provide over 60 business benefits in the following seven categories (Doughty Centre for Corporate Responsibility, 2011):

- Brand value and reputation
- Employees and future workforce (recruitment, motivation, retention, learning, and innovation)
- Operational effectiveness and efficiency
- Risk reduction and management
- Direct financial impact (investor relations and access to capital)
- Organizational growth
- Business opportunity

With significant growth in pension assets, indexing (see Section 6.3.1) has become a popular investment strategy. While indexing mitigates asset churning, the large number of investee companies held in indexed funds is difficult and costly to monitor. "This often leads to sub-optimal monitoring and analyst coverage of companies unless collective action is achieved" (Kirkpatrick *et al.*, 2011, p. 10).

Thus, there is a strong need for pension funds, particularly those with sizable indexed assets, to seek responsible corporate governance practices from their investments. Pension funds should support businesses that integrate responsible practices into their operations. Businesses that embrace such practices will survive and thrive; those that do not—think Enron, Massey Coal—may not.

6.2.2 Well-governed companies are more likely to respect workers' rights

Good corporate governance helps to promote accountability throughout the company's operations, including the company's obligations to respect the international human rights of workers. At the international level, there is a growing set of conventions and guidelines to protect workers' rights. Some have been ratified by global governing bodies and national governments, including:

- **International Labour Organization (ILO).** The ILO is the global umbrella for monitoring workers' rights and aims to ensure that it serves the needs of working women and men by bringing together governments, employers, and workers to set labor standards, develop policies, and devise programs (ILO, 1996).
- **UN Guiding Principles on Business and Human Rights.** In 2011, the United Nations Human Rights Council unanimously endorsed the UN Guiding Principles on Business and Human Rights, which is a set of guidelines for states and companies to prevent and address human rights abuses committed in business operations (UNWG 2014).
- **OECD Guidelines for Multinational Enterprises (MNEs).** The OECD Guidelines for MNEs aim to help businesses, labor unions, and non-governmental organizations (NGOs) by providing a global framework for responsible business conduct covering all areas of business ethics, including tax, competition, disclosure, anticorruption, labor and human rights, and environment. While observance with the guidelines is voluntary and not legally enforceable, adhering governments commit to promote the guidelines and increase their influence among companies operating in or from their territories (OECD, 2014).
- **UN Global Compact.** The UN Global Compact is a strategic policy initiative for businesses that are committed to aligning their operations and strategies with 10 universally accepted principles in the areas of human rights, labor, environment, and anticorruption. By doing so, business, as a primary driver of globalization, can help ensure that markets, commerce, technology, and finance advance in ways that benefit economies and societies everywhere (UN Global Compact, 2014).

6.2.3 It pays to give workers a voice in the governance of corporations, both as employee stakeholders and as investors

CEOs claim that their staff and employees are the most valuable "asset." According to TUAC:

> Workers' firm-specific investments are an essential source of corporate wealth creation through human capital development and intangible assets. Workers, as employees of the firm, however are equally exposed to firm-specific risk, including market and production risks but also occupational and health and safety risk. (TUAC, 2014a, p. 3)

Workers are stakeholders and investors, and their human "capital" should be stewarded like all other forms of capital.

Human Capital Management (HCM) encompasses:

> a broad range of corporate practices related to the management of employees, including, but not limited to, hiring and retention, employee engagement, training, compensation, fair labor practices, health and safety, responsible contracting, ethics, desired company culture, and diversity, both with respect to a company's direct employees and to the employees of vendors throughout the company's global supply chain. (HCM Coalition, 2014, p. 1)

Why, then, have workers not benefited from documented historical increases in productivity? Why have workers fallen behind while founder-owners and managers have become enriched? There is a strong history of literature praising the role of workers and the need for "high-performance" work systems that recognize their talent and innovation, dating from the works of management guru Peter Drucker.[6] Drucker, who coined the phrase "knowledge worker," said in a *Harvard Business Review* article in 1991:

> [Responsible] institutional owners ... maximize. But they do not attempt to maximize shareholder value or the short-term interest of any one of the enterprise's "stakeholders." Rather, they maximize the wealth-producing capacity of the enterprise. It is this objective that integrates short-term and long-term results and that ties the operational dimensions of business performance—market standing, innovation, productivity, and people and their development—with financial needs and financial results. It is also this objective on which all constituencies depend for the satisfaction of their expectations and objectives, whether shareholders, customers, or employees.
>
> (Drucker,1991)

6 See, for example, Appelbaum *et al.*, 2014.

More recently, the Human Capital Management (HCM) Coalition is working to "further elevate human capital management as a critical component in company performance." In line with research-based evidence demonstrating a correlation between strong HCM and shareholder returns, the coalition "engages with companies with the aim of understanding and improving how human capital management contributes to the creation of long-term shareholder value." A co-operative of 24 institutional investors representing over $2.3 trillion in assets, the coalition is led by the UAW Retiree Medical Benefits Trust (Hauser Center, 2015). Currently, the coalition is focusing its work on the retail industry, with plans to extend its services to additional industries such as food service.

Further, for good corporate governance to work, shareholders and managers need to treat workers as valued stakeholders, as illustrated in Box 6.2.

Box 6.2: Good corporate governance initiatives by a labor bank

Amalgamated Bank, New York's first labor bank, was born out of the principle to offer hardworking people and their family's access to affordable banking. Today the bank has nearly $38 billion in assets under trust, including over $13 billion in assets in its LongView family of funds. Of the latter, nearly $11 billion, or 89%, is in investment funds or vehicles that follow responsible investment guidelines. The bank is also a founding signatory to the PRI.

Through its LongView funds, the bank has undertaken many successful corporate initiatives and aggressive shareholder actions to hold corporations accountable to rigorous ESG standards while delivering on sound investment returns over the long term. In so doing, the bank has taken a strong stance on responsible investing, shareholder returns, golden parachutes, and other tools, to get corporations to return capital to investors and all stakeholders.

The bank has also begun to take stronger actions to protect workers in the garment industry after a number of successive accidents within the industry in Bangladesh. In 2013, as part of a coalition of institutional investors with combined assets of over $1.35 trillion, the bank called on fashion and apparel companies to better track their suppliers, ensure compliance with safety standards, and fully disclose their supply chains. The tragedies also spurred the bank's efforts to improve individual companies' manufacturing and supply chain policies. While the bank recognizes the initial progress made, it is focused on making a long-term commitment to bring about lasting change.

Source: Keith Mestrich, President, Amalgamated Bank, personal communications/interviews, August 14, 2014 and December 3, 2015.

6.3 Responsible investment approaches

Pension funds may implement responsible investments through a variety of approaches, from passive (such as screening out investments that run contrary to one's values or beliefs) to active (such as shareholder engagement and the integration of material ESG issues when arriving at an investment's intrinsic value). In discussing each of these approaches, we emphasize the use of active approaches that can enable pension funds to achieve enhanced engagement, impact, and financial performance, particularly in the long term. It should be noted that the approaches discussed are not mutually exclusive; rather, they can be combined to deliver a comprehensive responsible investment strategy.

6.3.1 Indexing

Indexing is a long-term passive investment strategy that seeks to achieve the risk–return attributes of a chosen index of securities. Investors can follow an indexed strategy though investments in separate accounts or pooled funds.

Indexing is an important investment strategy for many large institutional investors, particularly pension funds, whose portfolio performance is impacted not only by the performance of individual stocks, but also by the performance of the whole economy (Zanglein and Clark, 2001). However, indexing may lead to increased equity market volatility (Sullivan and Xiong, 2012).

Pension funds with an indexed investment strategy naturally lend themselves to incorporating responsible investment criteria in their investment portfolios. Passive investors can exercise their proxy voting rights through external investment managers or specialized service providers, or through in-house staff. While an indexed strategy is not suited to exclusionary screening (unless the assets are invested in an ethical index), divestments, or focused ESG integration, passive investors can nonetheless deploy activist strategies such as proxy voting rights and other shareholder actions to have their voices heard on a range of corporate matters, from financial and governance to sustainability (UNEP FI, 2011).

6.3.2 Proxy voting

When invested in the public equities of a company, shareholders obtain the right to vote on various corporate matters related to how a company is run,

Box 6.3: Active ownership by passive investors

The pursuit of active shareholder tools by large passive investors was trail blazed by CalPERS, though not without challenges, as illustrated by the following story:

> Prior to 1986, CalPERS had a commitment to a passive investments strategy; it did not vote its proxies. Furthermore its investment approach tended towards a long-term commitment of funds, with a high level of diversification. In 1986, alarmed at a downturn in stock that seemed to be caused by inept corporate management, CalPERS demanded corporate accountability but was routinely ignored by corporate management. The combination of a long-term investment horizon and a passive investment approach began to look like a recipe for disaster. As a result, CalPERS launched its first corporate governance campaign by targeting ten of the poorest-performing companies in its domestic stock portfolio for improvement. (Carmichael, 2005, p. 52)

This was the genesis for the CalPERS focus list, a list of the worst-performing companies that the fund tries to engage with and request improvements of, supplementing their efforts with shareholder resolutions that promote positive corporate governance change. In the past, the list was made public, whereas it is now kept private. In combination with active ownership strategies by the pension fund, such focus lists continue to make a positive impact in having shareholder voices heard and pressing nonperforming corporations to improve their performance.

The California State Teachers' Retirement System (CalSTRS), the second-largest public pension plan in the U.S.A. after CalPERS, has about 80% of its U.S. investments in passive investment strategies. In order to mitigate the risk associated with its investments, CalSTRS has developed a list of 21 risk factors that it requires to be included by its staff and external investment managers in their investment decision-making. Among the 21 risk factors are transparency and corporate governance, human and worker rights, and the environment. As noted by the pension fund, "this list is not exhaustive and does not attempt to identify all forms of risk that are appropriate to consider in a given investment transaction; however, they do provide a framework of other factors that might be overlooked." The risk factors are applied to the pension fund's investments in all asset classes, both within the U.S.A. and globally (DiChristopher, 2014; CalSTRS, 2015).

regardless of whether the investors pursue a passive or active management of their assets. In lieu of their physical presence at annual meetings where these matters get voted on, shareholders have the option to vote by proxy. In the case of pension funds, boards of trustees are responsible for deciding how these proxy votes should be managed. Trustees may delegate proxy voting authority to another fiduciary, such as an investment advisor or a specialized proxy voting consultant, or retain their ability to vote proxies in-house.

Box 6.4: AFL-CIO proxy voting guidelines

The AFL-CIO's *Proxy Voting Guidelines: Exercising Authority, Restoring Accountability* (AFL-CIO, 2012) is a comprehensive and excellent resource for capital stewards wishing to learn more about how to effectively exercise their proxy voting rights on issues of corporate accountability and governance, as well as social and environmental importance.

For pension funds and other institutional investors, proxy voting has emerged as a powerful tool for engaging in corporate governance matters. The DOL has included proxy voting rights as part of a pension fund's assets, thus requiring all votes to be cast according to the fiduciary duties of loyalty and prudence as applied to plan investments. Under ERISA, this requires the trustees and the voting fiduciary to make voting decisions that are in the long-term economic best interest of the plan participants and beneficiaries.

In addition, ERISA does not preclude fiduciaries from taking into account collateral impacts—such as those involving social and environmental concerns—for their proxy voting decisions as long as the voting fiduciary can articulate a clear basis for concluding that the proxy vote is more likely than not to enhance the economic value of the plan's investment before expending plan assets (U.S. DOL, 2008). The important point is that fiduciaries should establish plan documents that are in compliance with prevailing laws, comply with those documents in conducting their duties, seek independent advice where required, exercise oversight, and document all processes and procedures followed (AFL-CIO, 2012).

In order to perform their fiduciary duty as it relates to proxy voting, trustees may wish to adopt comprehensive written proxy voting guidelines similar to an investment policy. The guidelines should establish which fiduciaries—trustees themselves, delegated asset managers, or specialized proxy voting agents—have proxy voting responsibilities. While proxy voting guidelines are expected to provide advice to the voting fiduciary on a list of identified proxy issues, the guidelines do not necessarily need to direct managers or specialized agents in how the votes are ultimately cast (AFL-CIO, 2012).

As suggested by the AFL-CIO (2012), trustees and fiduciaries may include the following issues when developing comprehensive proxy voting guidelines:

- Board of director independence and expertise as well as limits to size and compensation.
- The independence and expertise of a company's auditors, including limits to non-audit services.
- An executive compensation structure that sets high performance objectives and incentivizes long-term corporate value creation. In addition, a structure that sets up an executive/employee pay ratio that is fair and commensurate with the value-added provided by each group.
- Issues related to changes in management such that any change will enhance the long-term economic best interest of the plan participants and beneficiaries.
- Matters of corporate responsibility such as labor and human rights, supply-chain code of conduct, equal employment opportunity, environmental practices, etc., that are important to the long-term economic success of a company.

Box 6.5: Engaged corporate governance

Wall Street Talk refers to active shareholder actions for engaging with management to improve corporate performance and ultimately the value of the investment. **Wall Street Walk** refers to shareholders simply divesting in the stock when dissatisfied with the company's performance (Zanglein and Clark, 2001). Since ownership in the company (and therefore investor say in financial and nonfinancial concerns) ceases to exist in a "walk" situation, trustees and fiduciaries are encouraged to engage in "talk" (via proxy votes, shareholder proposals, etc.) with the management of concerned companies.

Until the 1990s, many investors, particularly asset managers, either did not cast proxy votes or they reflexively voted with corporate management's recommendations (AFL-CIO, 2012). With DOL's formal position taken in 1988 that proxy voting rights are plan assets, trustees began to recognize the importance of proxy voting as a means of holding corporations accountable on a variety of financial and nonfinancial matters. As is evident from the example of CalPERS, even pension funds in passive investment strategies can positively impact corporate behavior by committing to a thorough proxy voting strategy.

Box 6.6: AFL-CIO Key Votes Survey

The AFL-CIO Key Votes Survey rates the voting practices of investment managers by surveying how they voted on proposals representing a worker-owner view of value. This worker-owner view emphasizes management accountability and good corporate governance. These proposals are assessed by the AFL-CIO proxy voting guidelines and managers are ranked by the percentage of votes cast in accordance with the guidelines. The most recent Key Votes Survey can be found at http://www.aflcio.org/Corporate-Watch/Capital-Stewardship/Proxy-Voting.

Many pension funds delegate the authority to vote their proxies to their investment managers or to a specialized proxy voting consultant. To assist the trustees of these pension funds, the AFL-CIO annually publishes its Key Votes Survey of investment manager proxy voting, designed to help pension fund trustees fulfill their fiduciary duty to monitor the proxy voting performance of investment managers. Since the AFL-CIO first started publishing the survey in 1997, investment managers have become more likely to vote independently of corporate management's recommendations.

6.3.3 Shareholder activism

> Nothing concentrates the mind of a corporate executive quite so sharply as a pointed inquiry from a large investor or outside director.
>
> (Robert Reich, Former Secretary, Department of Labor, quoted in McGurn, 1994, p. 4)

Shareholder activism refers to proactive actions by shareholders to influence the behavior of the companies in which they have invested—above and beyond proxy voting. In her book, *Pension Power*, Isla Carmichael defines shareholder activism as actions that are "directed at bringing about social change in the corporation's relationship with its shareholders, employees or community" (Carmichael, 2005, p. 49).

These actions can range from private letters or meetings with companies to formal shareholder proposals presented at a company's annual meeting. Given the role of pension funds as universal owners and the potential costs of untimely divestments, responsible trustees and fiduciaries can create better value for their investments, and in capital markets as a whole, through active engagement and dialogue, to the extent possible, with the companies they are invested in.

As with proxy voting, shareholder activism may include issues related to governance, such as CEO compensation, board of director selection, and mergers and acquisitions, as well as nonfinancial corporate sustainability issues such as human rights, diversity, and environmental pollution. Though shareholder proposals are nonbinding, through such actions trustees and other fiduciaries can bring attention to and support those issues that are expected to contribute to the long-term economic best interest of plan participants and beneficiaries. The DOL has endorsed shareholder activism by pension plan fiduciaries under ERISA, as long as the benefits of shareholder activism for the pension plan are reasonably expected to exceed the costs involved (U.S. DOL, 2008).

Box 6.7: Examples of shareholder activism

Michael Garland, Assistant Comptroller of Corporate Governance and Responsible Investment for the $160 billion New York City (NYC) Pension Funds, points to a long and proud history of shareholder proposal engagement by the funds in areas such as greenhouse gas emissions and political spending. The NYC Pension Funds are incrementally working to make companies more transparent and corporate boards more responsive.

For instance, among its many successful responsible shareholder initiatives, the NYC Pension Funds, along with CalPERS, led the public "VOTE NO" campaign in 2014 against the board of directors of Duke Energy after its coal ash spilled into 70 miles of a river in North Carolina. As Garland noted, this was the first time that owner investors decided to hold the board responsible over an environmental issue. While the board, composed of four representatives with no relevant experience in the committee they oversaw, was reelected at the company's annual meeting, "the circumstances served as a wake-up call to investors regarding the need for relevant director expertise to oversee environmental risk management in the energy industry" (NYC Pension Funds, 2014, p. 8). In another initiative, NYC Pension Funds led the Boardroom Accountability Project to give shareowners a choice in the election of directors of publicly held companies. To gain greater momentum, the project was initiated by submitting proxy access shareowner proposals to 75 companies simultaneously.[7]

In another example, Aviva, a large U.K.-based insurance company, at its annual meeting in 2012 lost support for its executive pay proposal by 60% of all votes, a result of shareholders' dissatisfaction with the firm's poor performance in recent years. Though nonbinding, the action led to a furor that ended in the resignation of the firm's CEO because of widespread opposition to his pay.

Overall, institutional investors have much bargaining power when it comes to affecting positive change among their investment holdings through shareholder proposals. According to a 2012 Deutsche Bank report, institutional investors filed 2,392 proposals between 1997 and 2009. Of these, 810 (33.9%) were withdrawn before the annual meeting—a reflection of a satisfactory agreement having been reached

7 Michael Garland, Assistant Comptroller for Corporate Governance and Responsible Investment at New York City Office of the Comptroller, personal communication/interview, December 17, 2014.

during private negotiations. In addition, labor unions submitted 2,726 proposals, of which 34.6% were withdrawn. Further, as the report notes:

> institutional investors filed more corporate social responsibility (CSR) proposals, which deal with environmental and social issues, than corporate governance proposals (1,244 vs. 1,115). Institutions were also more successful in negotiations on CSR proposals (42.4% withdrawal rate) than on corporate governance proposals (24.8%). Hence, institutional investors appear able to promote changes in corporate behavior pertaining to ESG issues.
>
> (DB Advisors and MUSBE, 2012, p. 5)

Rather than engage in the "Wall Street Walk" by selling their shares of companies, pension plans can help create value by engaging in shareholder activism to encourage good corporate governance and corporate responsibility. In particular, selling shares of companies with poor governance or irresponsible practices is not a viable alternative for pension plans who employ passive indexing strategies. As noted, these passive investors can still be "active" owners through shareholder activism and proxy voting.

6.3.4 Best-in-class or positive screening

Best-in-class or positive screening is the opposite of exclusionary or negative screening in that it seeks to make investments in companies that show leadership in ESG matters when compared with their peers. Instead of excluding investments in whole industries or sectors, this approach enables investments to be made in companies based on their track record in social and/or environmental practices—companies that may have otherwise been screened out under exclusionary approaches.

While exclusionary screens tend be more black and white, the best-in-class method requires the analysis of a company's practices in a variety of areas, such as environment, workplace diversity, and supply chain management, *vis-à-vis* its peers. This approach can be applied to small-, medium-, or large-capitalization companies. Through private equity or venture capital investments, it can also be applied to companies engaged in providing novel solutions to social and/or environmental problems, such as clean energy, waste management, products and services for under-served communities, and sustainable agriculture. In the case of public companies, the best-in-class method can help determine which companies in a particular sector or industry have better corporate policies (SocialFunds, 2016).

6.3.5 ESG integration

The integration of ESG considerations in traditional investment analysis to determine the intrinsic value of a company is perhaps the holy grail of responsible investment approaches. Rather than excluding companies with poor ESG performance or being limited to companies that appear better investments only in comparison with their poor-performing peers, pension funds can invest in businesses that are truly operating in a manner that is accountable to all stakeholders, particularly workers, and respectful of the environment and society.

To effectively integrate ESG considerations into the investment analysis process, pension funds should select ESG factors that are material to the financial performance of their portfolio and analyze them alongside traditional risk–return indicators. Once an investment has been made, pension funds may continue to actively engage with management on these material ESG issues through proxy votes and shareholder activism, as mentioned above, ensuring that their investments meet portfolio goals (Caplan *et al.*, 2013).

The establishment of the PRI in 2006 has galvanized tremendous support for the inclusion of ESG considerations in institutional investments. The PRI has created several working groups that are focused on various asset classes, providing tangible guidance and peer-to-peer examples on how to pursue responsible investing. One such working group is the PRI Listed Equities ESG Integration Working Group, which in February 2013 published

Box 6.8: Five stages of integrating ESG analysis into listed equity analysis

1. **Economic analysis:** understanding how ESG factors affect economic growth and macro themes, such as resource scarcity
2. **Industry analysis:** understanding how ESG factors influence consumer preferences and regulatory change, such as environmental legislation
3. **Company strategy:** understanding how a company manages ESG risks and opportunities, for example in supply-chain management
4. **Financial reports:** understanding how ESG factors impact on earnings growth, operational efficiency, intangible assets, and underlying cash flows
5. **Valuation tools:** understanding how analysts are integrating ESG considerations into valuation tools such as discount rates and economic value added

Source: PRI ESG Working Group, 2013

an excellent report on the application of traditional research methods to the integration of ESG factors in investment portfolios (PRI ESG Working Group, 2013). Box 6.8 provides five key stages through which pension funds may make ESG integrated investment decisions. Though applied to listed equities in the report, elements of this methodology may also be useful for other asset classes.

The value of this methodology is of course dependent on the quality of data available on ESG factors. Unlike financial data reporting by companies, ESG data is not yet reported in any consistent way, nor is the information generally audited. But efforts are under way to standardize the collection and reporting of ESG considerations (such as by the PRI and GRI discussed later).

6.3.6 Exclusionary or negative screening

Screening out investments based on one's ethics or values is the oldest and most basic way to engage in responsible investing. Depending on investor preferences and/or available investment products, investments may be screened out to exclude companies engaged in certain products or practices. Investors may either completely avoid investing in such companies or set a materiality threshold for exclusion, such as companies deriving more than 10% of their revenues from such activities. Investments may also be screened out to exclude companies with poor environmental and/or human rights records.

Exclusionary or negative screening of investments has a long history in the faith-based and socially responsible investor worlds. In addition to accommodating their moral considerations, some hope that by not investing in certain companies they may be able to put downward pressure on a company's stock price and/or upward pressure on its cost of capital. They may also be able to bring attention to the harmful effects of the companies' products and/or practices.

However, skeptics argue that because of the efficiency of capital markets, negative screens do not have an impact on the stock price or availability of capital for excluded companies. For every investor who sells shares based on a negative screen, there is an investor ready to buy undervalued shares. Moreover, public companies do not generally raise additional capital by issuing new shares. Instead, they tend to make capital investments out of retained earnings or by issuing corporate debt. For this reason, any changes in the company's stock price will not necessarily impact the company's access to capital.

For pension plan fiduciaries who must seek competitive risk-adjusted investment returns, the use of negative screens reduces the investable universe and impacts portfolio diversification. In addition, given the complex and global dynamics in which businesses operate today, few companies can claim to be 100% compliant with ESG best practices, further limiting investor options.

For example, tobacco screens are being used by nearly 200 ethical mutual funds (SocialFunds, 2016); however, tobacco stocks have tended to outperform the S&P 500 index (Randall, 2009). Pension plan fiduciaries who are interested in screening investments should first seek legal and financial advice to ensure they do not sacrifice investment returns. But this advice should also include a balanced discussion regarding risk.

Despite limited benefits, negative screening can be a useful approach for responsible investors who wish to apply ethical or moral considerations to their investment portfolio, especially in conjunction with best-in-class or positive screening as well as other active shareholders practices. In fact, some academic studies have found return advantages when negative screens have been combined with the best-in-class method over portfolios limited to negative screens or even conventional portfolios (DB Climate Change Advisors, 2012; Clark *et al.*, 2014).

6.3.7 Divestment

Divestment refers to the sale of an investment with the aim to influence corporate behavior or policy around a financial, governance, or ethical issue. The most famous example of a divestment campaign is the sale of stock by large institutional investors in companies doing business in South Africa in protest at the country's apartheid regime. More recently, a variety of public pension plans and university endowments adopted divestment policies for companies that did business in Sudan after the Darfur genocide. Because investors cannot directly influence the policies of entire countries that have systemic human rights abuses, country-level divestment campaigns may be the only viable strategy for some responsible investors.

Pension plan trustees may wish to consider divestment from companies who are listed and primarily operate in countries where there are systemic human and labor rights concerns. The International Trade Union Confederation (ITUC) publishes an annual Global Rights Index that provides background on workers' rights concerns in countries around the globe (ITUC, 2015). The ITUC Global Rights Index supersedes previous editions

Box 6.9: OECD's Principles of Corporate Governance (2015)

These principles (first published in 1999 and revised in 2004) have long been among the most influential sources of corporate governance guidelines for regulators, stock exchanges, investors, and companies worldwide, and continue to be referenced as a benchmark for good governance practices.

1. **Ensuring the basis for an effective corporate governance framework.** The corporate governance framework should promote transparent and fair markets, and the efficient allocation of resources. It should be consistent with the rule of law and ensure effective supervision and enforcement
2. **The rights and equitable treatment of shareholders and key ownership functions.** The corporate governance framework should protect and facilitate the exercise of shareholders' rights and ensure the equitable treatment of all shareholders, including minority and foreign shareholders. All shareholders should have the opportunity to obtain effective redress for violation of their rights
3. **Institutional investors, stock markets, and other intermediaries.** The corporate governance framework should provide sound incentives throughout the investment chain and provide for stock markets to function in a way that contributes to good corporate governance
4. **The role of stakeholders in corporate governance.** The corporate governance framework should recognize the rights of stakeholders established by law or through mutual agreements and encourage active cooperation between corporations and stakeholders in creating wealth, jobs, and the sustainability of financially sound enterprises
5. **Disclosure and transparency.** The corporate governance framework should ensure that timely and accurate disclosure is made on all material matters regarding the corporation, including the financial situation, performance, ownership, and governance of the company
6. **The responsibilities of the board.** The corporate governance framework should ensure the strategic guidance of the company, the effective monitoring of management by the board, and the board's accountability to the company and the shareholders

Source: OECD, 2015a

of the AFL-CIO Country Watch List that many pension plans incorporated into their investment policies for international equity investments.

Divestments need to be carefully planned as untimely stock sales can negatively impact portfolio performance. In addition, divestment is believed to have had limited impact on the stock market performance of target companies (Gregory, 2014). As with negative screens, pension plans considering a divestment should seek legal and financial advice to ensure they do not sacrifice investment returns. Because divestment is unlikely to impact the divested company's cost of capital, some consider divestment to be a less effective method of changing corporate behavior.

As a result, pension funds, in their capacity as universal owners, have been encouraged to engage in "Wall Street Talk" over "Wall Street Walk." As mentioned, once shares in a company have been sold, investors lose their ownership and voting rights, and hence a chance to affect positive corporate change through active ownership.

While the authors are not generally endorsing specific divestment campaigns, they do acknowledge the passions of students, citizens, and capital stewards engaged in the carbon divestment movement, which started in campuses and has grown rapidly in the offices of mayors, endowments, and institutional investors cross the country and globally. We are, with this *Handbook*, focusing more on the "invest" side of the divest/invest coin.

6.4 Takeaways

Corporate governance practices can impact the ability of companies to generate long-term shareholder value, which "is a key metric for assessing whether the corporation is effective and efficient in its activities" (Gregory, 2014). For this reason, the promotion of good governance and responsible business are important tools available to pension funds. Through proxy votes, shareholder activism, and the integration of ESG considerations in investment decisions, pension funds and their trustees can influence and improve corporate governance practices, and, by extension, the long-term value of the funds' assets.

6.5 References

AFL-CIO (The American Federation of Labor and Congress of Industrial Organizations) (2012). *AFL-CIO Proxy Voting Guidelines: Exercising Authority, Restoring Accountability*. Retrieved June 2, 2016 from http://www.aflcio.org/content/download/12631/154821/proxy_voting_2012.pdf.

Appelbaum, E., Bailey, T., Berg, P., & Kalleberg, A.L. (2014). *Manufacturing Advantage: Why High Performance Work Systems Pay Off*. New York, NY: Cornell University Press.

CalPERS (2006). *Corporate Governance: Core Principles & Guidelines*. Retrieved June 1, 2016 from http://www.globalsepri.org/UploadPhotos/200891217402733.pdf.

CalSTRS (2015). *Attachment A: Investment Policy for Mitigating Environmental, Social and Geopolitical Risks (ESG)*. Retrieved June 2, 2016 from http://www.calstrs.com/sites/main/files/file-attachments/esg_policy_and_21_risk_factors.pdf.

Caplan, L., Griswold, J.S., & Jarvis, W.F. (2013). *From SRI to ESG: The Changing World of Responsible Investing*. Retrieved May 18, 2016 from https://www.commonfund.org/wp-content/uploads/2016/01/Whitepaper_SRI-to-ESG-2013-0901.pdf.

Carmichael, I. (2005). *Pension Power: Unions, Pension Funds, and Social Investment in Canada*. Toronto, Canada: University of Toronto Press.

Cheffins, B.R. (2013). *The History of Modern U.S. Corporate Governance*. Cheltenham, UK: Edward Elgar Publishing. Retrieved June 20, 2016 from http://www.elgaronline.com/view/Research_Reviews/9781849807616/intro.xml.

CII (Council of Institutional Investors) (2013). About us. Retrieved June 2, 2016 from http://www.cii.org/about_us.

Clark, G., Feiner, A., & Viehs, M. (2014, October 20). *From the Stockholder to the Stakeholder: How Sustainability Can Drive Financial Outperformance*. doi:10.2139/ssrn.2508281.

DB Advisors and MUSBE (Maastricht University School of Business and Economics) (2012). *Corporate Engagement by Institutional Shareholders*. Retrieved June 16, 2016 from https://www.db.com/cr/en/docs/DBAdvisors_CorpEngagement_090113.pdf.

DB Climate Change Advisors (2012). *Sustainable Investing: Establishing Long-Term Value and Performance*. Retrieved June 2, 2016 from https://www.db.com/cr/en/docs/Sustainable_Investing_2012.pdf.

DiChristopher, T. (2014, November 18). Invest in funds that track major indexes: CalSTRS' Ailman. *CNBC*. Retrieved June 2, 2016 from http://www.cnbc.com/id/102196247.

Doughty Centre for Corporate Responsibility (2011). *The Business Case for Being a Responsible Business*. Retrieved June 2, 2016 from http://www.som.cranfield.ac.uk/som/dinamic-content/media/documents/Business%20case%20final.pdf.

Drucker, P.F. (1991). Reckoning with the pension fund revolution. *Harvard Business Review*, March–April, 106-114. Retrieved June 2, 2016 from https://hbr.org/1991/03/reckoning-with-the-pension-fund-revolution.

Gregory, H.J. (2014, December 1). Corporate governance issues for 2015. *Practical Law*. Retrieved June 2, 2016 from http://us.practicallaw.com/1-589-4503.

Hauser Center (2015). *Human Capital Management Coalition: Toolkit*. Retrieved June 2, 2016 from http://hausercenter.org/iri/wp-content/uploads/2012/05/HCM-Coalition-Toolkit.pdf.

Hawley, J.P., & Williams, A.T. (2000a). *The Rise of Fiduciary Capitalism: How Institutional Investors Can Make Corporate America More Democratic*. Philadelphia, PA: University of Pennsylvania Press.

——— (2000b). The emergence of universal owners: Some implications of institutional equity ownership. *Challenge*, 43, 43-61.

HCM Coalition (2014). *Human Capital Management Coalition: Questions*. Retrieved June 20, 2016 from http://hausercenter.org/iri/wp-content/uploads/2012/05/HCM-Coalition-Questions.pdf.

ILO (International Labour Organization) (1996). *Conventions and Recommendations*. Retrieved June 2, 2016 from http://www.ilo.org/global/standards/introduction-to-international-labour-standards/conventions-and-recommendations/lang--en/index.htm.

ITUC (International Trade Union Confederation) (2015). *ITUC Global Rights Index: The World's Worst Countries for Workers*. Retrieved June 2, 2016 from http://www.ituc-csi.org/ituc-global-rights-index-2015.

Kirkpatrick, G., Lehuedé, H., & Hoki, K. (2011). *The Role of Institutional Investors in Promoting Good Corporate Governance*. Paris, France: OECD.

McGurn, P. (1994). DOL Issues New Guidelines on Proxy Voting, Active Investing. IRRC Corporate Governance Bulletin. July/Aug. 1994, at 1, 4.

NYC Pension Funds (2014). *2014 Shareowner Initiatives: Postseason Report.* Retrieved June 18, 2016 from http://comptroller.nyc.gov/wp-content/uploads/documents/2014_Shareowner_Initiatives_Postseason_Report.pdf.

OECD (Organisation for Economic Co-operation and Development) (2014). Guidelines for multinational enterprises. Retrieved June 2, 2016 from http://mneguidelines.oecd.org.

——— (2015a). *G20/OECD Principles of Corporate Governance.* Retrieved June 2, 2016 from http://www.oecd.org/g20/meetings/antalya/Corporate-Governance-Principles-ENG.pdf.

——— (2015b). *OECD Principles of Corporate Governance.* Retrieved June 1, 2016 from http://www.oecd.org/daf/ca/corporategovernanceprinciples/31557724.pdf.

PRI ESG Working Group (2013). *Integrated Analysis: How Investors are Addressing Environmental, Social and Governance Factors in Fundamental Equity Valuation.* Retrieved June 2, 2016 from https://www.unpri.org/download_report/3950.

Randall, D.K. (2009). Sin stocks outperform over time, study says. *Forbes.* Retrieved June 26, 2016 from http://www.forbes.com/2009/10/21/sin-stocks-outperform-personal-finance-sin-stocks.html.

SocialFunds (2016). Screening your portfolio. Retrieved June 15, 2016 from http://www.socialfunds.com/page.cgi/article2.html.

Sullivan, R., & Xiong, J.X. (2012). How index trading increases market vulnerability. *Financial Analysts Journal,* 68(2), 70-83.

TUAC (Trade Union Advisory Committee) (2008). Labour and the OECD: the role of TUAC. Retrieved June 2, 2016 from http://www.tuac.org/en/public/tuac/0812_TuacRole.pdf.

——— (2014a). *TUAC Submission on the Review of the Principles of Corporate Governance.* Retrieved June 2, 2016 from http://www.tuac.org/en/public/e-docs/00/00/0E/49/document_doc.phtml (document "1403t_cg").

——— (2014b). The review process of the OECD Principles of Corporate Governance - Assessment by the TUAC Secretariat. Retrieved June 16, 2016 from http://www.tuac.org/en/public/e-docs/00/00/11/0D/document_doc.phtml.

UN Global Compact (2014). UN Global Compact homepage. Retrieved June 2, 2016 from https://www.unglobalcompact.org/index.html.

UNEP FI (UN Environment Programme Finance Initiative) (2011). *Responsible Investment in Passive Management Strategies: Case Studies and Guidance.* Retrieved June 2, 2016 from https://www.unpri.org/download_report/4005.

Unite Here! (n.d.). Card check and neutrality. Retrieved June 16, 2016 from http://unite-archive.library.cornell.edu/about/card.html.

UNWG (UN Working Group on Business and Human Rights) (2014). *The UN Guiding Principles on Business and Human Rights: An Introduction.* Retrieved June 2, 2016 from https://www.unglobalcompact.org/docs/issues_doc/human_rights/Resources/IntroToGPs.pdf.

U.S. DOL (U.S. Department of Labor) (2008). DOL Interpretive Bulletin 08-2. *Employee Benefits Security Administration, Labor.* Retrieved June 27, 2016 from http://webapps.dol.gov/FederalRegister/PdfDisplay.aspx?DocId=21630.

van der Velden, A., & van Buul, O. (2012). Really investing in the long-term: a case study. *Rotman International Journal of Pension Management,* 5(1), 50-57.

Zanglein, J., & Clark, D. (2001). *Capital Stewardship Certificate Program.* Silver Spring, MD: National Labor College.

7
Investing responsibly across traditional asset classes[1]

> For the HIT, there is no trade-off between ESG benefits and returns. The HIT's strategy is built on a cycle of sustainable investments, which begins when union pension plans invest capital in the HIT. This pension capital allows the HIT to finance multifamily development projects by purchasing government/agency multifamily construction-related securities. The securities help provide pension plan investors with competitive returns, while the projects create union construction jobs.
>
> Stephen Coyle, CEO, AFL-CIO Housing Investment Trust (HIT)

The foremost obligation of pension trustees is to invest plan assets in ways which may provide adequate retirement security to plan participants and beneficiaries (Croft, 2009). As discussed, ESG considerations can be material to investment performance, and institutional investors are increasingly using ESG analysis in their investment decision-making process.[2] When appropriately undertaken, ESG considerations can create sustained value (WBCSD and UNEP FI, 2010).

1 The *Handbook on Responsible Investment Across Asset Classes*, developed by David Wood and Belinda Hoff of the Boston College Center for Corporate Citizenship (Wood and Hoff, 2008), has been a very useful resource in the development of this chapter and the next. In addition, we relied on the PRI's implementation support for integrating responsible investments within a variety of asset classes. Many of these resources are available for free on the PRI's website (https://www.unpri.org), and we recommend trustees refer to these to increase their knowledge of responsible investments.

2 For example, see the list of signatories to PRI at https://www.unpri.org/signatory-directory/.

As discussed in Chapter 3, asset allocation is an important duty performed by trustee fiduciaries overseeing the prudent investment of plan assets. Asset allocation refers to the selection of appropriate asset classes for the investment of the fund's assets in relation to its investment objectives, risk tolerance and investment horizon.[3] A well-diversified portfolio consists of a range of asset classes in order to better spread investment risk.

In this chapter, we briefly discuss the traditional asset classes of public equities, fixed income, and cash, and how responsible investments can be incorporated into each. We present the characteristics of each asset class, and in each case explain the factors driving the realization of positive ESG impacts alongside tangible financial benefits. We also present examples of investment products and opportunities available to pension funds, alongside case studies of responsible investment practitioners.

The examples presented are by no means exhaustive, nor are we recommending them. Our sole aim is to help increase trustee knowledge of how traditional asset classes can support responsible investment strategies. In the next chapter, we follow a similar approach for responsible investment opportunities in alternative asset classes.

7.1 Public equity

Public equities consist of publicly traded stocks of corporations (issued in the form of common or preferred stocks) with market capitalization or market values ranging from nano-cap (<$50 million) to mega-cap (>$200 billion).[4] Generally, the larger the market capitalization, the lower the risk of investment and the smaller the potential returns.

Overall, public equities have a high return potential when compared with cash or fixed-income instruments, but they also exhibit significantly higher risk. At the same time, public equities offer high liquidity, the opportunity for long-term capital appreciation, income in the form of dividends, and portfolio diversification benefits.

Generally, public equities give investors ownership rights in the companies whose stock they own. As a result, shareholders obtain voting rights related

3 http://www.investopedia.com/terms/a/assetallocation.asp (retrieved June 21, 2016).

4 http://www.investopedia.com/articles/basics/03/031703.asp (retrieved June 21, 2016).

to corporate policy and governance (which can include ESG-related issues). These ownership rights are particularly important to pension funds in their role as universal owners who can wield the collective voting rights of numerous individual shareholders to positively influence corporate behavior.

7.1.1 Why make responsible public equity investments?

Public equity is the most commonly understood asset class for applying responsible investment strategies. Given its beginnings within religious groups, responsible investments in this asset class are often equated with negative or exclusionary screening. However, responsible investment approaches in public equities can be, and often are, applied in ways that go beyond exclusionary screens to deliberately integrate ESG considerations and active share ownership actions into investment decisions. According to the U.S. Forum for Sustainable and Responsible Investment's (SIF) 2012 trends report, the total value of responsible assets tracking all ESG factors (at approximately $3.4 trillion) far exceeds the value of those applying only exclusionary screens (at approximately $290 billion) (Voorhes *et al.*, 2012).

In terms of financial performance, on balance, active responsible investment approaches offer higher return advantages over exclusionary approaches (DB Climate Change Advisors, 2012; Clark *et al.*, 2014).[5] In addition, active approaches have been shown to not require trustee fiduciaries to trade their social and moral values for investment returns. As discussed, such approaches include the selection of best-in-class companies, integration of material ESG risks and opportunities into investment decisions, and post-investment active engagement by shareholders.

Various factors have contributed to the growing popularity of responsible public equity investments. Primary among these has been the demand for greater transparency and better corporate governance by institutional shareholders, particularly pension funds. In addition, seeing a rise in interest in ESG concerns from investors, asset managers have begun to offer responsible products and services that not only meet client demand, but also help these managers differentiate themselves from their peers (Calvert Foundation, 2012). Similarly, more and more corporations have come to view responsible operational behavior as not only good for their reputation, but also good for their financial bottom line.

As a result, ESG factors are increasingly seen as material to achieving an investment's intrinsic value (Roy and Gitman, 2012). According to a report

5 Please see Chapter 6 for more details.

by the International Integrated Reporting Council (IIRC), an increasing percentage of an investment's market value can be attributed to intangible assets including ESG factors. The report indicates that between 1975 and 2010, intangible assets increased from 17% of the market value of investments to 80% for S&P 500 companies (IIRC, 2011). Further, an increasing number of regulations now require public companies to disclose certain material ESG data as part of their reports to shareholders (Roy and Gitman, 2012). Popular financial data providers such as Bloomberg now also provide data on ESG factors and boast a large and growing number of ESG data providers and users (Bloomberg, 2015).

7.1.2 Opportunities in responsible public equities

In the previous chapter, we discussed various responsible investment approaches available to pension funds, from proxy voting and active shareownership to ESG integration. These approaches can be readily applied when investing in public equities. In this section, we focus on some of the broad product categories through which pension funds can access responsible public equity investments:

- **Pooled and mutual funds.** Pooled funds aggregate capital from various investors for investments in stocks, bonds, money market instruments, etc. Mutual funds are pooled funds, except a mutual fund is required to issue a prospectus under securities law.[6] Pooled and mutual funds can either be open or closed funds. For open funds, units in the fund can be bought or sold once a day based on the closing or opening net asset value (NAV); whereas for closed funds, trades are often not allowed until after a certain holding period, or allowed only in certain circumstances. As collective investment vehicles, pooled fund investments proportionately distribute the benefits and risks among investors.

  Generally, responsible pooled and mutual funds employ a combination of both exclusionary screens and positive screens when selecting investment opportunities. Many also use shareholder activism tools to have a greater positive impact on corporate behavior and operational policies. Some also support community

6 A prospectus is a "formal legal document, which is required by and filed with the Securities and Exchange Commission that provides details about an investment offering for sale to the public" (http://www.investopedia.com/terms/p/prospectus.asp, retrieved June 21, 2016).

projects by investing in community development banks, affordable housing, etc.

Given a wide range of responsible investor preferences and goals, a variety of funds have been developed whose mandate may range from a more broad-based ESG approach to funds that specialize in one thematic area (such as water resources). To enjoy diversification benefits, pension funds may opt to invest in a combination of available funds that collectively aim to meet their responsible investment goals.

Box 7.1: Responsible pooled funds

For example, labor-sponsored funds such as the Amalgamated Bank's LongView Funds, ULLICO's International Equity Fund and AFL-CIO's Equity Index Fund utilize active ownership strategies to hold public companies accountable on matters of shareholder importance. Other dedicated ESG-focused funds include the Calvert Equity and Calvert Bond funds and the Domini Social Equity Fund. Broad-based funds include funds such as the Vanguard FTSE Social index, which tracks the FTSE4Good U.S. Social Index, or the TIAA-CREF Social Choice Equity Fund (TISCX), which is an index-like fund that aims to replicate the risk characteristics of the Russell 3000 index while applying social screens maintained by the social-investment department at MSCI. Specialized thematic funds include green funds focused on environmental issues, such as the Green Century Balanced Fund, or community development funds, such as the CRA Qualified Investment Fund (Kathman, 2014).

When selecting a responsible investment fund, trustees and fiduciaries should conduct thorough due diligence on available products, just as they would for any other investments. Factors to consider should include the fund's fee structure, the fund manager's investment track record, and the fund's performance over the last few years. In addition, trustees should seek to understand the level of active shareholder engagement expected to be undertaken post-investment as part of the fund's overall responsible investment mandate.

- **Exchange-traded funds (ETFs) and notes (ETNs).** The underlying investments of ETFs and ETNs are some combination of stocks, bonds, and/or money market instruments. ETFs track an index or an index-like basket of assets. They trade on stock exchanges like common stocks, and investors can buy and sell ETFs as they would common stock. ETFs provide diversification benefits and liquidity, but they also limit investment choices to the composition of the index being tracked. ETNs combine features of both bonds and ETFs. These too can be traded on stock exchanges or held until maturity like a debt security.[7]

Because ETFs and ETNs track a basket of assets, they are impacted to a similar degree by market movements as the underlying assets. In addition, ETFs and ETNs can be complex and difficult to understand. Investors should be cautious, and thoroughly investigate the risks involved.

Unlike responsible pooled and mutual funds, responsible ETFs are barely a decade old.[8] However, there has been a gradual growth in the number of new ETFs, including those that focus on one or more ESG factors:

- The Global Alternative Energy ETF, which tracks the performance of a global universe of listed companies engaged in the alternative energy industry
- The Women In Leadership ETN that tracks the performance of the Barclays Women in Leadership Total Return USD Index, which only includes companies that, among other requirements, have a female CEO and/or at least 25% female members on the board of directors
- The more recent ALPS Workplace Equality Portfolio ETF that invests in both U.S. and global companies that support equality for LGBT employees in the workplace

A number of ETFs also focus on water infrastructure such as the PowerSharesWater Resources (PHO) ETF, which is the largest in this sector with $1 billion in investments.

Though many responsible ETFs and ETNs are currently small in size, and hence have higher fund expenses, their expansion reflects investor interest in supporting ESG considerations within various asset classes. As investors increase their allocations to such vehicles over time, the resulting economies of scale are expected to lower costs and further improve performance.

7 For ETFs, see http://www.investopedia.com/terms/e/etf.asp; for ETNs, see http://www.investopedia.com/terms/e/etn.asp (both retrieved June 21, 2016).

8 The first responsible ETF, the iShares MSCI USA ESG Select Index (KLD), was established in January 2005.

- **Direct public equity investments.** Direct public equity investments are held in investment portfolios through separate or segregated accounts. Direct investments allow investors to increase or decrease their allocation to particular companies without being bound to the composition of a pooled or indexed fund. Trustees and investment managers can therefore apply custom responsible investment criteria when selecting individual investments within an investment portfolio. Furthermore, direct investments may also provide greater opportunities for shareholder activism to trustees and their managers.

7.2 Fixed income

Fixed-income investments (also called bonds) consist of short- and long-term debt instruments with a fixed maturity and a fixed or adjustable return in the form of interest income. Fixed-income products are offered by a wide range of institutions, from national and local governments to private corporations and non-profit organizations. Bonds issued by governments and municipalities are often used to finance projects for the public good and therefore have an inherent social purpose. When issued by corporations, bonds are usually used to fund expansion projects. Depending on the credit standing of the issuer, bonds can range from being high-investment-grade bonds to non-investment-grade junk bonds or lower.[9]

7.2.1 Why make responsible fixed-income investments?

Despite recent credit market turmoil, fixed-income investments remain an integral part of pension investment portfolios.[10] A 2015 study of the top seven pension markets in the world reported aggregate allocations of 31% to fixed-income investments (Towers Watson, 2015). The study also reported a strong domestic bias in fixed-income allocation within the U.S. pension industry, with over 90% of the total fixed-income allocation invested in domestic

9 Fixed-income instruments can also include more complex products, such as derivatives, though these are beyond the scope of this chapter.

10 Fixed income investments have seen a great amount of turmoil in recent years as a result of the crash in the subprime housing market and the Eurozone sovereign debt crisis when debt issued by developed countries, historically considered a safer asset, underwent volatile swings in value.

bonds. Since fixed-income investments are generally made for income security, the primary goal of this asset class is seen as mitigating downside risk (PRI, 2011). The inclusion of ESG factors in fixed-income analysis can play an important role in mitigating this risk: "ESG factors can be material to both credit worthiness and investment performance" (PRI, 2013a).

Factors that form the backbone of traditional fixed-income analysis—such as credit risk, default risk, country risk, or litigation risk—can be significantly enhanced by incorporating material ESG considerations on a company-, industry-, or countrywide basis. For instance, by integrating governance considerations, such as levels of corruption in sovereign debt assessment, investors can better monitor the associated country risk of the sovereign issuer (this risk factor was one of the most important reasons for the start of the Eurozone debt crisis in 2009 (PRI, 2011), but one that was largely missed and/or ignored by traditional credit rating agencies).

In the past, the inclusion of ESG considerations in fixed-income analysis was limited to the impact of certain governance risk factors on an issuer's ability to repay its debt. However, as the PRI points out, environmental and social factors also present considerable risks to investors, in some cases having resulted in "credit rating downgrade, default, or even collapse of a company" (PRI, 2013b, p. 5). Enron, BP, TEPCO, and Lonmin are all examples of companies that suffered significant financial and reputational losses, to themselves, their bondholders, and their shareholders, due to a lack of investor attention to "issues outside traditional considerations of balance sheets and governance" in evaluating the companies' financial strength (PRI, 2013b, p. 5).

Despite negative precedence, credit rating agencies often do not adequately take into account ESG issues in the analysis of a fixed-income product's investment quality, perhaps due to a perceived lack of investor demand or evidence supporting the link between ESG factors and credit quality. However, case studies conducted by the PRI have shown high interest among institutional investors and managers in accounting for ESG issues in traditional credit analysis. The onus is, therefore, on investors and their consultants and managers to seek greater coverage of material ESG factors from investment managers and traditional rating agencies.

7.2.2 Opportunities in responsible fixed-income investments

Unlike equity investors, bondholders do not get a vote in relation to the management of companies to which they lend. It can therefore be difficult for bondholders to have an ongoing engagement with management on ESG issues. As such, large bondholders must undertake ESG-related due diligence upfront—that is, when the bond is about to be issued. This is when responsible investors can have maximum influence to incorporate terms friendly to ESG considerations and work to include them as part of the issuer's utilization of the capital raised (PRI, 2014).

Box 7.2: A responsible and competitive fixed-income strategy

The AFL-CIO Housing Investment Trust (HIT) is an open-end mutual fund that makes responsible fixed-income investments. The HIT's mission is to generate competitive risk-adjusted fixed-income returns by investing primarily in multifamily mortgage-backed securities, while providing affordable and workforce housing and creating union construction jobs. The HIT has applied responsible practices to its investments since inception in 1984 as a successor to the AFL-CIO Mortgage Investment Trust (MIT) fund. Since then, the fund has grown to over $5 billion in net assets, while financing 65,000 affordable housing units (99,000 total units) and creating 74,000 union construction jobs.

The HIT's primary investors include multiemployer pension plans, labor organizations, and public employee pension plans. These investors are attracted to the HIT because of the fund's ability to offer competitive fixed-income returns while achieving collateral benefits for labor and local communities.

For the HIT, there is no trade-off between ESG benefits and returns. The HIT's responsible investment philosophy supports its financial goals by taking less credit risk and investing in higher-yielding investments than the benchmark. The same philosophy supports its goals to provide union construction jobs, affordable and workforce housing, and community development through direct sourcing of construction-related multifamily mortgage-backed securities that together create a ripple effect in the local economies in which the HIT is invested.

Source: Interview and survey with AFL-CIO HIT, November 25, 2014.

Pension funds can make direct or indirect fixed-income investments in the following product categories such that invested assets target community development and/or environmental sustainability:

- **Corporate bonds.** Through investments in investment-grade corporate fixed-income securities, pension funds can target the responsible development and use of renewable energy, natural resources, community and economic development, affordable housing, etc. Pension funds may also choose to avoid investments in companies with poor corporate governance or a poor ESG track record. A majority of responsible investments in corporate bonds are through socially responsible pooled funds that either include investments based on certain positive criteria or screen out companies based on exclusionary criteria (Fraser, 2010).

Box 7.3: Typical responsible bonds

- The **Calvert Bond Portfolio (CSIBX)**, available to institutional investors, conducts ESG integration across sectors and holdings as part of its risk and opportunity assessment while seeking to provide as high a level of current income as is consistent with prudent investment risk and preservation of capital.
- The **Domini Social Bond Fund (DSBFX)** invests up to 10% of its holdings in community development finance institutions (CDFIs) that revitalize communities across the country.

- **Government bonds.** Government bonds can be bought domestically, such as U.S. Treasuries, and/or as foreign investments in the form of sovereign bonds. Government bonds can be issued to support the financing needs of a variety of government operations, including those that target specific investments such as infrastructure. Bonds that support the creation of public goods, such as schools and sustainable energy sources, may be particularly attractive to responsible investors (Wood and Hoff, 2008).

  When conducting sovereign debt analysis, funds will benefit from combining traditional credit analysis with material ESG considerations. The latter may include governance factors such as a country's corruption levels and legal and regulatory environment, social factors such as respect for labor rights and standards of health and education, and environmental factors such as climate change-related impacts (PRI, 2013b).

- **Municipal (muni) bonds.** Muni bonds include bonds issued by state governments, local governments, or quasi-government agencies. Pension funds do not generally buy local nontaxable muni bonds because they cannot take advantage of the tax breaks offered by these bonds. In addition, in some cases, the returns offered by such bonds may be too low to justify the investment of pension assets. However, taxable muni bonds, such as the Build America Bonds (BAB), can be more attractive to pension funds given the promise of higher yields, similar to the yields offered by corporate bonds.

  Appropriate muni bonds may, therefore, better meet the needs of pension funds seeking both reasonable returns and targeted regional, local, or community benefits. For example, pension funds may buy high-yielding muni bonds that fund a hydroelectric project or bonds that fund inner-city development. According to the Brookings Institution (Puentes *et al.*, 2013), the BAB program, if reinstated by Congress, would make muni bonds appealing to pension funds.[11]

- **Green bonds.** Green bonds are instruments that tie the proceeds of a bond issue to environmentally friendly investments. Green bonds are usually issued by international financial institutions that have a long history of providing numerous sustainable investment products in areas ranging from the environment to social development. The first green bond was issued in 2008 by the World Bank and these instruments have since seen tremendous interest from institutional investors.

  In 2012, $3 billion of green bonds were sold. In 2013, the number reached $10 billion (Economist, 2014), and in 2014, green bonds tripled to around $37 billion in assets. According to a recent study, the green bonds market is expected to reach $100 billion by the end of 2015 (Hulac, 2015).

  Green bonds have generally been investment grade, with the same credit profile of, and offering the same yield as, the issuer's conventional bonds, except that the issuer pledges to use the investment to finance environmental projects (Nicholls, 2013).

  Until recently, green bonds were issued primarily by multilateral financial institutions; however, they are now also being issued by corporations (see Box 7.4) and municipalities. Though there is currently a lack of commonly accepted, and enforced, verification and performance measurement tools to help better identify genuine green bond investments, investors may refer to the voluntary guidelines of the Green Bond Principles, and/or the Centre for International Climate and Environmental Research—Oslo (CICERO) investment framework (see Box 10.3) for help in this area.

11 The two-year BAB program was created by Congress in response to the dramatic effect of the 2007/8 financial market crisis on state and local government and entities' ability to issue debt. Established through the American Recovery and Reinvestment Act (ARRA, a.k.a. the "stimulus" bill) of 2009, the program authorized state and local governments to issue special taxable bonds that received either a 35% direct federal subsidy or a federal tax credit worth 35% of the interest owed to the investors, and was hugely successful.

Box 7.4: Private-sector green bonds

In March 2014, Toyota Financial Services, a division of Toyota Motors, sold a $1.75 billion bond to finance sales of zero-emission cars. The same month, Unilever, a consumer-goods company headquartered in the U.K., issued a £250 million ($416 million) green bond to fund expansion projects that will include clearly defined criteria on greenhouse gas emissions, water use, and waste disposal for the projects, and will outline a yearly reporting structure to provide full traceability of the funds raised.

7.3 Cash

Cash is part of the traditional asset classes of public equity and fixed income to which investors seek to allocate capital. Generally, cash investments account for 0 to 5% of total portfolio allocation. They are short term, and range from money held in checking and savings accounts to investments in money market instruments and certificates of deposit generally maturing within one year. Cash serves as a readily available source of money for general spending and/or as protection against emergencies, and, in the case of investors, provides a holding place for investments yet to be made.

As an asset class, cash offers very low risk and high liquidity, providing stability to the overall investment portfolio. On the other hand, it offers low returns and risks the loss of purchasing power in times of high inflation. Although pension funds typically hold only small amounts of cash that provide limited opportunities for responsible investments in this asset class, health and welfare plans and union treasuries (as well as other institutional investors, such as endowments) typically have significant cash management requirements.

7.3.1 Why make responsible cash investments?

Cash is perhaps the most underutilized asset class when it comes to allocations to responsible investments. Given its low yield and short-term nature, cash is viewed as a "defensive" asset class and accorded little attention by long-term investors (Hauser Center, 2011).

However, through its use by financial institutions that hold deposits for customers (such as banks, credit unions, and saving and loan institutions), cash investments can enable "access to finance for the broadest segments of society" (Hauser Center, 2011, p. 2). As such, when allocated by these institutions to low-income and under-served communities, cash can serve a strong social purpose by helping reduce social inequality. In addition, when deliberately invested for increased social benefits, such as through various community development finance institutions (CDFIs), cash enables responsible investors to actively seek environmental, community, and/or social impacts along with a financial return (Cates and Larson, 2010).

7.3.2 Opportunities for responsible cash investments

Investors wishing to utilize their cash allocations more responsibly can use one or both of the following approaches:

- Hold cash with or invest in financial institutions that make direct or indirect investments toward positive ESG impact
- Hold cash with or invest in financial institutions that follow an ESG approach in managing their own business activities

With limits on resources in the aftermath of the global financial crisis, financial institutions that still support reinvestments in local communities, and are themselves a responsible business, deserve the support of investors to create a cycle of reconstruction and development.

Box 7.5: A note on green banks

Green banks aim to bridge financing gaps for creditworthy clean energy and energy efficiency projects that can't scale up due to the lack of reasonably priced financing options in private capital markets. Three U.S. states, Connecticut, New York, and Hawaii, have already launched such banks, and many others are actively considering it. The New York Green Bank is the largest of these, seeking $1 billion in capitalization as of the writing of this *Handbook*. The banks have been able to leverage both public and private funds to drive investments into clean energy projects across their state. For example, Connecticut's Green Bank has attracted private capital by leveraging public funds by 10 to 1 (GreenBiz, 2014).

Many of the different instruments for responsible cash investments can be used to support community investing. While some of those listed below may be too small for very large pension plans, our intent is to showcase the application of responsible investments to a variety of asset classes. Further, as one source noted:

> community investing is a fragmented industry with various types of investment vehicles, maturities, and risk levels. Some CDs [certificates of deposit] and savings accounts have returns that are

competitive with those for traditional banks while other programs pay below-market rates. Because it's difficult to assign an economic value to the social benefits of community investing, it makes little sense to compare the returns from those programs with the returns for other investments. (Friend White, 2006)

As such, trustees may choose a responsible cash and community investment vehicle that best meets their return requirements for this asset class, keeping in mind that fiduciaries who are subject to ERISA are not permitted to sacrifice investment returns for social benefits.

- **Checking and savings accounts.** Everyday bank accounts such as checking and savings accounts offer the most basic responsible investment tool. These accounts can be held at financial institutions that are generally represented by big retail banks (but that are also responsible), at credit unions, or at depository CDFIs (NCIF, 2010).

  Under the Community Reinvestment Act (CRA) of 1977, regulated financial institutions have "continuing and affirmative obligations to help meet the credit needs of the local communities in which they are chartered." These institutions are rated on their compliance level with CRA requirements as "outstanding," "satisfactory," "needs to improve," or "substantial non-compliance" (NCRC, 2007). Ratings information, available to the public on the Federal Deposit Insurance Corporation's (FDIC) website,[12] can help pension funds deposit their assets with those banks that are actively supportive of the CRA and the communities in which they operate.

  In addition to the CRA ratings, corporate social responsibility (CSR) or other engagement reports published by big retail banks can provide insights into whether a given institution also integrates ESG issues into the way it does business. Such integration may include support for fair employment practices, firm-wide and board diversity, minimization of environmental footprint, and an active commitment to increase financing opportunities for local businesses and under-served communities.

  Another option lies in holding checking and savings accounts at credit unions, which by virtue of their organizational structure and non-profit business model seek to serve local communities. However, since the maximum insurance on credit union deposits is up to $250,000, they may not meet the needs of large institutional

12 https://www5.fdic.gov/crapes/.

Box 7.6: Labor's responsible financial institutions

- **Amalgamated Bank**, founded in 1923 by ACTWU, with branches in California, Washington, D.C., New Jersey and New York, has a history of active investments in affordable housing. Recently, the bank approved $100 million for investment in such housing in New York City. The bank is also exploring opportunities for a bold new fund, potentially in collaboration with New York City and/or state pension plans, which aims to invest over $1 billion in multifamily housing in the city.
- **AmalgaTrust**, a division of Amalgamated Bank, is a trustee on various real estate trusts and requires that all construction be accomplished with union labor. It also established a customized labor-friendly proxy voting program in 1996 and has participated since inception in the AFL-CIO Key Vote Survey for Pension Fund Investment Managers.
- The **Amalgamated Bank of Chicago**, founded in 1922 by ACTWU, is dedicated to serving America's working people. The bank offers new and innovative banking products and services to unions and union members in Chicago and across the nation. With significant union ownership, the bank remains one of only a handful of U.S. banks devoted to the labor community.
- The **Bank of Labor**, founded in 1924 by the International Brotherhood of Boilermakers, grew its roots deep into the labor community of greater Kansas City. Its original mission was to be a bank that working men and women could trust. The bank recently opened a branch in Washington, D.C.

investors such as pension plans. In this case, investing in larger certificates of deposit that are insured under the FDIC may be a better option as outlined below.

- **Certificates of deposit.** A certificate of deposit (CD) is a promissory note issued by a financial institution, entitling the investor to receive a fixed interest over a fixed term. The term on CDs generally ranges from one month to five years. Certificates of deposit offer a cash-based way to finance small businesses, microenterprises, non-profits, commercial real estate, and affordable housing in low- and middle-income communities.

  The Certificate of Deposit Account Registry Service (CDARS) can be used by institutional investors to create one large cash deposit that is placed in multiple banks while still qualifying for federal deposit insurance by the FDIC. The National Federation of Community Development Credit Unions offers a similar product for credit union CDs.[13]

13 See http://www.cdars.com and http://www.cdcu.coop.

- **Money market instruments.** These include money market accounts and money market mutual funds. The former are interest-earning savings accounts with FDIC-insured financial institutions, while the latter are managed by fund companies and do not offer any guarantee of investments even though they are viewed as risk-free investments (Loth, 2013). Money market accounts, such as the Pax World Money Market Account, deposit their assets in a community based-bank in Chicago that offers investors a liquid investment vehicle for holding their cash allocation while investing in social and community benefits (Pax World Investments, 2014).

7.4 Takeaways

Pension trustees are likely to be familiar with the types of traditional asset class and investment product we discuss in this chapter. However, they may be less familiar with the possibility of applying responsible investment strategies across these asset classes. As such, our aim in this chapter has been to increase trustee knowledge of the characteristics of each of these asset classes in relation to responsible investments, so that trustees may be able to include responsible investments within a diversified pension investment portfolio.

7.5 References

Bloomberg (2015). *Impact Report Update 2015*. Retrieved June 18, 2016 from https://www.bbhub.io/sustainability/sites/6/2016/04/16_0404_Impact_Report.pdf#page=11.

Calvert Foundation (2012). *Gateways to Impact: Industry Survey of Financial Advisors on Sustainable and Impact Investing*. Retrieved June 2, 2016 from http://www.calvertfoundation.org/storage/documents/Gateways-to-Impact.pdf.

Cates, R.S., & Larson, C. (2010). *Connecting CDFIs to the Socially Responsible Investor Community*. Retrieved June 2, 2016 from https://www.cdfifund.gov/Documents/Connecting%20CDFIs%20to%20the%20Socially%20Responsible%20Investor%20Commun.pdf.

Clark, G., Feiner, A., & Viehs, M. (2014, October 20). *From the Stockholder to the Stakeholder: How Sustainability Can Drive Financial Outperformance*. doi:10.2139/ssrn.2508281.

Croft, T. (2009). *Up from Wall Street: The Responsible Investment Alternative*. New York, NY: Cosimo Books.

DB Climate Change Advisors (2012). *Sustainable Investing: Establishing Long-Term Value and Performance*. Retrieved June 2, 2016 from https://www.db.com/cr/en/docs/Sustainable_Investing_2012.pdf.

Economist (2014, July 5). Green grow the markets, O. *The Economist.* Retrieved June 2, 2016 from http://www.economist.com/news/finance-and-economics/21606326-market-green-bonds-booming-what-makes-bond-green-green-grow.

Fraser, B.W. (2010, April 7). SRI bond funds a small but growing niche. *Financial Advisor.* Retrieved June 2, 2016 from http://www.fa-mag.com/news/sri-bond-funds-a-small-but-growing-niche-5308.html.

Friend White, C. (2006, February 3). The socially responsible investor. Retrieved June 2, 2016 from http://msmoney.com/what-is-a-prenup/womens-corner/millionairess/the-socially-responsible-investor/.

GreenBiz (2014, May 6). Green Bank Act gets a second chance. Retrieved June 2, 2016 from http://www.greenbiz.com/blog/2014/05/06/green-bank-act-gets-second-chance.

Hauser Center (2011). *Understanding Cash as an Asset Class Within a Theory of Responsible Investment.* Retrieved June 2, 2016 from http://hausercenter.org/iri/wp-content/uploads/2010/05/Summary-of-March-4-Cash-Convening.pdf.

Hulac, B. (2015, May 29). Moody's: green bonds will more than double to $100B this year. *ClimateWire.* Retrieved June 2, 2016 from http://www.eenews.net/stories/1060019301.

IIRC (International Integrated Reporting Council) (2011). *Towards Integrated Reporting: Communicating Value in the 21st Century.* Retrieved June 2, 2016 from http://integratedreporting.org/wp-content/uploads/2011/09/IR-Discussion-Paper-2011_spreads.pdf.

Kathman, D. (2014). Find the right socially responsible fund. *MorningstarAdvisor.* Retrieved June 2, 2016 from http://www.morningstar.com/advisor/t/86835856/find-the-right-socially-responsible-fund.htm.

Loth, R. (2013, May 24). Do money-market funds pay? *Investopedia.* Retrieved June 2, 2016 from http://www.investopedia.com/articles/02/120602.asp.

NCIF (National Community Investment Fund) (2010). *Doing Business with Community Development Banking Institutions: A Deposits Initiative.* Retrieved June 2, 2016 from http://hausercenter.org/iri/wp-content/uploads/2010/05/DepositsInitiative_Final.pdf.

NCRC (National Community Reinvestment Coalition (2007). *CRA Manual.* Retrieved June 2, 2016 from http://www.ncrc.org/images/stories/pdf/cra_manual.pdf.

Nicholls, M. (2013). Painting the bond markets green. *YourSRI.* Retrieved June 2, 2016 from https://yoursri.com/responsible-investing/newsletter/Topic%20of%20the%20month%20June%202013.

Pax World Investments (2014). Funds. Retrieved June 2, 2016 from http://paxworld.com/funds/home.

PRI (Principles for Responsible Investment) (2011). *Fixed Income Work Stream: Discussion Paper.* Retrieved June 2, 2016 from https://www.unpri.org/download_report/3983.

——— (2013a). *Sovereign Bonds: Spotlight on ESG Risks.* Retrieved June 18, 2016 from http://www.corporate-engagement.com/files/file/report%20SFIWG%202013.pdf.

——— (2013b). *Corporate Bonds: Spotlight on ESG Risks.* Retrieved June 2, 2016 from https://www.unpri.org/download_report/3829.

——— (2014, February 4). Fixed income the "neglected child" of responsible investment. Retrieved June 2, 2016 from https://www.unpri.org/page/fixed-income-the-neglected-child-of-responsible-in.

Puentes, R., Sabol, P., & Kane, J. (2013, August 28). Cut to invest: revive Build America Bonds (BABs) tó support state and local investments. Retrieved June 2, 2016 from http://www.brookings.edu/research/papers/2013/08/28-build-america-bonds-puentes-sabol-kane.

Roy, H., & Gitman, L. (2012). *Trends in ESG Integration in Investments: Summary of the Latest Research and Recommendations to Attract Long-term Investors.* Retrieved June 2, 2016 from http://www.bsr.org/reports/BSR_Trends_in_ESG_Integration.pdf.

Towers Watson (2015). *Global Pensions Asset Study: 2015*. Retrieved May 26, 2016 from https://www.towerswatson.com/en-US/Insights/IC-Types/Survey-Research-Results/2015/02/Global-Pensions-Asset-Study-2015.

Voorhes, M., Humphreys, J., & Solomon, A. (2012). Report on sustainable and responsible investing trends in the United States: 2012. Retrieved June 2, 2016 from http://www.ussif.org/content.asp?contentid=82.

WBCSD (World Business Council for Sustainable Development) & UNEP FI (UN Environment Programme Finance Initiative) (2010). *Translating ESG into Sustainable Business Value*. March 2010. Retrieved June 15, 2016 from http://www.unepfi.org/fileadmin/documents/translatingESG.pdf.

Wood, D., & Hoff, B. (2008). *Handbook on Responsible Investment Across Asset Classes*. Retrieved June 2, 2016 from http://ccc.bc.edu/index.cfm?fuseaction=document.showDocumentByID&nodeID=1&DocumentID=1170.

8
Responsible alternative investments

> Our pensions can be partners with government policy makers and public investments to build affordable worker housing, effective and efficient public transportation, energy efficient buildings, infrastructure that will improve communities' resiliency in the face of climate change, sea level rise and catastrophic weather events.
>
> Kirsten Snow Spalding, Ceres California Director

Today, many pension fund leaders are making responsible investments in the real economy in strategic industries and SMEs, affordable and workforce housing, and economic and social infrastructure, for example. Such investments can be made as part of the alternative investment asset class that includes the sub-asset classes of real estate, private equity, and infrastructure, among others. There are many good reasons for pension funds to invest in alternative investments, including portfolio diversification benefits and higher return potential. Most importantly, alternative investments generally require a long-term investment horizon, which aligns the attributes of this asset class with the long-term goals of pension fund investments.

Responsible alternative investments have witnessed strong growth over the last few years. The U.S. SIF reported an estimated $224 billion in responsible alternative investments in 2014, up from $69.8 billion in 2010 (Voorhes, 2012; Humphreys, 2011). As discussed, U.S. pension funds have traditionally classified investments that create collateral benefits as economically targeted investments (ETIs). More recently, a growing number of pension funds have designed investment policies that utilize the global ESG framework to make such investments. In addition, many foundations, high-net-worth individuals, and family offices are beginning to engage in impact investments as part of making responsible investments within the alternatives asset class. No matter what label is applied, such investments can provide an opportunity to create collateral benefits while also earning competitive risk-adjusted returns. Some investors choose to make much-needed investments in the real economy and achieve the same ends without worrying about the labels.

As with traditional asset classes, responsible alternative investments can provide not only competitive financial returns, but also positive ESG impacts. In this chapter, we discuss the alternative investment sub-asset classes of real estate, private equity, infrastructure, and commodities, and provide examples of responsible investment strategies for each. Hedge funds, derivatives, and some other sub-categories, such as farmland, are not discussed.

8.1 Understanding alternative investments

As mentioned, alternative investments provide important diversification benefits to pension investment portfolios. Due to their limited correlation with the traditional asset classes of stock, bonds, and cash, alternative investments exhibit risk–return characteristics that are different than traditional asset classes (CAIAA, n.d.). In addition, the long-term nature of alternative investment sub-asset classes of real estate and infrastructure, for example, aligns well with the long-term nature of pension fund liabilities.

Given generally higher return expectations from this asset class than from traditional asset classes, the risk potential is correspondingly higher. While successful alternative investments can hit "home runs," earning large profits, it is also true that some investments can fail. For example, the real estate crash of the early 1990s and the fallout from the dot.com collapse of the early 2000s resulted in many failed investments. Similarly, in the last financial crisis, many pension funds suffered big losses due to overexposure in high-risk hedge funds, real estate investments and leveraged buyout (LBO) funds.

Some alternative investments, such as certain types of private equity, real estate, and infrastructure, can be quite illiquid. The fiduciary duty of managing expenses can also be more difficult with alternative investments. External manager fee structures can be opaque, and many irresponsible external managers have been criticized for pocketing unreasonably high management fees. In addition, since alternative investments are generally traded infrequently, historical data on the risks and returns for alternative investments is limited. As such, "there may be no reliable measure of investment value at any point in time other than at termination, where the investment's value is the amount of the final liquidating cash flow" (CAIAA, n.d., p. 15).

In light of these characteristics, trustees should seek a thorough rationale from their pension funds' internal staff and/or external consultants to justify an allocation to alternative investments. Such a rationale should include a careful consideration of the risk–return attributes of each of the sub-asset classes within alternative investments before committing pension assets to them.

Further, pension funds that make in-house investment decisions regarding alternative investments require at-scale expertise. Such funds retain their own investment professionals who can provide due diligence, and execute and manage the investments. Typically, only large pension funds are able to do this, as it is difficult for smaller funds to maintain in-house capacity in specialized asset classes. For example, large public funds, such as the nearly $280 billion CalPERS in the U.S.A. and the $77 billion Ontario Municipal Employees Retirement System (OMERS) in Canada, manage varying degrees of their infrastructure investment portfolios in-house, while smaller funds such as the $11 billion New Mexico Education Retirement Board (NMERB) have outsourced these investments to specialized external managers (CalPERS, 2016; OMERS, 2015; NMERB, 2015).

When making alternative investments via external managers, trustees, with the assistance of their consultants, should carefully analyze the track record, professional capacity, and fee structures of the external manager in the applicable alternative investment category.

8.2 Alternative investments and their application to responsible investment strategies

Pension funds can make investments in alternatives in ways that positively impact each of the "E," "S," and "G" goals of their investment portfolio. These impacts include, but are not limited to:

- **The "E" in ESG**
  - Investing in and growing sustainable enterprises and sectors
  - Utilizing green and LEED building construction practices and Global Real Estate Sustainability Benchmark (GRESB) principles in real estate[1]
  - Deploying efficient and renewable energy and transportation practices
  - Modernizing older industries through waste and pollution reduction, and improving air and water quality
  - Furthering sustainable and smart growth transit-oriented development strategies
- **The "S" in ESG**
  - Creating or retaining good jobs, including increased training and apprenticeships for union members and residents
  - Providing fair wages and benefits, and ensuring safe and fair working conditions
  - Employing responsible contractor policies and card check neutrality, and furthering project labor agreements (PLAs) to ensure that workers have a voice on the job
  - Investing in affordable workforce and multifamily housing
  - Supporting responsible, high-road supply chains; avoiding low-road offshoring/outsourcing
- **The "G" in ESG**
  - Promoting good corporate governance practices in privately held companies
  - Ensuring an alignment of interests between general partners and limited partners
  - Seeking transparency and disclosure of alternative investment performance and fees

Below we discuss the primary characteristics of the alternative investment sub-asset classes of real estate, private equity, infrastructure, and commodities, and present responsible investment options in each.

1 GRESB provides ESG-based data for the global real estate sector. For more, please see Appendix C and https://www.gresb.com.

8.2.1 Real estate: developing and renewing the built environment

For institutional investors, real estate investments range from direct investments in residential and commercial rental properties to pooled investments in real estate private equity and mutual funds, publicly traded or non-traded real estate investments trusts (REITs), and mortgage-backed securities (Wood and Hoff, 2008). Pension funds can also invest in credit enhancement products, and they can loan their credit rating to a municipality or a state agency for a fee.

Real estate investments can be further categorized into property development and redevelopment investments. Property development refers to the financing and construction of new real estate stock. Property redevelopment, on the other hand, refers to improvements, upgrades, and expansions to existing real estate stock (Falconer, 1999). As such, property redevelopment may include the purchase of "distressed or under-valued properties for enhancement and holding or resale," offering great potential for the inclusion of ESG factors (Wood and Hoff, 2008, p. 63).

As an alternative asset class, real estate investments have a low correlation with traditional asset classes. In addition, real estate investments complement traditional stock and bond investments within the total portfolio by providing bondlike predictable income (rent) and equity-like growth (capital appreciation). Given a higher correlation with inflation, real estate investments also offer inflation protection.

While direct real estate investments provide more control and are expected to offer a higher payoff, these investments also present high risk, are illiquid, and require more specialized investment expertise. Investments in pooled funds, on the other hand, offer better liquidity and access to professional expertise, as well as diversification benefits when combined with other direct real estate investments in a portfolio. Because of their specialized nature, both direct and pooled real estate investments can result in high investment management fees. However, conventional private equity-style real estate funds usually tend to be the most expensive with a "2 and 20" fee model; we discuss this model in more detail in the private equity section.

8.2.1.1 Why make responsible real estate investments?

The inherent characteristics of real estate investments discussed earlier—such as the underlying hard assets that are built in a physical environment, longer holding periods for direct investments and non-traded REITs, and expectations of long-term, predictable income—offer opportunities to create and sustain positive impacts across the ESG spectrum alongside tangible financial benefits for real estate investments. As the *Handbook on Responsible Investment Across Asset Classes* notes:

> the built environment inevitably plays a role in the way humans relate to each other and to their natural surroundings. The goal for the responsible investor is to identify those areas where long-term social, environmental, and economic impacts can both impact and be created through the investment process. (Wood and Hoff, 2008, p. 56)

Building trades pension funds have long invested in real estate projects, creating housing and good jobs for union members and other citizens while generating returns for the funds' investments. These projects have included new construction and renovations of:

- Affordable and workforce housing
- Special needs housing, such as for the elderly and students
- Multifamily housing and multiuse facilities
- Commercial real estate, such as hotels and industrial and office buildings.
- Hospitals, retirement centers, and assisted living facilities
- Warehouses and industrial parks

As the scope of responsible investments has broadened to include a wide range of ESG impacts, pioneer pension funds have maintained the pace by not only investing in much-needed social real estate, such as low-income housing, and creating good jobs, but also reviving the U.S.A.'s urban centers while utilizing green building technologies. In addition, investors are now paying greater attention to governance measures such as transparency in real estate investments, and studies predict larger pay-offs from investments in sectors and regions that improve on such metrics (Jones Lang LaSalle, 2013).

Ultimately, these responsible investors are developing sustainable and resilient built environments that improve social and environmental health, increase operational efficiencies, and provide better investment returns in the long run.

Box 8.1: Best practices in responsible real estate

Multi-Employer Property Trust

The Multi-Employer Property Trust (MEPT) fund was established in the early 1980s with a commitment to achieving strong risk-adjusted returns for its pension fund investors while also using 100% signatory contractors and union labor on all of its buildings. Over the years, MEPT's strategy has evolved to include a commitment to sustainability, and the fund is a recognized leader in responsible property investing. MEPT invests in commercial real estate properties including multifamily, office, industrial, and retail assets. The fund currently owns approximately $7.3 billion in gross assets, all of which are managed responsibly in order to create a stable income stream and long-term value for its investors.

MEPT's primary focus is on achieving strong investment returns. However, responsible investing has always been a key part of MEPT's investment strategy; the fund's management team believes that ESG benefits, if properly applied to an investment, improve asset performance and lower investment risk. Accordingly, every asset that MEPT considers is vetted for ESG performance and enhancement opportunities.

Specifically, MEPT applies a responsible contractor policy to all of its investments, requiring the use of 100% signatory contractors and union labor on any construction that the fund pays for, including base building construction, tenant improvements, and capital expenditures. Since its founding in 1982, MEPT has created over 218 million job hours in the markets where it has invested. MEPT is the largest open-end real estate fund with this stringent of a responsible contractor policy. In addition, beginning in the 1990s, MEPT recognized that building and maintaining properties that are efficient and sustainable creates a competitive advantage in terms of attracting high-quality tenants, improves net operating income, and protects against obsolescence. As such, MEPT invests in development assets that are designed to achieve LEED silver certification or better, and its operating portfolio is included in the U.S. Green Building Council (USGBC) LEED certification program and benchmarked to the U.S. Environmental Protection Agency's (EPA) Energy Star program. As a result, MEPT owns 10 million square feet of LEED-certified and Energy Star-labeled properties.[2]

MEPT's investment approach has placed the fund at the top of the GRESB survey rankings for the last several years, including being ranked the #1 U.S. Diversified Fund and earning a "Green Star" in the 2014 survey. Concurrently, GRESB named MEPT's real estate advisor, Bentall Kennedy, the top firm in the diversified peer group in North America and globally for 2014.[3] In addition, Bentall Kennedy has received the Energy Star Partner of the Year award for the last five years.

2 Sarah Stettinius, Senior Vice President, Bentall Kennedy (U.S.) LP/MEPT, personal communication/interview, January 15, 2015.

3 MEPT achieved #1 ranking in the U.S. Diversified peer group among 36 funds; and #1 ranking among the 28 funds, recognized as funds in the NCREIF Fund Index—Open End Diversified Core Equity (NFI-ODCE) that participated in the GRESB survey. See also UNEP FI, 2012, and https://www.gresb.com.

Intercontinental Real Estate Corporation

Established in 1959, the Intercontinental Real Estate Corporation invests in nearly all aspects of commercial real estate, including offices, retail, multifamily, senior living, student housing, and hotels. The firm manages assets in excess of $4 billion on behalf of many Taft–Hartley retirement funds and unions, and all of its assets are invested following a general responsible investment framework. The firm claims that ensuring fair wages and benefits together with socially responsible stewardship is considered mission critical. In so doing, the firm supports neutrality agreements and the use of union labor for new and existing construction projects. In addition, the firm believes in smart and green construction, and includes a vast majority of LEED-certified assets within its investment portfolio.

For example, in the aftermath of Hurricane Sandy, the firm is developing two mid-rise apartment buildings in Hoboken, New Jersey, that are LEED certified, complete with green roofs, water re-filtration systems, and state-of-the-art "smart" parking garages, among other green features. In another example, the firm's portfolio of assisted living facilities has LED lighting on each of its nine buildings. Returns on this smart, green investment were achieved in the first three years, after which the savings realized have directly contributed to the bottom line.[4]

As Peter Palandjian, chairman and CEO, notes:

> By adhering to responsible investing we are able to keep buildings current, which has allowed us to push rents up and keep costs low. In addition, the higher-quality training of union labor, the surety of available union workforce, and the safety standards of all-union construction lead to higher-quality craftsmanship and faster delivery, all of which translate to better risk-adjusted investing.

These benefits are compounded given the firm's long-term investment bias, which allows it to realize higher cost savings and efficiencies over the course of the investment period.

8.2.1.2 Opportunities in responsible real estate

The PRI has defined responsible investments in real estate that recognize ESG considerations along with financial objectives as responsible property investments (RPI). Such investments go beyond minimum real estate construction requirements to include, for example, strategies such as energy efficiency and resource conservation.

For pension fund investors engaging in responsible real estate or infrastructure investments, an important element is the development and enforcement of a responsible contractor policy (RCP) that protects labor interests. As such, pension funds should aim to work with those managers who can assist in the implementation of the fund's RCP or who maintain their own RCP (Wood and Hoff, 2008).

4 Peter Palandjian, Chairman and CEO, Intercontinental Real Estate Corp., personal communication/interview, April 20, 2015.

Box 8.2: Responsible property investment: key attributes

The UNEP FI recommends that responsible property be implemented from the property planning, design, and development stages and continually practiced throughout the property's life-cycle. The key to managing and monitoring progress on these issues can be achieved through the implementation of systems for measuring and benchmarking performance. Key activities include, as sourced directly from the UNEP FI:

- Developing or acquiring properties designed with environmentally and socially positive attributes (e.g., low-income housing or green buildings)
- Refurbishing properties to improve their environmental and social performance (e.g., energy efficiency, on-site power generation, disability upgrades, natural light exploitation, or other environmentally and socially responsible improvements)
- Managing properties in environmentally and socially beneficial ways (e.g., green leases, resource use, and waste & recycling benchmarking practices to improve performance, fair labor practices for service workers, and environmentally friendly cleaning methods and products)
- Demolishing properties in a conscientious manner (e.g., reusing recovered materials on-site for new development)

Source: UNEP FI, 2016.

Box 8.3: Responsible contractor policy

A responsible contractor policy (RCP) is a document that establishes provisions for labor in relation to wages, worker health and safety, and manager neutrality in union organizing campaigns and training programs, among other labor concerns. An RCP can also be required for protecting the rights of workers engaged in an asset's operation and maintenance when these workers are not covered by existing regulations such as those that provide some protection to construction trade workers.[5] As such, RCPs can strengthen the collective bargaining power of all workers. RCPs can also help protect the value of investments by ensuring the use of qualified contractors with skilled employees to avoid project delays and potential liabilities.

RCPs apply to both real estate and infrastructure assets. We discuss RCPs in more detail in the infrastructure section. In addition, we provide examples of RCPs of pioneer pension funds, investment managers, and labor leaders both in subsequent sections of this chapter and in Appendix B.

5 For example, the Davis Bacon Act of 1931 protects construction workers in all federally funded or assisted road projects by requiring 'prevailing wage' rates. Though the Act does not require union hiring, it has helped equalize bidding for union- and non-union constructions contractors (Barnhart, 2013).

Some examples of responsible real estate investment opportunities include:

- **Energy efficiency.** Buildings, through their construction, use, maintenance, and demolition, contribute up to 30% to global annual GHG emissions and consume up to 40% of all energy (UNEP SBCI, 2009). Investments in energy efficiency improvements that can lower these emissions may result in operational cost savings that may in turn improve rental yields, reduce vacancies, and lead to higher capital values on real estate investments.
- **Urban revitalization.** There is a strong interest to invest in the revival of the U.S.A.'s urban centers and town squares, as economic, demographic, and resource shifts bring young, working, and retired people alike back to cities and towns.[6] This revival is targeting transit-oriented, walkable, service-rich, opportunity-dense communities with access to arts, education, and green spaces. Such revitalization "may create a healthy environment that improves real estate values across whole neighborhoods and increases tenant satisfaction and economic activity in commercial and residential real estate alike" (Wood and Hoff, 2008, p. 57).
- **Affordable housing development.** Responsible real estate investments can fill capital gaps in areas that otherwise might not be funded, such as workforce and low-income housing. Further, funding partnerships can be forged with governments and other like-minded investors to secure guarantees and lessen risk.
- **Union-based job creation.** Responsible real estate investments can create good union-based jobs that in turn participate in creating affordable housing and providing economic stimulus to local communities (AFL-CIO, 2015). Such jobs should support "fair labor practices, responsible contractor policies, and enhanced health and safety policies (that) may improve labor performance, mitigate against health problems and corporate reputation risks, and reduce the negative social externalities associated with poor labor practices" (Wood and Hoff, 2008, pp. 58-59). For example, four pension-capitalized fixed income/real estate funds (AFL-CIO HIT, AFL-CIO BIT, ULLICO, and MEPT) invested nearly $22 billion in responsible

6 For instance, see Doherty, 2013 and Mykleby *et al.*, 2016. Find out more about these trends at urban planning and policy centers, such as the Brookings Institution.

property investments between 1995 and 2010, creating 161,083 job years, according to a report from the American Rights at Work Education Fund (Wasser, 2011).

- **Green building construction and operation.** A green building incorporates environmental and health concerns and resource efficiencies throughout its life-cycle.[7] Green building technologies provide responsible pension fund investors with opportunities to lower consumption of resources and increase operational efficiencies that can over time translate into better returns on investments. According to a 2010 UNEP FI study, the green construction market in the U.S.A. generated $173 billion in GDP, supported over 2.4 million jobs, and provided nearly $123 billion in earnings to labor between the years 2000 and 2008 (UNEP FI, 2010).

8.2.2 Private equity: revitalizing the industrial commons

Pension funds and other institutional investors are increasingly investing in the area of private equity, which entails equity and/or debt investments in nonpublic companies (or, sometimes, buyouts of public companies that results in a delisting). Investments by early private equity firms were responsible for many notable business start-ups, including Digital Equipment Company (DEC) and Fairchild Semiconductor (which produced the first commercially practicable integrated circuit), and later helped finance the growth of Silicon Valley.

Private equity firms provide expertise and capital to the companies in which they invest and typically have a measure of control in the management of the investee companies. When private equity investments lead to the growth of innovative firms, provide good investment returns, and create and retain good jobs, for example, they can be an attractive investment strategy for responsible pension fund investors. As noted by Michael Psaros, Co-Founder and Managing Partner, KPS Capital Partners:

7 Green buildings are "certified" by groups such as Leadership in Energy and Environmental Design (LEED), an internationally recognized green building certification system developed by the U.S. Green Building Alliance. LEED provides third-party verification that a building or community "was designed and built using strategies aimed at improving performance across all the metrics that matter most: energy savings, water efficiency, CO_2 emissions reduction, improved indoor environmental quality, and stewardship of resources and sensitivity to their impacts" (Boston University, 2016; see also USGBC, 2016).

Box 8.4: Teachers helping communities

The American Federation of Teachers (AFT), which represents over 1.6 million workers in education, healthcare, and public service, supports many responsible investment initiatives that seek to benefit both the investment value of teachers' pension funds and the wellbeing of teachers and the communities they serve.

For example, AFT is spearheading a partnership to create shared prosperity in McDowell County, the poorest county in West Virginia, with the highest rates of heart disease, suicide, and drug overdose (a consequence of job losses during the coal industry downturn). The AFT's initiatives in the county include the revitalization of public schools in order to "keep the county's roughly 3,500 students from becoming any one of those statistics" mentioned earlier. The AFT is also building a livable village for the county's residents by focusing on the provision of social services, housing, and transportation. In the next 3–5 years AFT, in partnership with AFL-CIO HIT, is also embarking on increasing the stock of teacher housing to support teachers' ability to live and work in the county.

In another example, AFT has committed up to $15 million to Oregon's Cool Schools Initiative, a project to help finance energy efficiency and other upgrades to school buildings across Oregon. The funds will be made available in partnership with unions and ULLICO, a union-owned financial service provider discussed later in this chapter.

Source: Randi Weingarten, President, AFT, personal communication/interview, November 17, 2014; PBS Newshour, 2015; Siemers, 2011.

> We see the power in capital and labor working together with one another ... KPS's relationship with large industrial, transportation and service unions in the U.S. and Canada has contributed 25–33% of KPS's deal flow. Either you recognize that the union representing employees is critical to your success, or you compromise your ability to succeed.[8]

The managers of private equity firms are known as general partners (GPs). Investors, including pension funds, are called limited partners (LPs). Private equity investments tend to be risky but also offer a higher potential for returns than traditional asset classes. Such investments also tend to be relatively illiquid, with holding periods for portfolio companies typically between three and seven years. In addition, the fee structure can be very costly, generally based on a "2 and 20" model charged by most private equity firms and hedge funds. In this fee model, firms charge a flat management fee of 2% of total asset value (invested and committed capital) as well as an additional 20% on any profits earned.[9] More recently, the fee structure

8 Michael Psaros, personal communication/interview, January 11, 2015.

9 The flat management fee is charged on all capital, whether it is invested or committed. Committed capital is a contractual agreement between the GP and the

has been reduced by some firms to a slightly lower "1.4 and 17" model after coming under pressure from investors, particularly in the aftermath of the recent financial crisis (Economist, 2014a).

Private equity investments refer to a variety of products and strategies including:[10]

- **Venture capital.** This refers to investments in start-ups or small emerging companies. These "seed" and early stage investments are often made in companies that are either developing unproven technologies and/or targeting unproven markets, often in high-tech fields.
- **Growth capital.** Growth capital is used to expand a business or take advantage of opportunities requiring more capital than a company can generate from its cash flow or existing lenders or owners. It includes sizable privately placed debt and/or equity capital investments in small- to middle-market firms, spanning manufacturing, transportation, distribution, communications, and technology industries. Often, existing firms (and industries) are easier to evaluate for profits and productivity than venture markets.
- **Mezzanine financing.** This is a hybrid of debt and equity financing models that is typically used to finance the expansion of existing companies. Investors provide debt capital that gives them the rights to convert to an ownership or equity interest in the company under certain conditions. Given its structure, this type of financing is generally subordinated to debt provided by senior lenders such as banks and venture capital companies.
- **Leveraged buyout (LBO).** LBO investors acquire a large and often controlling stake in a company through the use of borrowed money to finance the acquisition. As a result, LBOs often have high debt/equity ratios. Such investments generally seek to invest in more mature companies and, if done right, can enable such companies to expand through capital investments and reorganizations.

LP "that obligates the investor to contribute money to the fund. The investor may pay all of the committed capital at one time, or make contributions over a period of time. This often takes place over a number of years" (http://www.investopedia.com/terms/c/committedcapital.asp, retrieved June 21, 2016).

10 For expanded definitions of terms referenced, please search investopedia.com.

Box 8.5: Identifying bad LBOs

The LBO structure involves borrowing a significant amount of money against the assets of the target company to then acquire the target company with the borrowed money. Bad LBOs happen when the private acquisition of a company is financed through excessive debt and cost cutting, with the goal of stripping and flipping the company to another buyer. Such investment structures have often led to large-scale job losses while also stripping the company of its core competences. In the 1980s, LBOs achieved notoriety when several prominent buyouts led to the eventual bankruptcy of the acquired companies. The debt/equity ratio in such deals was nearly 100% and the interest payments were "so large that the company's operating cash flows were unable to meet the obligation."[11] Pension funds should be particularly wary of investing in LBOs that intend to finance investments with large amounts of debt and without regard to the negative impacts of these investments on the investee company's workers and long-term viability.

- **Special situations.** Such investments are made due to a special situation in an attempt to "profit from a change in valuation as a result of the special situation, and is generally not a long-term investment." Special situation investments include opportunities arising as a result of spin-offs or carve-outs of larger companies, mergers and acquisitions, and bankruptcy proceedings.
- **Fund of funds.** Such a strategy involves pooled investments in other funds that in turn hold stocks, bonds or other securities. A fund of funds enables investors to make smaller investment commitments while gaining access to multiple funds with specialized knowledge and economies of scale. Fund of funds management fees are often high, however, given the embedded fees of multiple investment firms.

8.2.2.1 Why make responsible private equity investments?

Applying ESG considerations to private equity can offer opportunities for significant impact without sacrificing financial returns (Wood and Hoff, 2008). Given relatively long-term investment horizons and significant share ownership, private equity firms can exert a higher level of influence over their portfolio companies, as the PRI notes in its guide to investment in private equity:

11 http://www.investopedia.com/terms/l/leveragedbuyout.asp (retrieved June 21, 2016).

> Private equity has a long-term investment horizon, with the GP bridging the gap between company management and its beneficial owners. At its best, private equity is a stewardship-based style of investment and should benefit from increased focus on ESG issues. Responsible investment should be seen as a natural step for private equity investors. ... While an LP [i.e., the investor] cannot make, or materially influence, specific investment decisions, a distinction can be made between influencing a decision and influencing a decision-making process. As a result, in dispatching its fiduciary duties, an LP should monitor and, where necessary, engage a GP [i.e., the private equity firm] about the policies, systems and resources used to identify, assess and make investment decisions, including ESG risk management.
>
> (PRI, 2011a, pp. 4-5)

In so doing, pension funds can use active share-ownership strategies to directly engage with the private equity firms managing the funds' assets to encourage greater ESG adoption among investee companies.

In the past, private equity firms' engagement in ESG issues was limited to reputational risk management by ensuring that portfolio companies were compliant with applicable regulatory requirements (White, 2014). But that is changing. Mega-trends such as climate change, natural resource depletions, and population pressures have put the management of ESG-related

Box 8.6: Characteristics of private equity investments conducive to ESG considerations

- A business model that is focused on identifying and generating operational improvements, efficiencies, and cost savings
- An active ownership model that can make private equity investments agents of positive change
- Influence over portfolio companies through involvement in governance matters
- Ability to develop symbiotic relationships where one company's waste materials can be another company's raw materials
- An inherent desire for product differentiation and innovation, such that ESG-related strengths can act as a competitive advantage for portfolio companies
- Longer-term investment horizon that aims for value creation rather than short-term profit maximization (with the exclusion, generally, of the LBO model)
- A distinct focus on reputation and brand
- A culture of innovation that can help support the development of industries that are more sustainable (such as renewable energy) as global trends and force a transition away from traditional industries (such as coal)

Box 8.7: Responsible private equity advisors and managers

Hamilton Lane

A private market advisory and fund of funds investment management firm, and signatory to the PRI, Hamilton Lane represents a number of worker-friendly pension investors. The firm advises nearly $215 billion in assets, in addition to holding more than $37.5 billion in discretionary assets under management—about a quarter of the latter is on behalf of multiemployer pension funds.

Mario Giannini, CEO, notes that the firm has always been very attentive to labor relations and to the need to treat workers well as part of its investment process. The firm believes that if it can get both sides of an industry, i.e., management and labor, to agree to cooperate, the result is a win–win. The firm has also been active in promoting good governance and in building communication and trust between GPs and LPs. In addition, the firm engages in environmental sustainability, thereby including each of the "E," "S," and "G" considerations in its investment decisions. As such, all of the firm's managed assets—not just those represented by multiemployer pension investors—are viewed through the lens of responsible investments. The firm also supports responsible investments among clients in its advisory practice.

One of the important initiatives the firm has undertaken to increase the share of responsible investments has been to bring together GPs and LPs, including many union leaders, for an annual conference. The conference has led to increased engagement among the investment management, pension fund, and labor community around mutually advantageous outcomes.

Source: Mario Giannini, CEO, Hamilton Lane, personal communication/interview, October 31, 2014.

Pegasus Capital Advisors, L.P.

Pegasus Capital Advisors is a responsible private equity fund manager that began in 1996 and currently manages $2 billion in assets. The firm's investment thesis is focused on growth companies that are creating alternative business models in light of a global resource scarcity. Such companies can profit from the potential business opportunities around reducing waste, improving resource efficiency, and implementing the highest standards of ESG principles. The firm believes that a focus on ESG principles improves the bottom line for its investors and portfolio companies and acts as a significant risk mitigator. The firm also recognizes the need for a thoughtful approach to labor's role, i.e., the "S" in the ESG, in successfully accessing and implementing the above-mentioned opportunities. As such, it is starting a new infrastructure debt fund that will include provisions for labor, such as responsible contractor policies, combined with other responsible investment principles.

Source: David Pollak, Director of Marketing and Investor Relations, Pegasus Capital Advisors, November 26, 2014.

issues at the forefront of corporate value creation and profitability (Doughty Hanson & Co., 2011). In addition, growing investor concerns over the transparency, accountability, and impact of their investments, as well as increased government regulation in the aftermath of the recent subprime mortgage crisis, have led to increased investor interest in applying ESG considerations to private equity investment decision-making.

Recently, implementation support by the PRI has helped bring large numbers of institutional investors in line with the ethos of private equity investments that can be both profitable and responsible.[12] Though relatively nascent, interest in responsible private equity investments among GPs and LPs has ballooned in recent years as a result of the above factors.

8.2.2.2 Opportunities for responsible private equity investments

Trustees seeking responsible private equity investments may make direct investments in private companies or pooled investments as LPs in private equity funds. Responsible ESG considerations can also be applied across private equity strategies, such as through venture capital that supports innovative solutions to social and environmental problems, mid-level and mezzanine financing that helps such solutions grow to scale, and buyouts of public companies that may offer the potential to improve performance through the integration of ESG considerations within the acquired company. In addition, ESG considerations may be incorporated into private equity investments in the same way as active ESG screens are applied to public equity investments. As such, "Investors may choose to focus on those funds that invest in companies with better track records of environmental management, benefits provided to employees, and governance records" (Wood and Hoff, 2008, p. 52).

Trustees can choose to make private equity investments that include one or more of the following responsible investment strategies:

- **Theme-based investments.** Such investments are made in sectors and industries that employ market-based business models to achieve one or more ESG-related mission. These may include private equity investments in cleantech and renewable energy, waste management, water scarcity, investments in under-served communities, ESG-supported supply chain management, infrastructure, sustainable agriculture, responsible real estate, and responsible emerging market investments.

12 For more information, please see https://www.unpri.org.

Box 8.8: Employee ownership and empowerment

Employees are the foundation on which any business achieves profitability, sustainability, success, or failure. The skills, abilities, attitudes, and behaviors of employees are what a customer sees every time they use a firm's product or utilize its service. To transform the current workplace into one that is more participatory and that can be more successful in the marketplace, many people are exploring shared equity as a vital and essential means to higher-performing enterprises. If brought to scale, shared equity can also reduce income inequality.

Tens of millions of Americans own stock in their own successful company through employee ownership models. Some responsible funds, such as the KPS Funds, have structured buyouts in a way that provided partial ownership to workers through an employee stock ownership plan (ESOP), a structure provided for under U.S. law that gives tax advantages to the worker-owners. In another example, American Working Capital (AWC) has converted companies to subchapter S ESOPs, a special employee ownership status with additional tax incentives. More often, though, ESOPs have been viewed as an exit strategy, as retiring owners of family-owned firms can also receive tax incentives if a certain percentage of the firm is sold to employees.

There are also new democratic worker ownership initiatives across the country that are endeavoring to establish worker co-operatives (co-ops). A co-op is a business owned by its members; in the case of a unionized worker co-op, it is owned by represented workers employed by the business. Labor's access to group health and pension plans and worker training programs and protections can provide important market advantages for new co-ops.

These models offer a unique potential for responsible investment impacts (focused on the "S" in ESG), although, as always, prudence is advised when dealing with smaller business investments.

- **Minority-supportive investments.** Such investments may support private equity firms that promote diversity goals (such as toward women and minorities) in the hiring, management, and ownership practices of investee companies so as to create "positive spillover effects in the form of jobs, stable tax bases, and a healthier economic and social climate" (Wood and Hoff, 2008, p. 49).
- **Worker-oriented investments.** These investments can be targeted toward private equity firms and investee companies that view workers as valuable assets and that seek to ensure that worker interests are protected regardless of the private equity investment stage or strategy. In the case of private equity investments in real estate and infrastructure, pension funds can stress the inclusion of responsible contractor policies that promote fair labor practices, worker health and safety, and neutrality and card check provisions, among other labor concerns.

- **Geographically targeted investments.** As with real estate investments, private equity investments can be targeted to support urban and economic revitalization in neighborhoods that are "ready for redevelopment, but [where] information asymmetry and market biases have prevented private equity funds from taking advantage of opportunities that exist for market-rate investments that have particularly beneficial side effects" (Wood and Hoff, 2008, p. 50).

Box 8.9: Responsible growth and turnaround strategies

KPS Capital Partners, LP

KPS Capital Partners manages the KPS Special Situations Funds, a family of private equity funds with more than $5.7 billion in assets under management. The funds take controlling equity positions in distressed companies across a range of manufacturing industries.

Unlike many so-called turnaround private equity firms that strip and flip target companies for a quick profit, KPS sees itself as a "constructive" investor that takes a long-term approach and seeks to align the interests of management, employees, and all stakeholders in facing challenging operational situations.

The firm believes that a "commitment of significant time and resources, in conjunction with professional turnaround experience, is required to unlock the value of non-core, underperforming, or distressed businesses." The firm works with investors and companies who recognize that building sustainable equity value takes time and patience, leading to turnarounds that have resulted in the retention or creation of nearly 40,000 jobs.

Source: Michael Psaros, Managing Partner, KPS, personal communication/interview, January 11, 2015.

Blue Wolf Capital Partners, LLC

Blue Wolf Capital Partners is a private equity firm that takes controlling investments of $10 million or more in middle-market companies facing complex situations involving various stakeholders or financial, operational, or governance distress. The firm has approximately $500 million in assets under management, all of which are invested responsibly. Blue Wolf integrates ESG risk assessments into its investment process because it believes that responsible investments can help reduce portfolio risk, improve risk-adjusted rates of return, and add value to portfolio companies in a sustainable way.

Blue Wolf is a founding signatory to the PRI. The firm is actively engaged in promoting the integration of ESG in private equity markets through its role in the PRI's Private Equity Committee, which is focused on helping interested firms (GPs) and their investors (LPs) navigate responsible investment implementation and reporting (Musuraca, 2015).

Source: Michael Musuraca, Managing Director, Blue Wolf Capital Management, personal communication/interview, January 11, 2015.

8.2.3 Infrastructure: growing the clean economy

Infrastructure represents the "basic physical systems of a business or nation."[13] Infrastructure investments can be grouped into the following broad categories:

- Energy (power generation, storage, and distribution, and gas pipelines)
- Transportation (roads, seaports, airports, railways, bridges, and parking)
- Water (water networks, sewage facilities, and desalination plants)
- Communication (cable, telecom, and satellites)
- Social infrastructure (schools, hospitals, social housing, courts, and prisons) (Russell Investments, 2009)

Investments in infrastructure can be made directly or indirectly:

- **Direct investments in infrastructure.** These are project-based investments that allow investors to have greater control over the underlying asset. Direct investments require specialized knowledge based on project type and are riskier because of larger capital allocations to a limited number of projects. CalPERS and Canadian pension plans (such as the CPPIB, OMERS, and OTPP) have made many direct infrastructure investments that also included an assessment of ESG factors during the investment due diligence and monitoring process.
- **Indirect investments in unlisted infrastructure.** These are investments in private infrastructure companies or sub-sectors such as renewable energy. Investments in such assets are generally made through closed-end or open-end private equity funds that offer investors access to specialized knowledge and investment efficiencies. A downside of such investments can result from private equity-style high fees and short holding periods that are a mismatch with the long-term nature of pension funds. However, there has been a growth in successful responsible infrastructure funds in the U.S.A., Australia, and Canada that have primarily been born out of a demand by pension funds.

13 http://www.investopedia.com/terms/i/infrastructure.asp (retrieved June 27, 2016).

- **Indirect investments in listed infrastructure.** These are investments in publicly traded securities or debt of companies that own and/or operate infrastructure assets. Investments in listed infrastructure are usually accessed through pooled funds. Listed infrastructure investments offer diversification benefits across sectors, liquidity, and greater access to institutional investors of all sizes. However, because listed investments track the general equity/bond market, they have higher correlation with public equities and bonds, and may offer lower diversification benefits at the portfolio level. Such funds may also have complex management and fee structures.

Infrastructure investments can also be classified as early stage, growth stage, or late stage. Early-stage or "greenfield" investments include new developments that initially offer little or no revenue; growth-stage investments include expansion projects or privatizations of existing assets with some operating track record; and late-stage or "brownfield" investments include mature assets with a proven revenue stream (Beeferman, 2008).

Infrastructure investments are characterized as having long life-spans (usually 20–25 years or more), thus providing a natural alignment with the long-term liabilities of pension funds. Overall, infrastructure investments provide diversification benefits given their lower correlation with other asset classes. Such investments offer stable and attractive long-term returns and act as an inflation hedge. Many infrastructure assets also have a built-in ESG component—often projects, particularly greenfield ones, involve early environmental and social assessments to meet legal and regulatory requirements and prevent future litigation risks (PRI, 2011b).

Investing in infrastructure requires specialized investment knowledge. Since these investments tend to be project-based, each investment presents a unique risk–return profile.

A recent article in *The Economist* points to the lack of adequate attention to infrastructure assets from investors and money managers, who have "shied away, scared by the scale, complexity and political risk involved". Investments in emerging markets exacerbate these risks for foreign investors. Currently, only 0.8% of global pension capital is allocated to infrastructure investments, and there is an estimated trillion-dollar gap annually in global spending on basic infrastructure (Economist, 2014b).

In the U.S.A., infrastructure has been primarily financed through public debt offerings, which is the cheapest and most efficient source of funding, according to pension consultant Allan Emkin.[14] However, recent financial crises and a lack of political consensus have shrunk this financing source, resulting in public infrastructure spending levels that are at a 20-year low (Economist, 2014b). In its 2013 *Report Card*, the American Society of Civil Engineers estimated that $3.6 trillion is needed in infrastructure investments by 2020 to fill deficits in the nation's water systems, roads and bridges, electric grids, and social and civic infrastructure (ASCE, 2014).

Box 8.10: A note on project finance

Aside from fixed-income offerings, project finance is another strategy for capitalizing long-term infrastructure investments, including renewable energy and energy retrofit projects. The project finance structure is "based upon a non-recourse or limited recourse financial structure where project debt and equity used to finance the project are paid back from the cash flow generated by the project".[15]

8.2.3.1 Why make responsible infrastructure investments?

Increasing gaps in infrastructure spending present a big investment opportunity for private capital. Indeed, owing to their stable and attractive long-term returns, infrastructure investments are gaining popularity among pension funds and other institutional investors. In its report on alternative investments, the PRI points to significant growth in institutional investors' allocations to infrastructure—approximately 370% over the three years until 2011 (PRI, 2011b). This growth has been coincidental with the fact that infrastructure investments also have significant impacts on the local economy.[16]

Pension funds and their investment managers are seeking ways to integrate ESG considerations into infrastructure investments. Previously mentioned mega-trends such as population growth and climate change have made imperative the need for greater and smarter investments in infrastructure that are socially conscious, ethically developed, and/or utilize renewable resources. The recent credit crunch and large government budget deficits have necessitated the need for private capital to fill the spending gap

14 Allan Emkin, pension consultant, personal communication/interview, July 16, 2014.

15 http://www.investopedia.com/terms/p/projectfinance.asp (retrieved June 21, 2016).

16 Allan Emkin, pension consultant, personal communication/interview, July 16, 2014.

Box 8.11: ULLICO infrastructure fund (UIF) and responsible contractor policy (RCP)

The UIF is managed by ULLICO, the only labor-owned insurance and investment company in the U.S.A. As of the writing of this *Handbook*, the fund had raised nearly $360 million, primarily from pension fund investors, and completed $44 million of projects in water (San Diego-area water treatment plant project), wind (Hawaii wind farm), and solar facilities (a deal with Panasonic) in central California. Like other investment products offered by ULLICO, the UIF has been designed with the aim to deliver attractive and competitive returns to investors. As an ERISA fiduciary, the firm prudently invests assets with the goal of optimizing investment performance. At the same time, The UIF does not believe that there is a trade-off between ESG benefits and financial returns. In addition, unlike traditional private equity firms, UIF invests for the long term, approaching investments in infrastructure assets as public goods that are not meant to be traded frequently.

One example of a successful responsible investment is the UIF's investment in Rialto Water Services (RWS). RWS is a company jointly owned by UIF and Table Rock Capital. RWS entered into a 30-year concession agreement with the city of Rialto, California, to outsource and upgrade the city's water and waste-water facilities. The city will retain full ownership of the water and waste-water systems, water rights, and public authority for rate setting. Veolia Water North America will operate, maintain, and oversee upgrades to the water and waste-water system through a long-term contract with RWS. RWS received the New Infrastructure Project of the Year award from the North America Strategic Infrastructure Leadership Forum in October 2013.

A fundamental part of the UIF's investment objective is the inclusion of a strong responsible contractor policy (RCP). The policy covers union construction, union operations, and union sourcing for materials used in the construction of the project. The UIF claims to honor preexisting collective bargaining agreements and its RCP also includes neutrality agreements that allow workers to organize without interference.

Source: Edward Smith, President and CEO, ULLICO, personal communication/interview, November 24, 2015; ULLICO, 2014.

to update a country's crumbling infrastructure while boosting the economy, creating jobs, and engaging in sustainable development. Such responsible investment practices are the key to long-term risk reduction and potential life-cycle savings over the course of the life of infrastructure investments, according to pension expert Tessa Hebb (Hebb, 2014).

8.2.3.2 Opportunities for responsible infrastructure investments

Direct investments provide the best chance for incorporating ESG issues into the investment policies and procedures for infrastructure investments. For pension funds not able to access or not wanting to make direct investments, opportunities can be accessed by making indirect investments in investment managers that apply responsible strategies to pooled public

Box 8.12: Infrastructure innovations and ESG

- **Impact Infrastructure LLC**, based in New York, acts as an independent provider of clearinghouse services for the socially responsible investing community and high-impact infrastructure projects
- The **West Coast Infrastructure Exchange**, a partnership among the American states of Washington, Oregon, and California, and the Canadian province of British Columbia, focuses on spurring infrastructure innovation through an ESG lens.

equity and fixed-income products. In addition, responsible listed infrastructure investments can offer ESG integration opportunities similar to those discussed under the traditional asset classes of stocks and bonds.

Similar to responsible investment opportunities in real estate and private equity, trustees can undertake responsible infrastructure investments that focus on one or more of the following example strategies:

- **Cleantech infrastructure.** This includes investments in renewable sources of energy such as biomass, geothermal, solar, hydro, and/or wind-based infrastructure assets. In 2015, renewable sources of energy accounted for about 10% of the U.S.A.'s total energy consumption and 13% of its electricity generation (EIA, 2015). The current federal administration aims to increase the latter to 25% by 2025 (Obama and Biden, 2009). In terms of dollar allocations, a 2012 report by the Brookings Institution estimated U.S. federal government spending of more than $150 billion on cleantech infrastructure (including $100 billion in renewable energy alone) for 2009–14, more than three times the levels between 2002 and 2008. The report estimated that this level of federal spending will be able to leverage $327–622 billion in cumulative public- and private-sector investments in cleantech for the same time-period (Jenkins *et al.*, 2012).
- **Union-contracted infrastructure.** Such investments involve the development of roads, railways, ports, and other transportation infrastructure that pay fair wages for fair work and have met material environmental and community impact assessments.
- **Green infrastructure.** Per the U.S. Environmental Protection Agency (EPA), green infrastructure: "uses vegetation, soils, and other elements and practices to restore some of the natural processes required to manage water and create healthier urban environments" (EPA, 2016). Essentially, green infrastructure investments

Box 8.13: A note on public–private partnerships (P3s)

In a P3 model, private investors make investments in public assets such as highways and tunnels, courthouses, or water systems. P3s can have a wide range of structures/ arrangements in terms of which parties own the asset, which operate the asset, how the revenues that are generated are shared, and what portion of the project risks are borne by each partner. The arrangement selected defines the dynamics and the eventual success of the partnership (ICMA International, 2010). Certain P3s have come under criticism for promoting the privatization of public infrastructure assets while exposing pension funds to high risks. Where such partnerships involve investments through conventional private equity firms, the "2 and 20" fee model and three- to seven-year payout structures may not only erode investor returns, but also create a mismatch with the longer-term nature of both the infrastructure assets and pension fund liabilities. The privatization of public infrastructure assets may also result in an erosion of public services and worker protections.

Many of these concerns were heightened after the recent financial crisis, "when the small boom in infrastructure-fund investments in America erupted" (Barnhart, 2013, p. 6). Oft-quoted examples of P3 investments that failed during this time include the Chicago Skyway toll road and the Indiana Toll Road, which left investors "stuck with high leveraged investments yielding weak returns" while also negatively impacting union jobs and placing higher costs on the users of the assets (Barnhart, 2013, p. 6). Pre-financial crisis failures of P3s have included the South Bay Expressway near San Diego and the Southern Connector in Greenville County, South Carolina (Bathon, 2014).

To be successful, in addition to achieving strong and steady returns for the funds' investment portfolios, responsible infrastructure investments must ensure that labor and public interests are protected. Such considerations can help pension funds "shape workplace practices alongside laws, government regulations, and the collective bargaining of unions" (Barnhart, 2013, p. 10).

The AFL-CIO has adopted a position paper on infrastructure investments, supporting pension fund investments in this category as long as labor and other stakeholder interests are protected, and the control and ownership of the asset remains with the public. See Box 8.14 for AFL-CIO's best practice guidance when making such investments.

involve opportunities that explore the potential of urban green spaces in adapting cities to climate change (Gill *et al.*, 2007). In addition to investment opportunities, the operation and maintenance of green infrastructure present a significant opportunity to create entry-level jobs in the green sector (Sanchez *et al.*, 2013).

- **Investments in sustainable materials.** Materials used in the construction of real estate and infrastructure investments can have significant environmental and social impacts. Investment opportunities in this area may include the utilization of new types of concrete and pavement material, for example, that are more durable and environmentally friendly, translating into both operational efficiencies and better ESG risk management.

- **Infrastructure investment partnerships.** These are specific detailed agreements to invest private capital and/or public funding, allocating risks, benefits, and costs among multiple parties engaged in the development, expansion, and/or retrofit of environmental, social, transportation, and other public infrastructure.

In addition to the above, the PRI's report on *Responsible Investment in Infrastructure: A Compendium of Case Studies* (PRI, 2011b) gives investors and their managers additional practical examples on how to make responsible infrastructure investments.

Box 8.14: AFL-CIO goals for infrastructure investment

1. Address the need for maintenance, repair and expansion of U.S. infrastructure.
   - The American Society of Civil Engineers estimated in a 2009 report that our country needed about $2.2 trillion in infrastructure improvements over the next five years. U.S. infrastructure has fallen from first place in the World Economic Forum's 2005 economic competitiveness ranking to number 15 today.
2. Create good jobs in the construction industry, which is suffering from 17% unemployment, and to ensure that work in design, inspection, operations and maintenance that is currently performed by public employees remains in the public sector.
   - We encourage pension funds to invest in infrastructure projects that utilize union construction labor and protect the jobs, collective bargaining rights and working conditions of current employees. Certain types of infrastructure are currently privately owned and operated. We fully support pension fund investment in maintaining, improving and/or building these private assets.
   - With respect to public infrastructure, any investments must ensure that design, inspection, operation and maintenance continue to be performed by public entities and public employees. Local practices vary in reality with respect to the use of private-sector firms for phases of the development of certain types of infrastructure. Coordination with local representatives of the labor movement is essential to ensure that investments in rebuilding America's infrastructure do not come at the expense of the workers who have invested their careers in providing America with first-rate infrastructure.
3. Provide stable, risk adjusted returns for public pensions.
   - Private equity-type infrastructure funds have a poor track record in delivering the returns that would justify their fees and their use of leverage. We need a different model. The infrastructure asset class is more appropriately financed through

vehicles akin to fixed income instruments than to private equity, with long term stable returns.

4. Finance projects in a way that best protects the public interest.
   - Given that interest rates are at historic lows, and many public entities have considerable latitude to issue debt, bond financing is the best way to achieve this goal. Since tax exempt bonds are often not an attractive option for pension funds, Congress should reauthorize Build America Bonds (BABs), first authorized in the American Recovery and Reinvestment Act of 2009. The tax exemption on interest earned by BABs was replaced by a direct subsidy, which increased the interest earned by investors and made these instruments attractive for pension funds and other tax-exempt investors.
   - We will also explore pension fund financing of infrastructure through letters of credit. CalPERS and CalSTRS have facilities to issue letters of credit for floating-rate municipal bonds. Pension funds compete and collaborate with commercial banks, which also issue these letters of credit. In the aftermath of the financial crisis, the availability of letters of credit has diminished.
   - Given the recent turmoil in the banking community, there is an opportunity for public pension funds to provide a needed financial resource for state and local governments and earn a rate of return that is commensurate with their risk, while maintaining public control and ownership of public assets.
   - We oppose investments in public infrastructure that will result in private control or operation of public assets. Private equity investors in public assets typically demand a high rate of return and such provisions as lengthy contract terms, anti-compete clauses or guaranteed payments that are not in the public interest. We should work together to explore structures in which a public pension fund or group of public pension funds together holds majority control of an infrastructure asset.

Source: AFL-CIO, n.d.

Box 8.15: Examples of enforcement of RCPs by labor-friendly investment managers

The **UIF** ensures the enforcement of its RCP through regular reviews. If the fund becomes aware of noncompliance with its RCP by an operator, partner, contractor, or subcontractor at an investment, the fund begins by placing the noncomplying party on a probation watch list. If the noncomplying party does not modify its conduct after discussions with ULLICO, the fund will take into account this pattern of conduct when the noncomplying party's contract is under consideration for possible renewal, or will avail itself of any cancellation provisions in the contract, and put the contract out to bid.

The **AFL-CIO HIT** enforces its RCP through its labor relations staff, who work with the HIT's investment staff to obtain a written agreement to comply with the HIT's labor policy from every borrower to ensure that the developer and general contractor or construction managers will adhere to the union requirements.

8.2.4 Commodities

Commodity investments include investments in physical commodities such as metals or food commodities, investments in real assets such as farmland and timberland, and debt or equity investments in companies that invest in commodity-related businesses (Knoepfel, 2011). There are also investments in commodity derivatives. Like many alternative investments, commodities can provide a hedge against inflation and have little correlation with equity and bond markets, making them an attractive portfolio diversification tool. In addition, the potential for return can be high, based on supply and demand, exchange rates, and economic growth.

However, commodities markets, particularly physical commodities, can be highly volatile and, like other alternative investment sub-asset classes, require sophisticated investment knowledge. While commodity funds provide diversification at the portfolio level, the investments themselves are concentrated in a handful of assets, thus reducing the overall diversification benefit. Other risks include speculative trading, which can result in significant performance differences between the fund and the underlying commodity, as well as political and economic risks from foreign and emerging markets exposure (Fidelity, 2014).

Investments in commodities include the following broad categories:

- **Physical commodities** provide the "purest exposure" to the sub-asset class and include investments in gold and other precious metals, and, more recently, in industrial metals
- **Real assets** include investments in agricultural lands, forests, mines, etc.
- **Investments in commodity-related businesses** include debt and/or equity investments in companies that are engaged in commodity-related businesses
- **Commodity derivatives** are the most common type of vehicle used by investors to gain exposure to commodity investments, and include listed and over-the-counter contracts in futures, swaps, and hedge funds

8.2.4.1 Why make responsible commodity investments?

Macro trends discussed earlier—such as increased population, accelerated global demand, scarcity of natural resources, and climate change—have also all contributed to increased demand for commodities and therefore increasing institutional investor interest in this asset class. As of 2011, investments in commodities by institutional and retail investors were estimated at over $400 billion, compared with only $6 billion in 2001 (Knoepfel and Imbert, 2011).

The production and trade of commodities inherently involve a wide range of ESG issues such as human rights, pollution, waste management, and impact on biodiversity. Any negative impact on such ESG issues can pose a threat to the investment and reputation of investors in this sub-asset class (Knoepfel, 2011). Given a variety of available strategies for investments and their execution, the impact that responsible investors can eventually have varies greatly (Knoepfel and Imbert, 2011).[17]

8.2.4.2 Opportunities for responsible commodity investments

Though commodity investments are inherently exposed to multiple ESG factors, the concept of responsible investments in this asset class is still quite nascent. While it may be difficult to efficiently apply ESG principles to each of the categories detailed below, investor experience has shown that ESG factors can be made more compatible with this asset class if "certain best practices and precautions are followed" (Knoepfel and Imbert, 2011, p. 10).

Different types of commodity investment present different opportunities and challenges to responsible investors as follows:

- **Physical commodities.** Responsible investors can have both direct and indirect positive impact, though limited, on ESG issues in this category of commodity investments. To maximize this impact, one of the best options for investors is to support responsible supply-chain initiatives in the production of commodities. Another is to support fund managers that in turn support producers who have been certified to meet material ESG standards (Knoepfel and Imbert, 2011).
- **Real assets.** If invested internally, investments in this category allow greater responsibility over the ESG issues at stake. As such, responsible investors may be better able to conduct in-depth

17 The report *Responsible Investor's Guide to Commodities: An Overview of Best Practices Across Commodity-Exposed Asset Classes* (Knoepfel and Imbert, 2011) is an excellent resource for more information on the categories within this sub-asset class, discussing how responsible investors can participate in each to maximize their desired ESG impacts. Our insights in this section have borrowed heavily from this valuable resource.

environmental, social, and community-impact assessments prior to and after making the investment. If invested through external managers, investors may impose similar standards of care on the managers they choose to hire.

- **Debt or equity investments in commodity-related businesses.** Though not the most optimal way to achieve portfolio-level diversification, these investments offer an opportunity to effect positive ESG impacts through a range of strategies that are applicable to other public or private debt/equity investments. These include screenings, best-in-class investments, integration of ESG issues in stock or bond selections, and shareholder engagement and activism.
- **Commodity derivatives.** Given the structures of derivatives, the capacity of investors to effect positive ESG impacts through these instruments is indirect and limited. An important measure that responsible investors can take is to support increased transparency in both listed and over-the-counter contracts and among hedge funds. Investors may also promote standardized investment contracts that take into account minimum ESG standards (AMP, 2011). Most importantly, investors may set reasonable return expectations to prevent managers from having to chase those expectations and take undue risks (Knoepfel, 2011).

8.3 Protecting participants and beneficiaries when investing in alternatives

The allocation of workers' capital to alternative investments should be a strategy that aligns pension assets with the long-term nature of pension liabilities alongside achieving positive economic and ESG impacts. Pension assets should be invested in ways that lead to sustainable growth in the real economy, spurring businesses and jobs, not in ways that extract or hollow out the value of long-standing profitable companies, arbitrarily shedding jobs in the process. Pension assets should help build housing and civic properties that improve communities, not invest in exotic real estate securities that undermine household financial security. Pension assets should be invested in ways that improve the environment, not in ways that create toxic externalities that harm our communities and the climate.

Instead of responsibly engaging in alternative investments, however, consultants, managers, and trustees have often taken on riskier and short-term positions in this asset class. Indeed, as we look back on the crisis, it has become obvious that some of the practices of alternative investment vehicles contributed to the market crash (Croft, 2009), severely challenging the funding levels of retirement systems in the U.S.A. and globally.

As discussed in this chapter, alternative investments exhibit certain unique characteristics that make them very suitable for responsible investment strategies. However, the specialized knowledge required to make these investments, alongside limited or skewed data available on their performance, requires trustees to place greater reliance on consultants, investment managers, and other experts in the investment value chain. As a result, trustees might wonder, "How can I tell a consultant (or, money manager, lawyer, etc.) what to do when they know so much more than I do?" When such doubts arise, trustees should bear in mind that, even though they may have to rely on external experts to make these investments, it is the trustees who control the decision of hiring and monitoring these experts. As such, trustees need to be able to ask some hard questions of these experts, particularly as it relates to responsible alternative investments.

Below we summarize thoughtful approaches trustees can take and questions they can ask, zeroing in on four "hot" issues in the field:

8.3.1 Selecting responsible external managers

For pension funds without in-house expertise in alternative investments, selecting the right external managers is an important process.

As a first step, trustees should be aware of the investment managers and vehicles active in the desired alternative investment sub-asset class, so that they may prescreen managers for further due diligence. Trustees generally rely on the aforementioned consultants to help with this awareness. Consultants in turn tend to direct trustees toward those managers and investment vehicles in the databases they maintain. However, if a given consultant's database does not include managers with a responsible investment focus, trustees will not gain exposure to such managers unless they specifically ask for it. In such a situation, trustees should demand that their consultants provide information on firms that are characterized as responsible.

Second, trustees should conduct a thorough due diligence of the managers and vehicles they have prescreened. In so doing, trustees and their consultants should not only scour the expected performance and benchmark reports from these managers, but also ask to see concrete examples of projects the managers have invested in, including information on expected or achieved financial returns and ESG impacts. This is paramount. As Debbie Nisson, a ULLICO real estate professional, describes her approach, "I ask them to explain what they do, and how they do it."[18] In addition, trustees should assess whether the consultants and the managers describe the performance of alternative investments on a longer-term basis—five, 10 years (20, if available)—or whether they are focused on short-term quarterly returns. As mentioned, a short-term focus runs contrary to the pension fund's long-term investment goals.

Policy leaders and pension funds are calling for regulations and more transparency for many of the larger alternative fund vehicles. There have also been new financial standards and laws passed on the tax treatment of a number of investment vehicles (especially the low rates of capital gains taxes). These new taxation and regulatory actions could clearly affect potential returns. Trustees should urge their consultants and investment managers to research new and pending proposals for regulating alternative investment managers and report back on how each one, if enacted, would affect the risk and return of the fund's alternative investment holdings.[19] We discuss manager selection across asset classes in more detail in the next chapter.

8.3.2 Managing fees and expenses

An important consideration in managing pension investments is ensuring that the fees paid in relation to the investments are "reasonable."[20] As discussed, due to their specialized nature, alternative investments can result in generally high investment management fees.[21] Recently, pension

18 Personal communication/interview, December 11, 2014.

19 Comments in this section from Teresa Ghilarducci's contributions to Croft, 2009.

20 Please see Chapter 5 for more information on DOL's guidance regarding the Fair Costs Rule.

21 An article in *The Economist* identified the origins of the "2 and 20" formula popularized by private equity and hedge funds. In the 1950s, Alfred Winslow Jones, the manager of the first modern hedge fund, claimed that Phoenician merchants kept a fifth of the profits generated from their seafaring adventures and paid out the rest to their financiers. So Jones "finagle[d] a 20% cut from his backers." Other managers subsequently added a 2% annual charge on the assets they invested to arrive at the "2 and 20" formula that became the standard for both hedge funds and private equity (Economist, 2014a).

and institutional funds have begun to aggressively question the fees and expenses of conventional private equity and hedge fund managers (Clark, 2014). The New York City Comptroller, Scott Stringer, reported that New York City's five pension funds, over the past 10 years, paid more than $2.5 billion in fees to alternative asset managers, eye-popping numbers that were difficult to obtain. The office claims these and other fees wiped out many of the gains of the system (McGeehan, 2015).

Many investors have raised serious doubts over the prudence of extraordinarily large fees and investment opacity that exist among some alternative investment managers and vehicles. As *The Economist* notes, "Investors, who have long suspected that this arrangement enriches managers faster than their clients, are belatedly fighting back. ... Sovereign-wealth funds, for example, some of which have begun conducting their own buy-outs in-house, simply will not pay '2 and 20'" (Economist, 2014a).

As fiduciaries of workers' capital, trustees have the power to question the elephant in the room. Trustees should impress on their consultants to do comparative fee shopping when researching alternative investment managers. And they should negotiate lower fees or say no if a candidate's fee structure is outrageous. Trustees may also seek responsible fund managers whose fee models are more reasonable.

An example of investor action in this area is that of CalPERS, which divested all of its $4 billion worth of investments in hedge funds in 2014. The reasons for this divestment were primarily centered on high fees and the fund's desire to reduce risk and complexity in its investment portfolio.[22]

8.3.3 Ensuring positive economic and ESG impacts

Trustees should insist on the use and monitoring of ESG considerations to understand the impacts of the pension fund's investments on workers, the community, and the environment. For example, trustees may instruct their consultant and/or investment manager to report on the labor practices of the companies owned by the private equity limited partnerships in which the pension fund invests. Trustees can ask whether the employees of

22 While many institutional investors still view hedge fund strategies as having the ability to reduce risk and provide drawdown protection in investment portfolios, CalPERS' action sent shock waves through the financial community. Ted Eliopoulos, interim CIO at CalPERS, said that hedge funds were an expensive investment vehicle, and CalPERS paid out $135 million in hedge funds fees for the year ending June 30, 2014 (Marois, 2014).

investee companies are covered by collective bargaining agreements, and if not, why not. They can also ask the managers to quantify, company by company, how many jobs have been created and how many eliminated over the last three years. If consultants or managers do not know the answers, trustees should tell them to investigate and report back.

In real estate and infrastructure investments in particular, trustees can explore a number of protections for the public and working citizens, including responsible contractor policies, anti-privatization policies, opt-out, and other provisions that could be used to protect both the pension fund's investments and the interests of its participants and beneficiaries. Trustees may also ask whether real estate investors prioritize (with their developers) green building methods and other energy-efficient approaches.

In addition to a review of the environmental and social considerations mentioned above, trustees should require a review of the transparency and governance requirements of alternative investment vehicles. For instance, the International Trade Union Confederation (ITUC) has passed a resolution calling on trustees and fiduciaries of pension funds to be cautious when investing in private equity and hedge funds (ITUC, 2007a). The global confederation fears that pension funds that invest in LBOs, for example, do not understand what they are buying and cannot measure appropriately their risk exposure (ITUC, 2007b). Trustees, therefore, need to ensure that effective risk management strategies are applied when making alternative investments.

Special attention has been paid to private equity firms in recent years, given their large and growing impacts on the business sector. Since 2000, private equity-owned companies have employed some 7.5 million people, according to a recent book on the field, *Private Equity at Work* (Appelbaum and Blatt, 2014). Pension fund LPs account for about 35% of private equity capital, but have limited influence on their investments. In the worst cases—an extension of the "bad LBOs" story (Box 8.5)—private equity GPs load their investee companies with high debt and sell valuable assets, enriching themselves. A long list of famous companies have gone out of business or suffered major setbacks as a result of irresponsible private equity practices. In many other situations, bad private equity firms have run roughshod over the managers and stakeholders of their portfolio firms, ignoring workers' rights and ESG in general (Appelbaum and Blatt, 2014).

Box 8.16: CalPERS responsible contractor policy

Purpose

CalPERS invests in real estate primarily through outside investment managers. The CalPERS Responsible Contractor Program (RCP) Policy ("the policy") is intended to ensure that contractors, investors, managers, consultants or other participants selected by CalPERS to invest in real estate take prudent and careful action while managing the RCP. Additionally, use of this policy provides assurance that there is sufficient flexibility in controlling investment risks and returns while using contractors.

Introduction

CalPERS has a deep interest in the condition of workers employed by CalPERS and its managers and contractors. CalPERS, through the policy set forth in the current policy, supports and encourages fair wages and benefits for workers employed by its contractors and subcontractors, subject to fiduciary principles concerning duties of loyalty and prudence, both of which further require competitive returns on CalPERS real estate and infrastructure investments.

CalPERS endorses small business development, market competition, and control of operating costs. CalPERS supports many of the ideals espoused by labor unions and encourages participation by labor unions and their signatory contractors in the development and management of CalPERS real estate and infrastructure investments. CalPERS believes that an adequately compensated and trained worker delivers a higher-quality product and service. The Policy includes provisions for transition, monitoring, and enforcement.

RCP policy applies to

- Real estate or infrastructure investments in which CalPERS owns a greater than 50% interest. Other types of investment are not included (e.g., commingled funds, mezzanine debt, international investments) and housing development partnerships are exempted though voluntary compliance is strongly recommended, and
- Contracts over $100,000.

8.3.4 Protecting the freedom of association, and ensuring responsible contracting

As discussed, RCPs can be made a part of the investment criteria for certain alternative investment sub-asset classes such as real estate and infrastructure assets. In addition, RCPs can be applied both in the construction phase and in the ongoing management of assets.

Trustees can push for RCPs and worker-friendly policies in applicable alternative investments. By adopting such policies, trustees can start a productive conversation with their consultants and managers on the issue of responsible alternative investments. In addition, these policies can spell out the standards by which the pension fund expects its investment managers

Current policy

Designed by CalPERS staff, fiduciary attorneys, investment managers and labor stakeholders, the policy:

- Defines an RCP contract, an RCP investment, a responsible contractor and other terms;
- Sets fiduciary duties, competitive bidding, abidance by local, state and national laws and other principal requirements;
- States that CalPERS strongly prefers managers and contractors to hire Responsible Contractors to provide services to RCP Investments;
- Sets roles and responsibilities of investment managers, CalPERS staff and labor stakeholders;
- Sets transition enforcement, monitoring and administration requirements;
- Establishes that managers are responsible for communicating the policy to all contractors, maintaining written policies and procedures on the policy and monitoring and enforcing compliance of the policy;
- Requires managers to annually provide to CalPERS certification that they are in compliance with the RCP and an RCP report, which includes the number and dollar amount of RCP contracts;
- Requires managers to establish competitive bidding procedures and notify potential bidders of the policy; and
- Requires CalPERS, its investment managers and their contractors to remain neutral when union organizing activities of service personnel occur in the core real estate portfolio.

Source: CalPERS, 2015.

to evaluate and monitor potential investment projects. For sample guidelines, we recommend trustees contact their international trade union or similar authorities.[23]

Capital stewards can also encourage the use of card check neutrality and other positive labor–management engagement strategies by their private equity investments. In most card check and neutrality agreements, binding arbitration is included to quickly resolve conflicts.

23 For instance, see http://www.aflcio.org/About/Exec-Council/EC-Statements/Pension-Fund-Responsible-Contractor-Policy, http://ctwinvestmentgroup.com, or http://responsiblecontractorguide.com.

The pioneering pension consultant Allan Emkin acted as the CalPERS board's consultant to be part of the design of the first RCP policy for their real estate investments in 1995. Since then, public and multiemployer funds such as the Ohio Public Employees Retirement System (OPERS), CalSTRS, LIUNA, and SEIU, have also adopted RCPs. Other investors have promoted card check neutrality policies for operating company investments. Similarly, CalPERS, NYC Pension Funds, OPERS, and LACERA have adopted anti-privatization and opt-out policies.

8.4 Takeaways

Employment creation is one of the highest priorities of the global trade unions. According to the International Labour Organization (ILO):

> Persistent poverty, increasing income inequality and slow job growth—further exacerbated by financial and economic crises and climate change—are critical constraints on economic and social progress. Promoting inclusive job-rich growth is a central challenge for all countries today. With global unemployment at historically high levels, there has never been a greater need to put employment at the centre of economic and social policies. Even among those who work, the extent of poverty underscores the need for a far greater number of productive and decent jobs. (ILO, 2016)

Trustees and other capital stewards should explore the use of responsible alternative investments to catalyze job creation, create sustainable shelter, develop renewable sources of energy, and increase economic growth in partnership with governments and other investment allies.

In so doing, trustees and capital stewards need to seriously engage the management of the alternative investment funds in which they choose to invest. As already highlighted, alternative investments are complex and fraught with risk. In general, be wary, especially, of "market cowboys" from Wall Street. As such, trustees should first gain an understanding of how the alternative investment managers and vehicles operate. If trustees and/or their consultants do not clearly understand what the managers or vehicles do, they shouldn't invest. Second, trustees should assess whether or not the potential investments aim to stabilize and/or grow vital companies, provide necessary public infrastructure, protect labor and community interests, and respect the environment, among other positive impacts.

Trustees may also gain knowledge from the experiences of other pension funds active in responsible alternative investments. Trustees can learn how other pension funds exercise their influence and hold their managers accountable. Where trustees employ the same managers as other pension funds, they may be able to collectively influence the adoption of responsible investment practices—putting this influence to work for better investment outcomes.

8.5 References

AFL-CIO (The American Federation of Labor and Congress of Industrial Organizations) (2015). Union construction job creation. Retrieved June 4, 2016 from http://www.aflcio-hit.com/wmspage.cfm?parm1=1794.

AFL-CIO (n.d.). Internal Memo: Standards for Pension Fund Investment in Infrastructure.

AMP Capital Investors (2011, July). Commodities and energy: a responsible investment perspective. *Presentation for Responsible Investment Briefing 2011*. Sydney, Australia: AMP Capital Investors.

Appelbaum, E., & Blatt, R. (2014). *Private Equity at Work: When Wall Street Manages Main Street*. New York City: Russell Sage Foundation.

ASCE (American Society of Civil Engineers) (2014). *2013 Report Card for America's Infrastructure*. Retrieved June 4, 2016 from http://www.infrastructurereportcard.org.

Barnhart, B. (2013, March 28). Infrastructure partnerships: labor's evolving experience. Retrieved June 2, 2016 from https://www.americanprogress.org/issues/economy/report/2013/03/28/58147/infrastructure-partnerships-labors-evolving-experience/.

Bathon, M. (2014, September 22). Indiana toll road seeks bankruptcy as traffic declines. *Bloomberg Business*. Retrieved June 28, 2016 from http://www.bloomberg.com/news/2014-09-22/indiana-toll-road-seeks-bankruptcy-as-traffic-declines.html.

Beeferman, L. (2008). Pension fund investments in infrastructure: A resource paper. *Capital Matters*, 3, n.p.

Boston University (2016). What is LEED? Retrieved June 4, 2016 from http://www.bu.edu/sustainability/what-were-doing/green-buildings/leed/.

CAIAA (Chartered Alternative Investment Analyst Association) (n.d.) *CAIA Level I Core Book*. Retrieved June 27, 2016 from https://caia.org/sites/default/files/curriculum-download/CAIA%20L1%202015%20Chapt.%201.pdf.

CalPERS (2015). *Statement of Investment Policy for Responsible Contractor Program*. Retrieved June 20, 2016 from https://www.calpers.ca.gov/docs/policy-responsible-contractor-2015.pdf.

CalPERS (2016). Asset allocation and performance. Retrieved June 20, 2016 from https://www.calpers.ca.gov/page/investments/asset-classes/asset-allocation-performance.

Clark, S. (2014, November 21). Pension funds lambaste private-equity fees. *The Wall Street Journal*. Retrieved June 4, 2016 from http://www.wsj.com/articles/pension-funds-lambast-private-equity-firms-for-large-fees-1416562426.

Croft, T. (2009). *Up from Wall Street: The Responsible Investment Alternative*. New York, NY: Cosimo Books.

Doherty, P.C. (2013) A new U.S. grand strategy: why walkable communities, sustainable economics, and multilateral diplomacy are the future of American power. *Foreign Policy Magazine.* Retrieved June 5, 2016 from http://foreignpolicy.com/2013/01/09/a-new-u-s-grand-strategy/.

Doughty Hanson & Co. (2011). *Private Equity and Responsible Investment: An Opportunity for Value Creation.* Retrieved June 4, 2016 from http://assets.wwf.org.uk/downloads/private_equity_aw_lores_2.pdf.

Economist (2014a, February 8). Fees for hedge funds and private equity: Down to 1.4 and 17. *The Economist.* Retrieved June 4, 2016 from http://www.economist.com/news/finance-and-economics/21595942-cost-investing-alternative-assets-fallingslowly-down-14-and-17.

——— (2014b, March 22). Investing in infrastructure: The trillion-dollar gap. *The Economist.* Retrieved June 4, 2016 from http://www.economist.com/news/leaders/21599358-how-get-more-worlds-savings-pay-new-roads-airports-and-electricity.

EIA (U.S. Energy Information Administration) (2015). *Independent Statistics & Analysis. U.S. Energy Information Administration.* Retrieved June 21, 2016 from http://www.eia.gov/tools/faqs/faq.cfm?id=92&t=4.

EPA (U.S. Environmental Protection Agency) (2016). What is green infrastructure? Retrieved June 20, 2016 from https://www.epa.gov/green-infrastructure/what-green-infrastructure.

Falconer, K. (1999). *Prudence, Patience and Jobs: Pension Investment in a Changing Canadian Economy.* Ottawa, Canada: Canadian Labour Market and Productivity Centre.

Fidelity (2014). About commodity investing. Retrieved June 4, 2016 from https://www.fidelity.com/learning-center/investment-products/mutual-funds/about-commodity-investing.

Gill, S.E., Handley, J.F., Ennos, A.R., & Pauleit, S. (2007). Adapting cities to climate change: the role of the green infrastructure. *Built Environment,* 33(1), 115-133.

Hebb, T. (2014, November 6). Sustainable infrastructure. Retrieved June 17, 2016 from http://www.impactinfrastructure.com/blog/SustainableInfrastructure/.

Humphreys, J. (2011). *Sustainability Trends in U.S. Alternative Investments.* Retrieved June 2, 2016 from http://www.ussif.org/pubs.

ICMA International (2010). Public–private partnership structures and arrangements. Retrieved June 4, 2016 from http://icma.org/en/international/resources/insights/Article/101962/PublicPrivate_Partnership_Structures_and_Arrangements.

ILO (International Labour Organization) (2016). Employment promotion. Retrieved June 20, 2016 from http://www.ilo.org/ankara/areas-of-work/employment-promotion/lang--en/index.htm.

ITUC (International Trade Union Confederation) (2007a). Resolution on private equity and hedge funds. Brussels. Retrieved June 4, 2016 from http://www.ituc-csi.org/IMG/pdf/_2GC_Resolution_on_Private_Equity_and_Hedge_Funds_June_2007-2.pdf.

——— (2007b). *Where the House Always Wins: Private Equity, Hedge Funds and the New Casino Capitalism.* Retrieved June 4, 2016 from http://www.ituc-csi.org/IMG/pdf/ITUC_casino.EN.pdf.

Jenkins, J., Muro, M., Nordhaus, T., Shellenberger, M., Tawney, L., & Trembath, A. (2012). Beyond boom and bust: putting clean tech on a path to subsidy independence. Retrieved June 4, 2016 from http://www.brookings.edu/research/papers/2012/04/18-clean-investments-muro.

Jones Lang LaSalle (2013). *The Advancement of Real Estate as a Global Asset Class.* Retrieved June 4, 2016 from http://www.joneslanglasalle.com/ResearchLevel1/JLL-Real-Estate-as-a-Global-Asset-Class.pdf.

Knoepfel, I. (2011). *Responsible Investment in Commodities: The Issues at Stake and a Potential Role for Institutional Investors.* Retrieved June 4, 2016 from http://www.onvalues.ch/images/publications/11-01_RI_commodities_Jan2011_v02.pdf.

Knoepfel, I., & Imbert, D. (2011). *The Responsible Investor's Guide to Commodities: An Overview of Best Practices Across Commodity-Exposed Asset Classes*. Retrieved June 4, 2016 from https://www.unpri.org/download_report/3831.

Marois, M.B. (2014, September 15). Calpers to exit hedge funds, divest $4 billion stake. *Bloomberg*. Retrieved June 4, 2016 from http://www.bloomberg.com/news/articles/2014-09-15/calpers-to-exit-hedge-funds-citing-expenses-complexity.

McGeehan, P. (2015, April 8). Wall Street fees wipe out $2.5 billion in New York City pension gains. *The New York Times*. Retrieved June 4, 2016 from http://www.nytimes.com/2015/04/09/nyregion/wall-street-fees-wipe-out-2-5-billion-in-new-york-city-pension-gains.html?rref=nyregion&_r=0.

Mykleby, M., Doherty, P., & Makower, J. (2016). *The New Grand Strategy: Restoring America's Prosperity, Security, and Sustainability in the 21st Century*. New York, NY: St. Martin's Press.

NMERB (New Mexico Education Retirement Board) (2015). *1st Quarter 2015*. Retrieved June 27, 2016 from https://www.nmerb.org/pdfs/2015Q1IPA.pdf.

Obama, B., & Biden, J. (2009). The Obama–Biden Plan. Retrieved June 4, 2016 from http://change.gov/agenda/energy_and_environment_agenda/.

OMERS (Ontario Municipal Employees Retirement System) (2015). *2014 Annual Report*. Retrieved June 27, 2016 from http://www.omers.com/pdf/omers-2014-annual-report-english.pdf.

PBS Newshour (2015, February 3). Schools in rural West Virginia aim to improve students' prospects. *PBS Newshour*. Retrieved June 4, 2016 from http://www.pbs.org/newshour/bb/schools-rural-west-virginia-aim-improve-students-prospects/.

PRI (Principles for Responsible Investment) (2011a). *Responsible Investment in Private Equity: A Guide for Limited Partners* (2nd ed.). Retrieved June 4, 2016 from https://www.unpri.org/download_report/6223.

——— (2011b). *Responsible Investment in Infrastructure: A Compendium of Case Studies*. Retrieved June 4, 2016 from https://www.unpri.org/download_report/3784.

Russell Investments (2009). *Russell OpenWorld®: Listed Infrastructure Investing*. Retrieved June 27, 2016 from https://russellinvestments.com/-/media/files/emea/institutions/brochures/brochure-listed-infrastructure-investing-2008-11.pdf.

Sanchez, A., Quinn, A., & Hays, J. (2013). *Staying Green and Growing Jobs: Green Infrastructure Operations and Maintenance as Career Pathway Stepping Stones*. Retrieved June 4, 2016 from http://gfa.fchq.ca/focus/water/staying-green-and-growing-jobs-green-infrastructure-operations-and-maintenance-as-career-pathway-stepping-stones/.

Siemers, E. (2011, November 11). Teachers union invests $15M in "Cool Schools". Retrieved June 4, 2016 from http://www.bizjournals.com/portland/blog/sbo/2011/11/teachers-union-invests-15m-in-cool.html.

ULLICO (2014). Making an impact on Infrastructure: Q&A with Jeff Murphy, managing director Infrastructure Fund. *Ullico Bulletin*. Retrieved June 4, 2016 from http://ullico.com/newsroom/bulletin-2014-3-4.

UNEP FI (UN Environment Programme Finance Initiative) (2010). *Green Buildings and the Finance Sector: An Overview of Financial Institution Involvement in Green Building in North America*. Retrieved June 4, 2016 from http://www.unepfi.org/fileadmin/documents/CEOBriefing_greenbuildings.pdf.

——— (2012). *Responsible Property Investment: What the Leaders Are Doing* (2nd ed.). Retrieved June 2, 2016 from http://www.unepfi.org/fileadmin/documents/Responsible_Property_Investment_2.pdf.

——— (2016). Responsible Property Investment work stream. Retrieved June 22, 2016 from http://www.unepfi.org/work-streams/property/rpi/.

UNEP SBCI (UN Environment Programme Sustainable Buildings & Climate Initiative) (2009). *Buildings and Climate Change: Summary for Decision-Makers*. Retrieved June 20, 2016 from http://www.unep.org/sbci/pdfs/SBCI-BCCSummary.pdf.

USGBC (U.S. Green Building Council) (2016). LEED. Retrieved June 4, 2016 from http://www.usgbc.org/leed.

Voorhes, M., Humphreys, J., & Solomon, A. (2012). Report on sustainable and responsible investing trends in the United States: 2012. Retrieved June 2, 2016 from http://www.ussif.org/content.asp?contentid=82.

Wasser, M. (2011). *Creating Good Jobs for Our Communities: Pension Dollars at Work*. Retrieved June 4, 2016 from http://www.jwj.org/wp-content/uploads/2013/12/110316creating_good_jobs_for_our_communities_pension_dollars_at_work.pdf.

White, B. (2014). *ESG in Private Equity: A Fast-Evolving Standard*. Retrieved June 4, 2016 from http://research.insead.edu/2014/09/WhiteZeisbergerPrahl.html.

Wood, D., & Hoff, B. (2008). *Handbook on Responsible Investment Across Asset Classes*. Retrieved June 2, 2016 from http://ccc.bc.edu/index.cfm?fuseaction=document.showDocumentByID&nodeID=1&DocumentID=1170.

Section IV: Implementation and measurement

9
Selection and implementation of desired responsible approaches

> Pension funds should develop an investment policy which includes an understanding of stewardship objectives and risks. This policy should encourage the incorporation of financially material extra-financial risks within investment decisions and the exercising of stewardship responsibilities such as engagement and voting. Pension funds should select investment managers, across all asset classes, which act as responsible investors and hold them to account for adhering to the fund's own policy and expectations.
>
> *Responsible Investment Guide 2013*,
> National Association of Pension Funds (U.K.)

Previous chapters have emphasized the link between the long-term nature of pension investments and the impact of material ESG factors on the long-term financial value of these investments. We also discussed the role of pension funds as universal owners who own a significant share of the economy and are therefore impacted by changes in broader economic themes, from financial, such as interest rates and growth, to nonfinancial, such as natural resource scarcity or the impacts of climate change.

Taken together, these links underscore the importance of including ESG considerations in active share ownership practices for long-term benefits to plan participants and beneficiaries. As noted by the National Association of Pension Funds (NAPF), "there is an increasing awareness that if one company does well at the expense of others, a widely diversified investor may well pick up the costs as well as the gains" (NAPF, 2013, p. 4).

In this chapter, we discuss how trustees may develop, implement, and monitor a responsible investment (RI) policy. Such a policy should be based on the material ESG risks and opportunities expected to impact the financial value of plan assets, and consequently, the economic, social, and environmental wellbeing of worker-owners.

The following steps may be applied across asset classes. Where trustees have an opportunity to practice active ownership approaches, either internally or through external managers, both the financial and nonfinancial outcomes of the RI policy can be enhanced:

1. Develop an RI policy based on material ESG risks and opportunities
2. Build internal expertise and/or select external managers
3. Execute on material ESG themes and engage
4. Monitor performance and fine-tune policy

Box 9.1: A note on the role of investment consultants

Investment consultants provide a range of services to pension funds in the allocation and management of a fund's assets. These services may include developing an investment policy statement (IPS), assisting in asset allocation decisions, selecting external asset managers, and helping with portfolio performance evaluation. Some consultants may also assist trustees with managing the fund's proxy voting process and engaging in active ownership practices.

Consultants exert much influence on the investment decision-making process of pension funds, particularly for smaller funds who may not have an in-house chief investment officer (CIO) or adequate trustee and/or internal staff knowledge of investments. As a result, consultants are often seen as "gatekeepers" to the integration of ESG factors in the investment of pension assets (Voorhes, 2009, p. 4).

For pension funds that engage with a consultant, the most important step should be to ensure that the consultant's beliefs and philosophy with regards to responsible investments are similar to those articulated by the fund in its own investment beliefs statement. If a pension fund does not have a responsible investment beliefs statement, then the search for the appropriate consultant should be based on the consultant's ability to help the fund formally articulate these beliefs.

As advised by the UN Investor Network on Climate Risk, in selecting consultants who understand the link between ESG considerations and the financial value of investments, asset owners should ask a range of in-depth questions that go beyond the "check-box" approach (Snow Spalding *et al.*, 2012). These questions should probe the consultant on their responsible investment beliefs and their process for enabling the integration of ESG factors that are material to the fund's investment goals, among other criteria.

Once an appropriate investment consultant has been selected, they can help trustees develop and/or implement part or all of the steps of an RI policy discussed in this chapter.

9.1 Develop a responsible investment (RI) policy

As a first step to investing responsibly, trustees should develop a written RI policy, either as part of the fund's overall investment policy statement (IPS) or as a stand-alone policy. The RI policy should be rooted in a clear understanding of the fund motivations for pursuing a responsible investment strategy. It should incorporate material ESG risks and opportunities applicable to the industries, asset classes, and/or geographies in which the pension fund is invested. Such a policy, like the rest of the IPS, can serve as a governing document that can help protect the long-term interests of plan participants and beneficiaries as it relates to responsible investments. In developing this policy, trustees may consider the following factors and questions:

9.1.1 Understand the drivers for pursuing a responsible investment strategy

As we have stressed, achieving competitive long-term returns to meet current and future retiree benefits is the primary objective of pension fund investments. Related to this financial objective is the need to lower the long-term risks of pension investments so that retiree benefits may be better secured. Since ESG concerns, such as reduced worker rights, environmental degradation, and corporate mismanagement, have a bearing on the financial value of investments, trustees may be motivated by the need to account for the long-term investment risks of such factors. In addition, trustees may be motivated by the desire to enable plan participants and beneficiaries to retire in a sustainable, humane world, where basic rights and dignity are not sacrificed, nor scarce resources squandered, in the production of financial benefits. Understanding and articulating these drivers upfront is important and represents the foundation of an effective responsible investment strategy: "The assets pension funds own and have oversight of can play an important role in determining the future society member's face and thus, the real value of their retirement income" (NAPF, 2013, p. 5).

9.1.2 Develop an investment beliefs statement

In order to pursue a consistent responsible investment strategy, trustees should establish a clear link between incorporating ESG considerations into investment decision-making and the financial performance expectations from their pension investment portfolio. This link should be clearly articulated in a formal investment beliefs statement that complements the fund's RI policy and overall IPS.

Though we have cited reports documenting otherwise, the perception that ESG considerations detract from the financial performance of investments is an oft-expressed concern of key players in the pension investment value chain. Trustees should therefore seek to understand and clarify such concerns through research and peer-to-peer learning. The resulting investment beliefs statement will enable the clear communication, implementation, and accountability of the fund's RI policy with internal staff, investment consultants, and/or external investment managers. Most importantly, it will ensure the continuation of the fund's responsible investment goals beyond the current generation.[1]

9.1.3 Identify the scope of the RI policy

Trustees should determine whether the RI policy is to be applied to the entire portfolio or to specific industries, asset classes, and/or geographies. This will depend in part on the material ESG risks and opportunities to which the fund is exposed through the types of asset class and geography in which it is invested.

9.1.4 Identify material ESG risks and opportunities

The RI policy should aim to manage those factors that are important drivers of the fund's investment risks and returns while limiting focus on factors that are not material to the fund's financial value. In this way, the RI policy can be used to "select better managed companies that can mitigate risks and exploit opportunities" (NAPF, 2013, p. 17).

Some common material ESG factors include:

- **Environmental**
  - Climate change
  - Energy efficiency
  - Water scarcity
  - Pollution and waste management

1 The Initiative for Responsible Investment (IRI), housed at the Harvard Kennedy School, put forth an excellent working paper on responsible investment beliefs statements (IRI, 2011), which provides guidance and examples to institutional investors on developing such statements.

Box 9.2: Responsible pension consultants

To help trustees see how they can work with their consultants to incorporate responsible strategies into their investment portfolios, we provide examples of strategies undertaken by Marco Consulting Group (MCG), led by Jack Marco, and Pension Consulting Alliance (PCA), led by Allan Emkin.

MCG provides investment consulting and fiduciary services to investors with total assets worth $160 billion. The firm helps its clients select investment products and investment managers that not only provide solid investment returns, but also social and other economic benefits. MCG claims that, from the day a client agrees to engage the firm's services, a thorough review of the plan takes place and options for responsible investing are presented to the client for their consideration. A client's investment portfolio can have various levels of responsible investing, ranging from a completely responsible portfolio to select investments in responsibly managed portfolios. Clients can also utilize the firm's investment proxy services to engage companies whose stock they own to bring about responsible change without changing the investment mandate. As such, depending on a client's needs, the firm helps to incorporate the desired level of responsible investments into the client's investment portfolio.

PCA advises clients with total assets in excess of $1.1 trillion. Of this, $950 million represent pension assets. As a signatory to the PRI, PCA reports that it has a number of clients that are industry leaders in the areas of corporate and social responsibility. In instances where clients have been new to responsible investing, PCA has worked with the clients to craft and execute their custom responsible investment policy and beliefs.

For example, PCA worked with one client, the Oregon Investment Council (OIC), through the process of determining and publishing its investment beliefs on the hiring of a new CIO. The process of achieving consensus on investment beliefs is extremely important, so that the policy-makers "own" the beliefs and are able to adopt a responsible policy consistent with such beliefs to help guide investment decisions. During this process, Allan Emkin conducted interviews with the CIO, Treasury staff and all OIC members to elicit member and staff beliefs, ideas, and biases. Staff and council were asked to fill out a preliminary investment beliefs questionnaire that consisted of 56 "investment viewpoints" in 12 belief-related categories. The respondents were asked to indicate their level of agreement with an investment viewpoint on a scale of 1 to 4. PCA scored the survey responses from all 14 participants and ranked the investment viewpoint scores. Investment viewpoint rankings formed the initial basis for the new set of OIC investment beliefs.

The investment beliefs project continued with a presentation of survey results at a workshop. Taking into account the questionnaire data, views expressed during the interview process and feedback from the workshop, PCA further consolidated the investment beliefs into statements that PCA believed to be reflective of OIC thinking. The project then went to the consensus building stage. Negotiation of consensus beliefs required additional dialogue between OIC members and the CIO, a process that was facilitated by PCA. Once consensus was achieved, beliefs were encoded into clear, simple and accountable statements that will guide the revision of OIC's investment policy and implementation documents (Marco and Emkin, 2014).

Source: Jack Marco, chairman, Marco Consulting Group, personal communication/interview, December 8, 2014; Allan Emkin, Managing Director and Founder, Pension Consulting Alliance, personal communication/interview, November 4, 2014.

- **Social**
  - Human rights
  - Worker rights
  - Health and safety
  - Supply chain management
- **Governance**
  - Board independence and diversity
  - Executive compensation
  - Shareholder rights
  - Auditor independence

9.1.5 Establish protocols for active engagement approaches

In asset classes where trustees and other fiduciaries can engage in active ownership approaches, the RI policy should also include the types of approach and the extent of engagement that may be employed by the plan's internal and/or external investment management teams. In public equities, for instance, desired engagement may range from voting proxies to taking direct shareholder actions that seek to actively monitor and/or influence corporate behavior. In private equities, the engagement is likely to be through the private equity firm (GP), which has a measure of influence on the companies it invests in.

Appendix B provides links to RI policies and investment beliefs statements developed by various pension funds for reference by trustees and fiduciaries.

9.2 Build in-house expertise and/or select external managers

Once trustees have developed an RI policy, the next step is to implement this policy. Just as with a traditional IPS, so an RI policy may be implemented internally and/or through external investment managers. As such, trustees may either help build internal staff capabilities to implement a part or whole of the RI policy in-house, or select external managers for the same. Each scenario is discussed in more detail below, with examples of pension funds that have taken either approach.

9.2.1 Build, to the extent desired, in-house expertise to implement RI policy

The extent of internal expertise that trustees wish to develop will depend on the level of internal engagement and control desired in regards to RI policy. If the goal is to have better control over the resulting financial and nonfinancial outcomes, trustees may be well served to build in-house investment management expertise for specific asset classes or for the entire portfolio.

In general, in-house expertise can help augment organizational capacity and more effectively manage costs related to ESG analysis and implementation. This is particularly true for larger pension funds, who may be able to enjoy economies of scale by managing more of their investments in-house as opposed to with one or more external managers.

Box 9.3: Examples of funds with strong in-house investment capacity

Large Canadian pension funds such as the Ontario Municipal Employees Retirement System (OMERS), Canadian Pension Plan Investment Board (CPPIB), and the Ontario Teachers' Pension Plan (OTPP) are often praised for their prudent, long-term, and activist pension investments that have generated strong returns for their retirees. One of the reasons cited for the success of these funds has been the strength of their in-house investment teams (Groenewegen and Smith, 2014). For instance, the OTPP, which had approximately $153 billion in assets as of December 31, 2014, manages about 80% of the portfolio internally. Similarly, it has been reported that CPPIB and OMERS each has as many as 800 staff to "find attractive investments, put together bid proposals and close the deals" (Jordan *et al.*, 2012). The resulting economies of scale, as reported by the CPPIB, have reduced the cost of outsourcing investments to external managers by 10–15%.

Until recently, the trend in the U.S.A. had been to mostly outsource pension investment decision-making to external managers because of lack of in-house talent development. However, this trend is reported to be changing, buoyed by "control and fees" (Bradford, 2014).

For instance, CalSTRS, which had $184 billion in pension assets as of August 31, 2015, established its first social investment policy as far back as the 1970s. The pension fund, which is a signatory to the PRI, works to integrate ESG considerations into all its investment decisions. Rather than exclusively relying on external advice, CalSTRS is seeking to build strong internal expertise in each of the "E," "S," and "G" considerations. Presently, the fund has an internal staff of nine focused on responsible investments and spends roughly $2.5 million per year toward the initiative. Cognizant of a potential lack of internal congruency in relation to responsible investments, CalSTRS has also been actively educating its entire staff of 120 to bring them in line with the ethos of the pension fund's responsible investment goals.[2]

2 Christopher Ailman, CIO, CalSTRS, personal communication/interview, December 1, 2014.

In another example, in August 2014, the North Carolina Retirement System reached $90 billion in assets and also won approval from state legislators to hire additional staff so that it may manage more of its assets internally (as of September 30, 2013, the fund managed 30% of its assets internally).

It is important to note that building in-house investment expertise, whether in traditional or responsible investments, can be a slow process, and that economies of scale may not be achieved immediately. These challenges are even greater for smaller pension funds. Therefore, a patient and step-by-step approach is recommended. As the OTPP reports, the fund took "baby steps" in moving more of its assets to in-house investment management since its establishment in 1990 with $20 billion in assets (Bradford, 2014).

In addition, when building in-house expertise, the most important decisions that trustees will make are with regards to the cost savings and the structure of the investment management and governance teams. Aside from recruiting appropriate talent to the organization and creating a nimble investment team, trustees should also focus on improving the fund's internal governance structure as discussed in previous chapters. Such a structure should establish a clear long-term vision and mission for the plan in relation to ESG management, be backed by strong leadership at the board and management level, and allow for quick responses to any conflicts or opportunities encountered.

More often than not, trustees may employ a combination of in-house and external management of their ESG and broader investment goals.

Box 9.4: Appointing a chief investment officer (CIO)

The role of a CIO within a pension fund includes developing the IPS and engaging in asset allocation, manager selection, and performance evaluation in relation to the fund's investments. A 2007 study by pension governance experts Clark and Urwin identified the presence of a CIO as critical to the success of pension fund investment outcomes.

Large pension funds often have the resources to hire an in-house CIO who may also be able to direct a fund's responsible investment strategies under appropriate oversight by trustees. Smaller funds, however, often outsource the functions of the CIO to external service providers such as investment consultants. As mentioned, in selecting investment consultants for the implementation of a responsible investment strategy, trustees should be cognizant of the consultant's capabilities in relation to ESG risk management. In addition, an appropriate oversight structure should be put into place so as to mitigate the agency separation issues discussed earlier (Clark and Urwin, 2007).

TABLE 9.1 Advantages and disadvantages of in-house expertise and external managers

	In-house expertise	External managers
Advantages	• Generally cost-effective • Economies of scale • Better alignment with goals • Better control over outcomes • Opportunity to attract and increase talent pool	• Can be selected according to specific mandate/asset class • Better access to global markets through local presence • Access to high-quality talent pool • Wider skills base
Disadvantages	• Gradual—building expertise and coherence will take time • Limited local presence in global markets • Narrower skills base	• Generally higher costs • Less bargaining power • Potential for weaker alignment with fund's stated goals

9.2.2 When selecting external investment managers, determine the managers' approach to ESG integration

A number of pension funds hire external managers to invest a part or whole of their assets. This is especially true of smaller funds that lack the resources to, or do not want to, build an in-house investment team. Whether the ESG mandate is expected to be managed by an existing manager and/or by a new manager, trustees should seek to understand whether the manager has an RI policy, what it entails, and how it is incorporated into the manager's investment decision-making processes. Such an understanding may be developed through targeted requests for proposals, questionnaires, and interviews.

Ultimately, the manager's approach should be aligned with the fund's ESG goals. Trustees should gauge whether the manager has insights on material ESG risks and opportunities for the sectors, asset classes, and geographies in which the pension fund is invested, and whether the manager is capable of addressing the same. They should also determine whether or not the manager votes proxies and engages in shareholder activism on behalf of its pension clients. To assess the manager's commitment, trustees may seek examples where ESG factors have influenced final investment decisions by the manager. They should also determine whether the manager shows flexibility with regards to the evolving needs and understanding of the fund's ESG goals and investment mandate.

Just as with an internal investment management team, so the number of dedicated staff at the external manager and their level of expertise in the area of ESG management and implementation is important. Trustees should also pay attention to the manager's track record on ESG implementation and impact.

If a manager does not have an active RI policy or approach, trustees should determine whether the manager is able to incorporate the pension fund's own RI policy into its decision-making processes for the fund's investments. Conversely, trustees may consider utilizing the external manager's RI policy as long as it meets the fund's responsible investment goals. Finally, trustees should look to select those managers with whom they can actively engage, once the investment is made, through periodic updates and active ownership practices.

9.3 Execute on ESG themes and engage

If a plan's RI policy is implemented in-house, the investment team can undertake the following steps to align the RI policy with their investment decision-making process:

- **Screening.** In selecting potential responsible investment opportunities from a large universe of viable investments, the internal team may conduct a combination of top-down (selecting specific sectors and geographies across the entire portfolio or for certain asset classes that align with the plan's ESG and overall investment policy) and bottom-up (selecting companies that have a record of operating sustainably within the identified sectors) analysis.
- **Due diligence.** Once the investment universe has been narrowed down to investments of interest, the focus should shift to in-depth financial valuation and material ESG impact analysis to determine which investments will best meet the plan's financial and ESG goals.
- **Investment.** When due diligence is completed and an investment is made, the team should keep an eye on the outcomes expected vs. outcomes achieved and scale up or scale down the investments accordingly.

When trustees select external investment managers for the implementation of their RI policy, the investment process and decision is delegated to the manager. However, delegation does not absolve trustees of oversight responsibility. In fact, it increases the need for adequate monitoring of the external manager with the plan's established mandate.

Whether the RI policy is implemented internally or externally, trustees have the ability to exercise active ownership approaches that can enhance the fund's financial and ESG goals. As discussed previously, active ownership tools such as proxy voting and shareholder proposals can be used to engage constructively with underlying portfolio companies, positively influencing corporate governance as well as environmental and social outcomes. Trustees should advise their investment teams of these tools and actively engage in their implementation in tandem with the managers.

Box 9.5: Example of a responsible asset manager

The Dutch pension plan PGGM sums up its responsible investment approach as a combination of the following:

1. Fundamental financial analysis
2. ESG integration
3. (3) Active ownership

PGGM believes that active ownership allows for "strategic increases or decreases in the stake of a company to stimulate ESG advancements, actions that could substantially leverage the credibility and effectiveness of active ownership in a way that external ownership services cannot" (van der Velden and van Buul, 2012, pp. 51-52).

9.4 Monitor performance and fine-tune policy

Regardless of whether the RI policy is implemented internally or through external managers, trustees should take adequate steps to follow up on the impact of the policy. This is particularly important when one or more external managers have been selected to implement the policy. Trustees should therefore develop a process to hold the external managers accountable to the fund's policy and expectations as outlined below. In addition, trustees should continue to fine-tune the fund's RI policy in keeping with evolving circumstances and lessons learned.

9.4.1 Monitor performance

If the fund's RI policy is invested internally, trustees are able to exercise greater control over the implementation and outcomes of that policy through regular oversight and reviews. Similarly, as part of their monitoring

Box 9.6: Examples of responsible investment monitoring

Amalgamated Bank's LongView Funds regularly communicate with institutional clients on their corporate governance program, current engagements, and projects, and often collaborate with clients and similar investors on core issues of concern. The bank provides regular reports to all clients that detail how it votes its proxies alongside a rationale for each of the votes. The reports also include a review of any shareholder engagements the bank has led or participated in.

Similarly, **MCG** regularly monitors the investment managers it helps select for its clients in order to ensure compliance with the clients' investment goals, particularly in relation to responsible investments. The firm believes that continual monitoring of the portfolio characteristics and qualitative conversations about ESG issues are the best way to monitor and evaluate the success of a manager in meeting clients' responsible investment guidelines.

activities of external managers, trustees should request scheduled periodic updates from the asset manager(s) on the financial and ESG performance of the portfolio companies, sectors, asset classes, and/or geographies that are material to the plan's long-term success. When conducting due diligence and selecting external managers, trustees can set up expectations upfront for a monitoring schedule that may include formal tools (such as quarterly reports) and/or informal tools (such as telephone calls) to request information from managers.

For issues arising between reporting periods that may be of material importance to the fund, trustees should establish protocols for receiving notifications from the external manager on a timely basis. Conversely, if trustees identify new risks and opportunities, they should be able to alert the external manager on these issues and receive an update on its consideration by the manager.

Overall, trustees should endeavor to determine the effectiveness of their managers' investment decisions in relation to the RI policy and hold the managers accountable to the same throughout the duration of the investment.

9.4.2 Fine-tune RI policy and outcome expectations

As mentioned above, just as with traditional investments, so investments made with an ESG mandate should be evaluated on a scheduled basis. Based on the evaluation, trustees and their investment management teams should continue to refine the understanding and application of their ESG-linked investment beliefs and processes to strengthen the quality of the investment analysis, asset allocation decisions, and outcomes.

Box 9.7: Collaborating with like-minded investors

Trustees may share the knowledge they gain from the implementation of their RI policy with their peers as well as among their internal and external managers. Such knowledge sharing is likely to improve the ultimate outcomes of their own policy and promote greater responsible investments within their peers. Indeed, as noted previously, collaborations among pension funds have been shown to increase the success rate of environmental/social shareholder engagements (Dimson *et al.*, 2014). For smaller pension funds in particular, collaborations with other like-minded pension funds can be an effective way to access responsible investment opportunities and expertise.

For example, collaborations on large investment deals, particularly in infrastructure projects, have been a hallmark of the investment success of top Canadian pension funds. By co-investing with like-minded, long-term investors, pension funds such as the CPPIB, OMERS, and OTPP have been able to not only access large-sized deals, but also leverage the in-house expertise of the each of the participating funds (Dyck and Virani, 2012). Similarly, signatories to the PRI have engaged in a number of collaborative initiatives on ESG issues through the PRI Collaboration Platform (previously the PRI Clearinghouse) that gives signatories "enhanced power and legitimacy" when engaging with a company on ESG issues (Piani, 2013).

9.5 Takeaways

In implementing responsible investment strategies, trustees should develop and document a comprehensive RI policy that complements their overall IPS. Trustees may also work with appropriate financial and legal advisors who can help them develop an RI policy, make asset allocation decisions and select responsible investment managers. In order to have better control over their fund's investments, trustees may consider building and delegating greater investment responsibilities to in-house investment teams.

Whether investment decisions are executed by in-house teams and/or external managers, appropriate oversight procedures should be established so that the agency separation issues prevalent in weak pension fund governance structures are mitigated.

Finally, pension funds, particularly smaller funds, can benefit from collaborations with like-minded funds that are actively engaged in responsible investments.

Box 9.8: Support for trustee education

Formally created by the AFL-CIO's Executive Council in 1998, the AFL-CIO's Capital Stewardship Program "seeks to ensure that funds invested on behalf of working families are invested and managed in working families' long-term best interest. The AFL-CIO and its affiliates, working with our trustees, are committed to organizing our funds to be active, responsible stewards of worker capital" (AFL-CIO, 1998). According to the AFL-CIO, "Capital stewardship is about helping trustees manage pension and employee benefit plan assets with the goal of enhancing the economic value of their plan's investments," and that "Capital stewardship recognizes that the long-term, sustainable performance of any investment requires mutually beneficial co-operation among all those involved in a business" (AFL-CIO, 2016).

In addition, the Service Employees International Union (SEIU) Capital Stewardship Program (created in 2000), helps facilitate partnerships between the SEIU and the trustees, administrators, advisors, and investment managers of its members' pension assets, which represent over 15% of all U.S. pension assets. The program advocates for prudent, responsible, and financially sound investment policies. To achieve its goals, the Program "helps elect and appoint effective trustees, educates and provides technical support to union trustees, promotes responsible investment and proxy voting policies, and builds close working relations with the investment consultants and managers of our members' pension funds" (SEIU, 2016).

9.6 References

AFL-CIO (The American Federation of Labor and Congress of Institutional Organizations) (1998). Capital stewardship program. Retrieved June 4, 2016 from http://www.aflcio.org/About/Exec-Council/EC-Statements/Capital-Stewardship-Program.

——— (2016). What is capital stewardship?. Retrieved June 4, 2016 from http://www.aflcio.org/Corporate-Watch/Capital-Stewardship/What-Is-Capital-Stewardship.

Bradford, H. (2014, August 18). North Carolina revs up internal management. *Pensions & Investments*. Retrieved June 4, 2016 from http://www.pionline.com/article/20140818/PRINT/308189975/north-carolina-revs-up-internal-management.

Clark, G.L., & Urwin, R. (2007). *Best Practice Investment Management: Lessons for Asset Owners from The Oxford–Watson Wyatt Project on Governance*. doi:10.2139/ssrn.1019212.

Dimson, E., Karakas, O., & Li, Xi. (2014). Active ownership. *Review of Financial Studies*, 28(12), 3225-3268. Retrieved May 25, 2016 from http://papers.ssrn.com/sol3/papers.cfm?abstract_id=2154724.

Dyck, A., & Virani, A. (2012). *Buying into the 407: The Syndication Protocol as a New Model for Infrastructure Investing*. Retrieved June 4, 2016 from http://www.rijpm.com/admin/article_files/Case_Study_Buying_into_the_407_final.pdf.

Groenewegen, J., & Smith, S. (2014, January). *The Leading Role of Canadian Pension Funds at Home and Abroad*. Retrieved June 4, 2016 from https://www.osler.com/en/resources/governance/2014/capital-markets-report/the-leading-role-of-canadian-pension-funds-at-home.

IRI (Initiative for Responsible Investment) (2011). *Working Paper: Investment Belief Statements.* Retrieved June 21, 2016 from http://hausercenter.org/iri/wp-content/uploads/2012/05/Investment-Beliefs-Statements-10-2011.pdf.

Jordan, P., Hopkins, A., & Kim, S. (2012, January 12). The surprising strength of Canada's pension funds. *Reuters.* Retrieved June 4, 2016 from http://www.reuters.com/article/2012/01/12/us-pensions-idUSTRE80B1C620120112.

NAPF (National Association of Pension Funds) (2013). *NAPF Responsible Investment Guide 2013.* Retrieved June 4, 2016 from http://www.plsa.co.uk/PolicyandResearch/DocumentLibrary/~/media/Policy/Documents/0308_NAPF_Responsible_Investment_guide_2013_DOCUMENT_2.ashx.

Piani, V. (2013). *Introductory Guide to Collaborative Engagement: How Institutional Investors can Effectively Collaborate in Dialogue with Companies.* PRI. Retrieved June 21, 2016 from https://www.unpri.org/download_report/8528.

SEIU (Service Employees International Union) (2016). All about retirement security. Retrieved June 27, 2016 from http://www.seiu.org/cards/all-the-educational-resources-you-need-to-be-a-leader.

Snow Spalding, K., Cleveland, S., & Pears, S. (2012). *Incorporating Environmental, Social and Governance Factors Into Investing: A Survey of Investment Consultant Practices.* Retrieved June 4, 2016 from http://www.ceres.org/resources/reports/incorporating-environmental-social-and-governance-factors-into-investing-a-survey-of-investment-consultant-practices.

van der Velden, A., & van Buul, O. (2012). Really investing in the long-term: a case study. *Rotman International Journal of Pension Management,* 5(1), 50-57.

Voorhes, M. (2009). *Investment Consultant and Responsible Investing: Current Practices and Outlook in the United States.* Retrieved June 4, 2016 from http://www.ussif.org/files/Publications/Investment%20Consultant%20FINAL.pdf.

10
Criteria for evaluating responsible investment performance

> Values can be linked to value.
>
> Kimberly Gladman,
> Managing Director, Research, JUST Capital

Once investments are made, trustees and fiduciaries of pension assets will want to evaluate the performance of these investments against the goals of the fund. For pension funds invested responsibly, these goals include achieving adequate financial returns on invested assets, alongside positive ESG impacts such as improvements in corporate governance, the creation of well-paying jobs, reductions in greenhouse gas emissions, and the development of much-needed infrastructure.

Due to the variety of responsible investment approaches, there has been limited consensus on the metrics that should be used for measuring ESG impacts. This problem is further complicated by investors assigning different weights to specific ESG issues based on the importance of those issues in their overall portfolio. However, as noted, tremendous strides are being made by global sustainability reporting and responsible investment programs, such as the PRI, the Global Reporting Initiative (GRI), the Global Real Estate Sustainability Benchmark (GRESB), the Sustainability Accounting Standards Board (SASB), and the Global Initiative for Sustainability Ratings (GISR), to standardize ESG data collection and reporting.

In this chapter, we briefly discuss the challenges related to sustainability ratings, and provide some key criteria that trustees should consider and impress on their investment teams, internal and/or external, when evaluating the performance of their pension portfolio against its investment goals.

10.1 Sustainability ratings, rankings and indices

In recent years, there has been a proliferation in the availability of ESG ratings, rankings, and indices, as well as providers—a result of greater investor demand for the inclusion of ESG considerations in investment decision-making. The ESG data can be used to inform the investor's investment policy statement (IPS), make comparisons between companies, select stock based on a best-in-class strategy, and engage with management on issues material to the investors, among other uses. A majority of providers are focused on reporting data for publicly traded companies, while a small number provide data on privately held companies.

This proliferation of ESG data, however, has been accompanied by a lack of consistency in data collection methodologies, differences in the number and types of indicator collected, and limited depth in the evaluation of the indicators, particularly social and labor standards, by providers.

For instance, per a 2012 study of sustainability rating providers presented at the 2015 ITUC Workers' Capital Conference, some providers collect sustainability data on companies through publicly available information, while others do so through tailored questionnaires (Richter, 2015). According to the GISR, there are currently over a hundred sustainability agencies administering questionnaires to thousands of companies globally, seeking information on specific areas of concern or across the ESG spectrum (GISR, 2015a). The 2012 study also found that while providers incorporated and analyzed environmental and governance issues in depth, "they usually do not go beyond the formal commitment of the company" in matters related to social and key labor indicators (Richter, 2015, p. 3).

As a result of the above, there has been increased "survey fatigue" among companies and, in the absence of standard data-collection methods and indicators, reduced reliability and usefulness of the reports for investors.

To counter these shortcomings, organizations such as the GISR, launched in 2011, are working to apply a consistent standard for measuring sustainability performance across different providers. More importantly, with ESG data collection and reporting being driven primarily by investor demand, pension trustees can play an important role in pushing providers to strengthen the types of indicator collected and the evaluation of those indicators material to their investment policy. For instance, pension plans tracking the percentage of workers covered by collective bargaining agreements in a company within a certain industry would benefit from knowing

TABLE 10.1 **Sample list of indicators covered by a ratings provider**

Issues	Indicators	Business behaviors
Environmental	• Environmental strategy and ecodesign • Pollution management (prevention and control) • Development of green products and services • Risk management related to the affect on biodiversity • Sustainable water management • Rational energy consumption • Management of atmospheric emissions • Waste management • Management of local pollution • Impact of transport and distribution • Environmental impact on the overall life-cycle of products and services	• Integration of environmental factors in the supply chain • Product safety (process and use).
Social	• Respect for the fundamental human rights and safeguarding measures • Promotion of labor relations • Respect for the freedom of trade unions and right to collective bargaining • Nondiscrimination • Exclusion of child labor and forced labor • Promotion of social dialogue • Encouragement of participation • Reorganization policy • Care for individual career planning and professional availability • Quality of remuneration • Improvement of safety, health, and prevention • Working hours policy • Contribution to economic and social development of the territories of establishment and their human communities • Social impact of products or services • Contribution to causes of general interest	• Information to customers • Responsible customer relations • Sustainable relationships with suppliers • Integration of social factors in the supply chain • Product safety (process and use)
Governance	• Efficiency of the board of directors and associated committees • Effectiveness of internal controls and audit systems • Respect of shareholders' rights and transparency and efficiency in executive remuneration • Integration of CSR into corporate governance structures and processes	• Prevention of corruption • Prevention of anticompetitive practices • Transparency and integrity of influence strategies and practices

Source: GISR, 2015b.

the change in this percentage over time and from being able make comparisons with the industry average (Richter, 2015, p. 4).

10.2 Key criteria for responsible investment evaluation

To enable trustees to effectively navigate a plethora of available ESG data, we have distilled responsible investment evaluation into seven key criteria:

10.2.1 Focus on long-term performance evaluation

As emphasized, pension funds are long-term investors that start collecting contributions when individuals enter the workforce and may not pay out benefits until 30–40 years later. The investment value of pension assets is therefore impacted by long-term economic trends and ESG considerations that manifest many years into the future. In general, pension fund trustees, like other long-term investors, are advised to not get "overly concerned with short-term fluctuations in value, since trading based on short-term volatility could sidetrack your long-term goals" (FINRA, 2014). When evaluating responsible investment performance, therefore, trustees should keep in mind the long-term goals of their pension investments as they relate to the wellbeing of workers and their beneficiaries.

10.2.2 Factor in economic impacts on the broad economy

As universal owners, pension funds should evaluate the performance of their investment portfolios based on the impacts of their investments on the broad economy. Such an evaluation should include externalities, i.e., "the financially or economically measurable impacts that a company may have on employees, communities, ecosystems, or other stakeholders" (Gladman, 2011). These externalities can be positive or negative, and correspondingly can have a positive or negative effect on the financial value of pension assets.

10.2.3 Evaluate material ESG factors

In previous chapters, we discussed how pension fund trustees should focus on material ESG factors when incorporating responsible investment strategies. The materiality of ESG factors refers to the significance of the factors in

Box 10.1: Economic impacts of investment decisions

As noted by Gladman (2011):

> a state pension fund may hold stock in a company whose toxic emissions cause illness in state residents and pollute its parks, thereby imposing costs on the state's health system and reducing state tax revenues from the tourism industry. The company's pollution may even harm, directly or indirectly, other companies in the state pension fund's portfolio. Seen from the perspective of the state as institutional investor, pension fund returns from this company's stock may not look as positive after accounting for these related costs. Alternatively, a company that invests in employee education and training may raise the long-term earnings potential of its workers, resulting in higher future tax payments from those individuals to cities and states that may hold the company's securities in their funds.

Indeed, recent studies on the impacts of responsible property funds, for example, have confirmed that by investing in responsible property funds that specialize in deploying the highest-performing contractors, utilizing team approaches, and crafting trades knowledge and talent, pension funds can play a vital role in creating good jobs and stimulating and strengthening local economies. Below, we provide more details on the impacts of two such pension-financed investment funds.

Multi-Employer Property Trust (MEPT)

MEPT has spent a total of $7.5 billion since 1982 in responsible property, which has translated into $15.9 billion in economic activity. Consequently, 118,000 jobs have been created, $6.6 billion in income and benefits has been earned, and $526 million in tax revenue has been generated. The direct economic impacts of the $6 billion in "hard costs" on contractors and building trades' workers include:

- 42,450 jobs
- 81.8 million hours of work
- $2.6 billion in wages and benefits
- $130.9 million in state personal income taxes paid by union workers

Source: Podzena and Josephson, 2014.

AFL-CIO Housing Investment Trust (HIT)

The HIT has invested $12.4 billion over the past 30 years in responsible property investments. In addition to delivering competitive financial returns, the HIT's investments have directly generated 74,131 union jobs (or 149.2 million hours of work), $4.9 billion in wages and benefits for union workers, $318.8 million in tax and fee revenues for state and local governments, and $952.2 million in tax revenues for the federal government.

As of December 31, 2014, the HIT's investments had demonstrated the following (direct and indirect) fiscal and economic impacts:

- 157,321 total jobs across industries (or 303.8 million hours of work)
- $24.5 billion in economic benefits for local communities, including $9.6 billion in personal income
- $989.6 million in state and local taxes and $2.1 billion in federal revenue

Source: AFL-CIO, 2015.

terms of their impact on an investment's risk and return attributes. Just as certain financial indicators are more relevant to specific industries or companies, so certain ESG factors are more applicable to particular industries or companies. For example, as noted by Gladman (2011):

> a financial ratio like inventory turnover may be crucial for one firm and irrelevant to another. Similarly, some firms are affected by their relationships with repressive overseas governments or the rise in water scarcity, while others are not; for some firms, the number of work hours lost each year due to accidents is a key indicator while for others it is of lesser importance.

As such, when evaluating the performance of their responsible investments, pension trustees should focus on the key indicators related to their responsible investments in each industry.

10.2.4 Select the right benchmark

The success of an investment portfolio is often evaluated against a benchmark. Generally, market indices tracking a broad asset class, such as large capitalization stocks, or a narrower segment within an asset class, such as technology stocks, are used as benchmarks (PIMCO, 2014). Choosing the right benchmark is very important to avoid drawing the wrong conclusions (FINRA, 2014). As such, the appropriate benchmark should reflect the types of investment owned within the investment portfolio. In addition, the underlying riskiness of a benchmark should be evaluated against the established risk tolerance for the benchmarked assets.

Within responsible investments, benchmarks used primarily include the following (SRI Connect, 2014):

- Exclusionary indices that screen out "sin stock" sectors or companies

Box 10.2: Different benchmarks for different responsible investment approaches

The Dow Jones Sustainability Index (DJSI) family, which applies a best-in-class approach, includes companies that are ranked high in relation to corporate sustainability within their industry. The Vanguard FTSE Social Index (VFTSX), however, chooses to include only those companies that have been selected based on religious or ethical considerations.

- Broad sustainability indices that use a best-in-class approach by "filtering a conventional market index through broad-based sustainability screens"
- Thematic indices that use a bottom-up approach to specifically select companies "exposed to specific activities or issues." These may include companies with a focus on renewable energy, clean technology, etc.

To enable an apples-to-apples comparison, a strategy that uses exclusionary screens should compare its results with a benchmark that excludes companies based on the same criteria as the strategy. If a strategy combines different responsible investment approaches, it should similarly compare results with a benchmark that does the same.

As noted, however, excessive reliance on a benchmark is cautioned against. This is especially true in times of market downturns when a selected benchmark may show negative returns. Performing in line with the benchmark is no solace when pension assets are not able to meet promised retiree benefits. As such, trustees should be more focused on achieving returns—financial and ESG-based—that are in alignment with the pension fund's long-term benefit payments to its workers and retirees.

Box 10.3: Some useful ESG data sources

- The **Global Reporting Initiative (GRI)** provides a standardized reporting framework that is used by a number of companies globally to disclose the ESG impacts of their operations (https://www.globalreporting.org)
- The **Sustainability Accounting Standards Board (SASB)** develops sustainability accounting standards to help public corporations disclose material, decision-useful information to investors (http://www.sasb.org)
- The **Global Real Estate Sustainability Benchmark (GRESB)** provides ESG-based data for the global real estate sector (https://www.gresb.com)
- The **Centre for International Climate and Environmental Research–Oslo (CICERO)** conducts independent, research-based evaluations of green bond investment frameworks to determine their robustness in meeting institutions' environmental objectives (http://www.cicero.uio.no/en/)
- The **Green Bond Principles** are voluntary process guidelines that recommend transparency and disclosure of the green bond market by clarifying the approach for issuance of a green bond (E&E Publishing, 2014)

Further examples of both for-profit and non-profit ESG data providers are listed in Appendix B.

10.2.5 Use a combination of research sources

In order to get a full picture of their investments' ESG impacts, trustees and fiduciaries should seek information from a variety of company-specific and sector-specific research reports such as ESG ratings, greenhouse gas emissions and carbon footprint reports, and corporate governance scores. Financial data providers such as Bloomberg and MSCI have also begun to provide ESG performance data. For instance, Bloomberg's ESG data service provides ESG performance data on over 10,000 companies side by side with other fundamental financial data on these companies (Bloomberg, 2015).

In addition, many public companies now issue annual corporate sustainability reports (CSRs) that can be gauged for the ESG impacts of the companies' operations. CSRs may not currently offer a standard format for evaluation, although the SASB and GRI are creating standardized accounting and reporting tools to enable public companies to disclose ESG data in a consistent format.

10.2.6 ESG performance evaluation is an iterative process

Like any other evaluation exercise, the evaluation of an ESG strategy is a continual improvement process. Just as trustees may begin with applying responsible investment strategies to a part of their pension investment portfolio, so the evaluation of the impact of these strategies may be undertaken step-by-step and eventually applied to the pension fund's entire responsible investments.

10.2.7 Not everything that counts can be counted

Finally, we note that certain positive practices by companies may not readily lend themselves to financially quantifiable metrics. These practices, however, may still be important to pension funds in their role as universal owners and their objective to provide a safe and decent retirement to the plans' participants. As noted by Gladman (2011):

> [some] investors do not want to hold retailers whose overseas factories employ children or subject workers to harassment or violence; they do not want their manufacturing companies to deplete the drinking water of communities in the developing world; and they don't want the fast food chains they hold to build restaurants next to ancient ruins or on indigenous sacred sites. It may not be possible to make a "business case" for the prevention of labor abuses, drought, and

cultural destruction, but responsible investors also see themselves as citizens and human beings who have broader interests than the simple maximization of profit.

In such cases, trustees may still be able to take factors such as collateral benefits into consideration, so long as they do not sacrifice investment returns.

10.3 Takeaways

This chapter provides trustees with some basic criteria to use when evaluating the impact of their responsible investment strategies. In line with our recommendations for the development and implementation of an RI policy for pension funds, we recommend that trustees evaluate the performance of such a policy based on long-term investment principles. We also recommend that trustees focus on measuring what matters, while recognizing that not everything that matters can be measured.

10.4 References

AFL-CIO (The American Federation of Labor and Congress of Industrial Organizations) (2015). *A Detailed Overview of the AFL-CIO Housing Investment Trust: Its Fixed-Income Strategy and Fund Performance Winter 2015*. Retrieved June 5, 2016 from https://www.aflcio-hit.com/user-assets/Documents/special_reports/hit_overview_115.pdf.

Bloomberg (2015). Markets: Equities. *Bloomberg Professional*. Retrieved June 5, 2016 from http://www.bloomberg.com/professional/markets/equities/.

E&E Publishing, LLC (2014). *Green Bond Principles, 2014*. Retrieved June 5, 2016 from http://www.eenews.net/assets/2015/05/14/document_cw_01.pdf.

FINRA (Financial Industry Regulating Authority) (2014). Evaluating investment performance. Retrieved June 5, 2016 from http://www.finra.org/investors/evaluating-investment-performance.

GISR (Global Initiative for Sustainability Ratings) (2015a). Why GISR. Retrieved June 5, 2016 from http://ratesustainability.org/about/why-gisr/.

——— (2015b). Product profile: Vigeo. Retrieved June 5, 2016 from http://ratesustainability.org/hub/index.php/search/at-a-glance-product/15/72.

Gladman, K. (2011). Ten things to know about responsible investment and performance. *GMI Ratings*. Retrieved June 27, 2016 from http://www.integrity-research.com/ten-things-to-know-about-responsible-investment-and-performance/.

PIMCO (2014). Benchmarks: basics. Retrieved June 21, 2016 from http://europe.pimco.com/EN/Education/Pages/BenchmarksBasics.aspx.

Podzena, R., & Josephson, A. (2014). *The Economic Impacts of MEPT Investments across the United States*. Portland, OR: ECONorthwest, Inc.

Richter, M.S. (2015, September). *Labor Standards in Sustainability Ratings: How Well are they Incorporated.* Retrieved June 4, 2016 from http://www.workerscapital.org/files/A.2-CWC_08Sep15_CCOO_.pdf.

SRI Connect (2014). SRI indices: types & usage. Retrieved June 5, 2016 from http://www.sri-connect.com/index.php?option=com_content&view=article&id=610&Itemid=1154.

Conclusion: Renewing the real economy, restoring retirement trust

> We have far more retirement assets under management than any other country in the world and when properly invested in real assets, they can be leveraged as a cornerstone to rebuild infrastructure and drive economic stability. To realize this opportunity, we need political leadership, new financial tools for investors and regulatory balance that will ensure prudent but flexible reinvestment in our own country.
>
> Landon Butler, Founder, Landon Butler & Company, and Co-Founder, Multi-Employer Property Trust (MEPT)

As investors, trustees and the stewards of workers' capital stand at the threshold of the most transformational economic changes in a generation. It is time for such investors to step up as active asset owners that have a long-term perspective rather than a short-term focus. By teaming up with labor innovators, entrepreneurs, progressive governments, and allied investors to scale and solve the big economic, social, and environmental problems of our time, the stewards of *our money* could have unprecedented impacts in the next decade (Shah, 2013).

Paradoxically, it has become more difficult to manage pension funds due to a number of factors. These include recurring financial crises and resulting market volatilities, increasing capital markets and regulatory complexities, and a greater number of players in the investment value chain that have placed greater scrutiny and demands on trustees. In surveys of pension fund trustees by David Wood and Jay Youngdahl at the Harvard Initiative for

Responsible Investment (IRI), there are signs that it has been a hard time to be a trustee:

> The result has been a perfect storm of financial, economic, and political challenges ... Broader debates over the nature of retirement security, and the commitment that funds themselves represent to retirement security, have become a fundamental part of their work of financial stewardship ... [Q]uestions about [pension management matters] can become divorced from the fundamental purpose of the funds themselves, and run the risk of placing undue burdens on investment returns to make up for shortfalls created by political decisions about funding. (Wood and Youngdahl, 2011, p. 4)

To effectively meet these challenges requires, more than ever, better pension fund governance, greater transparency around investments, and improved risk management. More than ever, trustees need to secure better investment knowledge and training for themselves while ensuring ongoing due diligence of the advisers and managers of the plan's assets. More than ever, trustees need to be able to ask hard questions and challenge conventional market wisdom that often promotes a short-term focus over long-term value creation.

As Wood and Youngdahl assert, responsible investment on the part of trustees can be a way to build a coherent theory that addresses these challenges and capacity to better link the funds' financial strategies with their long-term purpose.

However, Global Unions argue that even though the PRI movement has had a positive impact, voluntary guidelines and agreements failed at preventing the worst economic downturn since the Depression.[1] Pension and institutional investors were, in fact, characterized by some as "absentee landlords" of "ownerless corporations" leading up to the market crisis (NAPF, 2013, p. 5). Unfortunately, the economic shocks worrying trustees

1 Ron Blackwell, the former Chief Economist of the AFL-CIO, believes that corporate social responsibility and standards of responsible investment are not alone sufficient to affect corporate behavior. A more robust design for corporate accountability can be represented as a pyramid. The foundation is adequate corporate regulation to align the private purposes of business with the social purpose of corporations to create wealth. Next comes unconflicted corporate governance. The next layer is the recognition of workers' rights to organize and bargain collectively to balance power between employers and employees. Only with these layers of accountability in place can voluntary corporate responsibility statements and socially responsible investment agreements play their role (personal communication/interview, December 8, 2015).

have not ended with the last crisis. And though the pension promise was constructed decades ago, that promise is at risk today. We need to restore the trust and the promise.

As such, pension trustees need to go beyond labels and exercise caution—both in the selection and ongoing due diligence of their responsible investment strategy. Trustees need to set up an investment strategy that supports the pension fund's long-term mission and investment beliefs. They need to ensure that the consultants and managers of plan assets, as well as the companies and projects that use these assets, are not simply paying lip service to important issues that may be material to the plan's investment value. They need to make their long-term investment objectives clear to the consultants and managers, and they need to monitor these players effectively. They also need to appropriately incentivize these players to engage in long-term value creation rather than chase short-term trends—whether in traditional or responsible investments:

> At least one thing should no longer be in any doubt—that responsible investment is not a mystery. It is a living and breathing part of making investment decisions. It is not an "add-on" or something separate. It is simply doing things better.
>
> Azhar Abidi, Director Responsible Investment, Industry Funds Management (IFM) Investors (Aalbu *et al.*, 2011, p. 5)

In this *Handbook*, we have tried to provide a practical overview of doing well by doing good. In so doing, we reviewed:

- The history of responsible investment, and labor's pioneering role in that history
- Good pension fund governance and corporate governance practices
- The principles and regulations promoting responsible investments, and the evolution from ETIs to ESG
- The correlation between incorporating ESG considerations and the positive impact on companies' operational performance and share price value
- How the investment of workers' capital can be targeted, across asset classes and for the long term, to generate competitive financial and economic returns alongside ESG benefits

- How trustees can engage with consultants and investment managers to question the status quo and implement a responsible investment strategy

In this concluding chapter, we reiterate the key principles advocated in this *Handbook* to protect and regrow workers' capital. We discuss the importance of worker-owners engaging with bosses, and talk about the split roles of worker-owners as shareholders and stakeholders. We also explore long-term investment strategies that can put workers' capital to work for their ultimate benefit.

Understanding risks in the new, fast-moving economy we live in

As John Evans, Chief Economist of ITUC, reminded us in 2013:

> On 15 September 2008 the merchant bank Lehman Brothers filed for bankruptcy, triggering a series of events that led to the worst financial crisis and global recession since the Second World War. The G20 was thrust into prominence as the central economic policy coordination forum in the near financial meltdown of 2008. In its first year of meeting, at the Leaders' Summit, the G20 showed the necessary political will to avert a second Great Depression. The ILO estimated that this coordinated action of 2008 and 2009 saved nearly 30 million jobs. An ambitious Financial Action Plan was adopted at the London Summit in April 2009. The then G20 Chair, Gordon Brown, said "never again will the financial sector be in control of the real economy". After strong pressure from the international labour movement in September 2009 in Pittsburgh, the G20 committed to "putting quality jobs at the heart of the recovery".
>
> However, in 2010, the G20 governments panicked in the face of resurgent financial markets and prematurely shifted from supporting global growth, jobs and economic rebalancing to cutting public expenditure and excessive austerity. The result, five years later, is that the "recovery" has not materialized. (Evans, 2013, p. 3)

Frédéric Hanin, a professor of Laval University in Montreal, said that the 2008 financial crisis was one manifestation of the instability of short-term "financialization" (Hanin, 2010). Working families and communities absorbed the risks of financial experimentation, and suffered tremendously, because our governments promoted the financial deregulation policies that contributed to the crash, and our governments were often hands-off as the economy fell down around them (Hanin, 2010). Or, worse than hands off, governments created a cure that made the disease worse, as pointed out by Evans.

Historian Kevin Phillips wrote that, in the mid-1900s, manufacturing drove about a quarter of U.S. GDP and was double the size of financial services. In recent times, the quotient has flipped, as financial sectors overtook manufacturing (Croft, 2009). "Global finance has altered the underlying logics of the industrial economy and the inner workings of democratic society" (van der Zwan, 2014, p. 99).

A report from the McKinsey Global Institute said that these unsustainable trends—most notably the growing size and leverage of the financial sector itself—propelled much of the financial deepening that occurred before the financial crisis. "Financing for households and corporations accounted for just over one-fourth of the rise in global financial depth from 1995 to 2007—an astonishingly small share, since providing credit to these sectors is the fundamental purpose of finance" (Lund *et al.*, 2013, p. 2).

These trends, sometimes called "financial engineering" (Rossman and Greenfield, 2006), are condemned by the Global Unions. Financial engineers have created a battery of risky financial products. Our general guidance to trustees has been to avoid highly risky, complex products if managers and consultants can't explain them.

The fallouts from the casino economy-fueled 2008 crash were horrific: lost jobs, lost assets and pensions, ravaged wages and benefits, and increased debts for working Americans. The poverty level among Americans rose and retirement savings for working people fell dramatically. The bank bailouts crowded out real stimulus, and contributed to deficits and austerity programs across countries (Hebb and Sharma, 2012). Financialization and globalization were factors in recent market crises, and led to the inexorable rise of income inequality, which spiked after 2008.

Ongoing challenges remain in the U.S.A.:

- Business investment in equipment, software, and structures declined in the 2000s, growing just 0.5%, less than a fifth of the 1980s and a tenth of the 1990s (Stewart and Atkinson, 2013)
- Federal housing funds have been cut; meanwhile, small business development, employment, and retraining, and antipoverty programs were cut or dried up

- There is a $3.6 trillion deficit for infrastructure, as our nation's water systems, roads and bridges, electric grid and civic infrastructure have rusted or fallen apart, according to repeated warnings from the American Society of Civil Engineers (ASCE, 2014)
- An extra $500 billion is need to sustainably modernize school buildings alone over the next decade, according to the U.S. Green Building Council (USGBC, 2013)

Due to budget crises that spread across cities and states, pension funds and other institutional investors have begun trying to meet these challenges through the investment of their assets in these critical areas. In some cases, they have become more active investors in the growth and sustainability of our cities. Governments once assumed this role for the public but, after the financial market crash and bank bailouts, governments suffered tighter budgets and adopted austerity measures. The result is a radical shift away from the public investment of the past, when inner-city urban revitalization was seen as a public good, to private investment with its attendant set of property rights and renters' profits, according to Tessa Hebb and Rajiv Sharma. This skewed development is said to be the latest wave of financialization of our cities (Hebb and Sharma, 2012).

We must be cautious of the rush toward "liberating" retirement funds for infrastructure investments and everything else needed in a society that is not paying for its basic needs. What are the antidotes to speculation and financialization? It is prudence—still the core fiduciary duty of responsible pension investors (Carmichael, 2005)—along with long-term investment horizons and a reemphasis on risk assessment. We cannot allow the next investment frenzy to obliterate our common sense and fiduciary obligations that should be investing in the long-term interests of pension beneficiaries.

This "new normal" requires the intervention of responsible investors and communities, unions, firms, and economic stakeholders, to secure a more stable economy and to sustainably regrow our cities (Hanin, 2010). It takes more than a village, you might say, to guard against capital schemes that repeat failures of the past. It takes a global coalition.

Below, we reiterate the key principles discussed in this *Handbook* to help trustees more effectively manage their pension funds within the new realities of the economy.

Paying attention to good corporate governance and ESG risk

Good governance is important not only in terms of managing companies efficiently, but in ensuring that companies pay workers a living wage, respect their right to organize, and pay attention to their health and safety. Shareholders and stakeholders alike must also play a watchdog role, as mistakes can cost lives.

On April 24, 2013, Rana Plaza, an eight-story garment factory near the Bangladeshi capital Dhaka, collapsed, killing over 1,100 workers and injuring 2,500 more (Burke, 2014). It was one of the most tragic industrial disasters in modern memory and focused Western attention on the terrible safety conditions that underlie the global garment industry. The U.S. public came to understand workplace safety only after a similar disaster, the Triangle Shirtwaist Factory fire tragedy in Manhattan, killed 146 garment workers, mostly women, a century ago. Dozens of American workers have continued to die, even in modern times, from mining and drilling disasters in recent years. These include the BP offshore oil derrick explosion in the Gulf of Mexico, the largest environmental disaster ever, and the Massey Energy mine explosion in West Virginia, both in 2010.

Activist pension funds, as referred to earlier, joined human rights coalitions to demand supply chain transparency in the Rana Plaza case. In the Massey disaster, shareholder anger from a coalition of pension funds over safety and risk management failures forced the firm's board of directors to strip the former CEO of his board chairmanship position (Lublin and Maher, 2010). Don Blankenship, the longtime CEO of Massey, was later indicted on charges that he violated or covered up critical federal mine safety rules at the company's Upper Big Branch Mine prior to the explosion that killed the miners (Ward, 2014). This allowed for responsible shareholders to play a significant role in restructuring the company. As we mentioned earlier, a jury of his peers in West Virginia ultimately convicted Blankenship, a rare verdict in a coal state where Blankenship had been accused of rigging the courts.

As Michael Garland, Assistant Comptroller for Corporate Governance and Responsible Investment at New York City Office of the Comptroller explained:

> Ultimately, the company was a Rorschach Test for everything that can go wrong in business. The firm had a long history of egregious health, safety, and environmental problems that led to fines and investor-led lawsuits. This tells us why companies with environmental practices in

> place are more sustainable. It is not just about values, it is about protecting and creating long-term value. At minimum, it is about managing risk.[2]

In another example of activist strategies by pension funds, the New York City Pension Funds launched a Boardroom Accountability Project in 2015, submitting proxy access shareowner proposals to 75 companies at once (Stringer, 2015). The purpose of this project is to give shareowners a true voice in how corporate boards are elected at every U.S. company. As Garland noted:

> Shareowners deserve a voice on the boards of the companies they own. The pension funds are working to collectively make companies more transparent. If a shareholder has 3% or more ownership in the company, he or she should have right to nominate up to 25% of the board, and have that cited in proxy ... It is all about long-term investors and making boards responsive.[3]

The responses from the targeted firms have been strong.

> There is also major risk to those managers that ignore ESG. You can see how you can get on the wrong side of a story very quickly. Just look at the examples of the sweatshops and supply chains in India and the recent factory deaths. BP, after the Gulf oil spill accident, lost billions of dollars. Nike had some problems in 2008, admitting its Chinese supply chain suffered from a lack of transparency, problems with wages, and the use of underage workers.[4]

Capital stewards, along with policy leaders, are also concerned about excessive executive compensation, a much contested topic. In some countries, legislators have passed laws requiring companies to hold "say-on-pay" votes, publish CEO/worker pay ratios, or limit bonuses (CWC, 2015; Bloxham, 2011). The AFL-CIO's Executive Paywatch website warns that, even as many companies argue that they cannot afford to raise wages, the nation's largest companies are earning higher profits per employee than they did five years ago (AFL-CIO, 2014).

Despite these pushbacks on the current system of executive accountability, we have a long way to go. In *Profits Without Prosperity*, University of Massachusetts (Lowell) economics professor William Lazonick documented that through the massive use of share buybacks, CEOs and top executives

2 Personal communication/interview, December 17, 2014.

3 Personal communication/interview, December 17, 2014.

4 Ana Lei Ortiz, Managing Director, Hamilton Lane Advisors, personal communication/interview, July 24, 2014.

are extracting value, instead of creating value, for their firms, stakeholders, shareholders, and society. Between 2003 and 2012, "publicly-listed firms in the S&P 500 used a colossal amount of their earnings—54 percent or $2.4 trillion—to buy back their own stock" (Lazonick, 2014). The consequences of these share buybacks were net disinvestment, loss of shareholder value, crippled capacity to innovate, destruction of jobs, runaway executive compensation, and windfall gains for activist insiders. Instead of the long-proven "retain-and-reinvest" approach, which contributes to "sustainable prosperity," this short-sighted practice leads to employment instability and income inequality (Lazonick, 2009, 2014; Denning, 2014).

Paying attention to long-term investing and worker-stakeholders

Leading up to the financial markets crash, institutional investors, according to author Jim Hawley, failed on most accounts to implement well-established corporate governance principles in most alternative investments, and failed to integrate risk analysis with governance, especially in the financial sector. Indeed, universal investors rushed into the same risky, reckless debts and all-too-often fraudulent investment schemes as most other market players (Hawley, 2009). The investments in very risky assets were caused by the "rush to alpha," as it is called. After the financial markets crash, the U.K. government asked for an analysis of how U.K. businesses could return to a more sustainable, innovation-driven growth model that builds value and creates jobs. The *Kay Review of UK Equity Markets and Long-Term Decision Making*, cited earlier, said:

> The interests of beneficiaries are largely interests in long-term absolute performance. The concern of asset managers—and the basis on which they are monitored by many asset holders, and by advisers to asset holders and retail investors—is short-term relative performance. This misalignment of incentives creates many problems.
>
> Returns to beneficial owners, taken as a whole, can be enhanced only by improving the performance of the corporate sector as a whole. Returns to any subset of beneficial owners can be enhanced, at the expense of other investors, by the superior relative performance of their own asset managers. Asset managers search for alpha, risk adjusted outperformance relative to a benchmark. But savers collectively will earn beta, the average return on the asset class.
>
> (Kay, 2012, pp. 41-42)

The Kay Review addressed the importance of long-term investment as a critical first step in good corporate governance, and provided a set of voluntary guidelines for institutional investors and companies. The critical distinction between alpha and beta in the report was echoed by Dennak Murphy, a former co-director of the SEIU Capital Stewardship program, who put it this way in a presentation to pension trustees: "Ultimately, pension fund returns mirror the returns produced by the overall economy ... Risk of a failed or sluggish economy is the greatest risk facing pension investors today. Some investment practices help strengthen and grow the economy; others do not" (Murphy, 2012).

But, as Hawley asked, who will watch the watchers? Pension trust boards are supposed to play that role, monitoring investments for prudence and appropriateness. However, shareholder interests should not be exercised at the expense of other key stakeholders. As such, trustees and worker-owners need to be the catalyst to realign incentives with longer-term investment horizons for consultants, asset managers, and other players in the investment value chain.

In "Making sense of financialization," Natascha van der Zwan (2014) argues that the ascendancy of the shareholder value orientation in the pension community is a factor in causing financialization.[5] Clearly, responsible shareholder value is a foundation of good governance, especially when capital stewards fully consider all of the components of ESG. But in the following case, the focus on "shareholder primacy" went too far.

A shareholders' campaign in 2013–14 to break up Timken Steel, a modernized, profitable firm in Canton, Ohio, forced the split of the company into two components. It was led by Relational Investors, an activist hedge fund founded by protégés of T. Boone Pickens (the corporate raider), and CalSTRS, a signatory of PRI. Multiple news accounts of the battle acknowledged the firm was well structured and well managed, had low debts and a healthy pension. The articles relayed the fears of the family, workers, and local citizens that the split was unnecessary and might result in Wall Street predators taking over the two firms and relocating or closing them.

5 This view is growing among the stewards of financial markets. For instance, "Andy Haldane, the Bank of England's Chief Economist, has said that the UK's shareholder model of corporate governance is holding back business investment and hurting economic growth. ... The TUC has long argued that the priority given to shareholder interests within the UK's corporate governance system contributes to economic short-termism and lower investment" (Williamson, 2015).

We have praised the responsible investment practices of CalSTRS in the *Handbook*. In the above case, however, the shareholder activists needed to pay more attention to growing companies sustainably, and to the "S" in ESG, not arbitrarily breaking them up to "unlock value and drive share prices higher" (Schwartz, 2014). The company had been a longtime good employer and generous corporate citizen for Canton: the hedge fund pocketed $188 million, a huge profit, within a matter of weeks of the split, after owning a small portion of the stock for only two years.

The United Steelworkers, who represent 2,300 Timken workers in Ohio, have had a long and decent relationship with the family and managers of the hundred-year-old firm, and opposed the breakup. The lead trustee from the teachers' union reportedly opposed the CalSTRS board vote that led to the split, all to no avail. The European Trade Union Confederation (ETUC) argues that hostile takeovers (and similar actions) generally do not lead to long-term value creation (Vitols and Kluge, 2011). Time will tell whether the breakup of Timken benefited long-term investors or whether it destroyed synergies and made the company more vulnerable to an economic downturn (Schwartz, 2014).

In addition to effectively intervening in corporate restructuring, as cited in Chapter 1, the Steelworkers Union has bargained for years to place worker representatives on corporate boards, such as on the board of USX, the parent company of U.S. Steel. This level of engagement improves communications among the board, managers, and stakeholders of the company. Perhaps we might want to look, once again, to Europe, where German works councils provide a stiffer voice for worker stakeholders on the job. In a companion piece to "Making sense," the author closely examined the works councils' "stakeholder" model as a more balanced and productive form of governance (van der Zwan, 2011). This successful strategy of company "codetermination," long the envy of U.S. policy wonks, has, after all, performed well against that of U.S. companies for the last several decades. It is important that capital stewards hunt for more balance between shareholder and stakeholder models of corporate governance, instead of exclusively chasing alpha.

There have also been, in the ramp up to infrastructure investments, a number of cases where pension-controlled infrastructure managers have invested in other countries. While they may have been PRI signatories and obliged to invest responsibly in their home countries, they have sometimes avoided those covenants when making investments across borders. These stories are embarrassing; investors should maintain solidarity in our transnational developments.

The financial markets disasters of the last 15 years have only added to the overriding obligation for responsible investors to separate from the financial "herd," which plowed (and lost) trillions of dollars into ill-advised, unsustainable, and sometimes illegal investments. The negative impacts of these events, along with human rights abuses, environmental disasters, and climate change, bolster the view that extra-financial risks must be taken into account when investing. Workers are stakeholders in businesses as well as shareholders and owners. Workers are citizens and taxpayers who can influence courts and elections, as van der Zwan points out. It is important to amass all those powers to restore the pension promise and the irrevocable trust.

Rebuilding cities, revitalizing our industrial commons, growing the clean economy

More than 200 years ago, U.S. citizens and entrepreneurs supplied the capital for and built the Erie Canal. Over the next two centuries, our nation built a remarkable economic and technological infrastructure that included highways, railroads, civic buildings and schools, space travel, high technology, and bio-medical and renewable energy breakthroughs. U.S. pension funds have been partners in many of these innovations, particularly since the middle of the 20th century.

But U.S. ingenuity has stalled in recent years. While the U.S.A. seeded the beginnings of the solar industry, it has since ceded its growth, expansion, and mainstreaming to Asia. As recounted by Harvard Business School professors Gary Pisano and Willy Shih, U.S. corporations gave away the manufacturing of semiconductors and flat-panels to China in the 1990s (Pisano and Shih, 2009). The experience gained by the Chinese in making computer chips and television screens, however, taught them how to process ultra-pure, crystalline silicon into wafers and to apply thin films of the silicon onto large glass sheets. Consequently, China has captured 70–80% of the world's solar panel industry production in just a few short years (Stokes, 2010). China and other countries, including high-wage Germany, have captured numerous industries over the last three decades that were considered nonessential (partly explaining the loss of 6 million U.S. manufacturing jobs since 2000).

In spite of harsh realities faced by working families in past years, caused by our country's short-sightedness, historic new movements are sweeping the land that bode well. “Making it in America” has become a popular new slogan, from the White House to the local coffee house. While supporting fair trade, consumers want to buy safe, high-quality U.S.-made products. Many economy watchers believe there are signs of a new “manufacturing renaissance” emerging, part of the so-called “re-shoring” phenomenon. And there is a vivid sense that Americans are concerned about climate and the environment, and they are adopting and investing in sustainable solutions.

In addition, important demographic shifts are tipping the scale in favor of responsible investment strategies. Millennials and boomers alike are moving back to the city, even Rust Belt cities, and are moving into transit-friendly multifamily housing. People are rethinking urban sprawl and highways to nowhere, and they are reviving and rehabilitating downtowns and urban neighborhoods, and supporting bike lanes and high-speed trains. People want to harness renewable energy, and they are installing solar panels on their roofs and other smart-house advances. They want to support community-minded companies and worker-owned co-operatives. They want to buy local produce, and they have launched urban agrarian campaigns. They want the national chains to utilize ethical supply chains and also source more products locally. And there is a new movement—across cities and states—to pay workers a living wage.

Capital stewards are poised to invest in these hopeful and more durable new future developments. They can invest in new paths, as we suggest in this *Handbook*, that rebuild our cities, revive jobs-producing industries, and bolster the clean economy, and they can mount aggressive actions to mitigate or prevent climate change. As part of a “paying it forward” approach, responsible investors are collaborating with new community apprenticeship programs that provide career ladders for young people and people of color, and they are supporting new community benefits agreements that share the dividends from investment and economic development. In light of these trends, opportunities for responsible investment have enjoyed a manifold increase. We summarize some of these below.

Rebuilding the built environment

Americans are becoming post-suburban, with up to 60% wanting walkable, service-rich, transit-oriented, opportunity-dense communities rather than car-dependent suburbs. The peak of the largest two demographic groups will overlap in the home-buying market from 2014 to 2029. Millennials, with new families, will be looking for starter houses. Boomers, looking to

Box 11.1: Responsible investors in the real economy: putting workers to work

- **Affordable housing, mixed use.** The AFL-CIO HIT's subsidiary, Building America CDE, made a unique investment in Paseo Verde, a multiuse project that will revitalize a distressed neighborhood in North Central Philadelphia near Temple University. This affordable housing and retail complex was built with 100% union labor and boasts the utilization of new LEED construction, renewable energy sources, and transit-oriented development strategies. The project bridges the perceived gap between "sustainable" and "affordable," citing Paseo Verde's green roofs, permeable paving, solar panels, and wallet-friendly rents.
- **LEED commercial.** The MEPT developed 1900 16th Street, a 17-story 400,000 square foot office building in Denver that earned LEED Gold (Core and Shell) certification in 2010 and subsequently received LEED Commercial Interior certification for 100% of the building's space. In 2014, the building achieved LEED Platinum (Existing Building) certification, making it the only LEED Platinum (EB) building in Colorado and one of only 175 globally. In addition, MEPT's investment in this new construction project generated 2.2 million job hours and over $330 million in economic activity in the Denver community.
- **Private capital.** The KPS Special Situations Fund invested in several unionized transportation and auto projects, including HHI, a supplier of forged and machined steel automotive part components with 16 plants in the Midwest. KPS turned around the industry group, comprised of five formerly bankrupt firms that were facing liquidation, saving 3,200 union jobs, with a plan to add another 1,000. Earlier, KPS restructured a bankrupt transportation company with factories in St. Cloud and Crookston, MN, and Winnipeg, Manitoba. The investment at New Flyer Industries saved the jobs of 1,800 union members, who design and manufacture hybrid transit buses and their parts for North America.
- **Infrastructure.** In its first couple of years, ULLICO's Infrastructure Fund accomplished four infrastructure investment deals, including a water and wastewater project in Rialto, California; a wind project in Hawaii; a solar project with Panasonic on their properties; and reinvested in an energy pipeline. These projects have also yielded good union jobs.
- **Renewable energy.** North Sky Capital helped orchestrate the nation's largest fuel cell project in San Diego, which will provide an additional 4.5 MW of generating capacity to the city. Billed as the nation's largest integrated fuel cell project, it won an award from the California Public Utilities Commission.

downsize from their larger single-family homes to something more manageable, will be looking for a similar product in similar places. That is, they want single-family, townhouse, live–work, condo, and apartment types of housing. The strongest growth in housing will be multifamily housing, according to the Kansas City Fed. In all, the demand is estimated to be three times the demand for housing after World War II (Doherty, 2013).

There is also a boom in green construction and sustainably built environments. According to the U.S. Green Building Alliance, in 2016, an estimated 40–48% of new non-residential construction by value will be considered green, representing to up to $145 billion. More than 13.8 billion square feet of building space is LEED-certified (as of August 2015). Of all non-residential building starts in 2012, 41% were green, as compared with 2% in 2005—this includes all commercial, residential, industrial, and infrastructure construction (USGBC, 2016). The rapidly dropping costs of renewable energy and smart building technologies are leading to the proliferation of net-zero-energy buildings globally.

As we assert, pension funds have become large economic impact investors in cities, led by affordable and workforce housing investment stalwarts. In extraordinary success stories such as King's Cross in London, spurred by the BTPS; Collingwood Village in Vancouver, B.C., capitalized by Concert Properties, a labor-sponsored investment fund; and the Cardiff Bay Project in Wales, purchased by the British Steel Pension Fund,[6] responsible capital stewards are not only making smart, sustainable property investments, they are regenerating entire parts of cities. They are building new mixed-use urban villages, connected to transit hubs, and centered around recreational amenities and parks, and creating new master-planned communities that revive brownfields and bring people back to the city:

> Urban growth is key to future development. Eighty percent of Americans now live in cities, and the trend toward urbanization will continue. Long-term sustainable investment opportunities lie in the massive amount of change our cities are about to undergo. Cities will intensify; homes and work will become transit-oriented in the face of rising oil prices. Demographics will drive change, as will innovation. We can expect changes in energy use, new infrastructure, and "green" jobs that result from our push to greater sustainability. Each of these changes provides an opportunity for savings to be put to work in advancing long-term sustainable growth.
>
> (Hebb and Sharma, 2012, p. 485)

6 Purchased from Aviva Investors' Igloo Regeneration Fund which, with its "Footprint" sustainable investment policy, was one of the first responsible property funds.

Revitalizing our industrial commons

After decades of irrational mergers and acquisitions, which failed to create value,[7] and over-leveraged mega-buyouts, many of which failed, the next market myth to fall may be offshoring, as reports are exposing the hidden costs, secretive tax havens, and other damages to our economy (Bivens, 2005; Urry, 2014). "Re-shoring", a reaction to offshoring, has been gaining momentum. Companies are re-shoring production because of internationally rising wages, production and shipping costs around the globe, supply chain disruptions, poor product quality, industrial espionage, etc. In other words, companies are now recalculating the costs and rethinking the purported advantages of offshoring (McCormack, 2013). The trade crisis is not over, but there has been a real shift in the corporate and economic gestalt in recent years.

In 2009, the fate of the American auto industry was in doubt, jeopardizing nearly a million jobs in the supply chain. Since the U.S. government's turnaround efforts, which began phasing out "gas-guzzlers," the domestic auto sector is regrowing and becoming much more energy efficient. The ripple effect across the supply chain has been immediate, setting off a revived auto "industrial commons" in support of a more productive and sustainable industry. "Industrial commons" refers to a foundation of knowledge and capabilities (technical, design, and operational) that is shared within an industry sector, such as "R&D know-how, advanced process development and engineering skills, and manufacturing competences related to a specific technology" (Pisano and Shih, 2009).

Responsible private capital investment houses such as KPS are turning around and recombining newly viable transit manufacturing industries, such as New Flyer Industries and Motor Coach Industries, deploying at-scale workers' capital that is bringing back part of our auto manufacturing sector. This recent large-impact transaction created a new, Earth-friendly transit bus company in North America and secured over 3,500 mainly union jobs. Large labor-sponsored funds such as the Solidarity Fund in Quebec, with $10 billion in workers' capital, have partnered with 2,467 firms and created or maintained 176,040 jobs, primarily industrial jobs, since 1990 (Fonds de solidarité, 2016).

7 Wharton School Professor Martin Sikora estimated that "one-third of mergers create shareholder value, whereas one-third destroy value, and another third don't meet expectations" (Wharton School, 2005).

As regional and national policy leaders have come to recognize the innovation advantages and the energy- and cost-efficiency of the industrial commons approach, there is a deeper recognition of the importance of systems, supply chains, and infrastructure that connect our markets, as Patrick Doherty has noted. These same policy leaders are identifying regional industrial commons across the U.S.A., and advocating that planning, development, and investment resources be deployed in ways that align with these value chains. This approach makes our industries and advancements in technology more resilient (Doherty, 2013).

Some have called the renewed interest in domestic manufacturing nothing less than a manufacturing renaissance. There are numerous reports, even, of a rebound of the Rust Belt. While it may be too early to say that the North is rising again, these new developments should inspire capital stewards from across the country because all sections of it will benefit. It's OK to invest in industry again, and responsible investors have been ahead of the pack in this regard.

Growing the clean economy

The most serious environmental challenge of our lifetime—global warming and climate change—is facing capital stewards. To avert irreversible climate change, the International Energy Agency says $36 trillion is required in new investments by 2050 (Hargreaves, 2012). Already unprecedented storms have devastated coastal areas across the globe, including New York City. Climate change and extreme weather could cost the world more than 3% of GDP by 2030, according to Richard Trumka, President of the AFL-CIO (Trumka, 2014).

In his 2014 speech at the Investors Summit on Climate Risk, Trumka noted:

> We have the technology to reduce building emissions by 50%. At the AFL-CIO headquarters, we have deployed many of these technologies in a retrofit project financed by the International Brotherhood of Electrical Workers National Pension Fund, and we put engineers, carpenters, glazers, electricians, and plumbers to work doing it.
>
> (Trumka, 2014)

Under its Green Jobs Initiative, the HIT has invested over $1.5 billion in 51 projects, including both energy-efficient retrofit and LEED-certified projects. Together with projects that received funding from HIT's subsidiary, Building America, 59 projects represent over $3.78 billion of development, approximately 18,730 union construction jobs, and 21,661 housing units (AFL-CIO HIT, 2016).

In fact, growing market preferences for lower-cost and dependable renewable energy, and other sustainable products and processes, are providing an integrative solution for residential and commercial construction, industrial production, and infrastructure development, an integration that is seeping into all asset allocation classes. These preferences have resulted in the following positive impacts (Bloomberg New Energy Finance, 2016):

- The energy productivity of the U.S. economy has increased by 13% from 2007 to 2015, and by 2.3% since 2014
- Total U.S. investment in clean energy in 2014 topped $56 billion, five times more than a decade ago
- With energy efficiency financing having the potential to grow from $20 to $150 billion annually, over a million jobs would be created
- Energy intensity for U.S. commercial buildings dropped by more than 40% since 1980
- According to specialists at the U.S. DOE, the net present value of retrofitting only a part of the commercial real estate market alone is $57 billion over the next decade or so
- The world has invested over $2.5 trillion in clean technology over the last decade

Activist pension funds such as ABP and PGGM have invested hundreds of millions of euros in dozens of sustainable energy projects through sustainable investment vehicles such as the Ampère Equity Fund, managed by Triodos Bank. These projects have included wind parks on land and at sea and biomass power stations in various western European countries. Along with the IFM projects in Australia, responsible capital stewards have been building the largest wind-power sites in Europe and Australia. Many of these investors have worked hard to empower the communities in the design and operation of these large projects.

Increasingly, unions are working with their members, signatory companies, and community partners to develop new training and business development opportunities in the clean economy. One of the most advanced initiatives is that taken by the International Brotherhood of Electrical Workers (IBEW), which has collaborated with its signatories through the National Electrical Contractors Association (NECA). In addition to managing some of the most successful solar and wind energy training and installation programs in the U.S.A. for its apprentices, NECA-IBEW has launched new financing platforms for its contractors. The NECA Energy Conservation and Performance Platform claims to further energy retrofit projects by seamlessly integrating the inclusion of best-practice project surety, project finance structuring, and project funding solutions into the project development process (NECA, 2016).

Paying it forward: navigating toward a sustainable world

As American Federation of Teachers President Randi Weingarten explains, our country is facing a retirement crisis. She believes it will be a crisis that will outstrip wages and the health economy.[8] Irresponsible finance markets helped to create this pension crisis. They caused intractable problems in our economy, harmed working families and their communities, and dramatically undermined the retirement security of Americans.

While there are many causes that contributed to this crisis, the collapse of middle-class jobs and the spike in "Roaring Twenties" levels of income inequality have cut the legs out from under our commons, so to speak, preventing a return to sustainable economic growth (Robert F. Kennedy Human Rights, 2015). The OECD fully analyzed this threat, and came to the conclusion that the gap between rich and poor is at its highest level for 30 years, and that it has a negative and statistically significant impact on subsequent growth (OECD, 2014).

These drags on economic growth and other global disruptions have affected financial markets and prevented a return to a more sustainable and "normal" economy. As the RFK Compass Program notes: "The conventional view that fiduciaries can make investment decisions based solely on narrow economic criteria, omits critical risk variables" (LACERS, 2011).

Capital stewards must face head-on the challenges of living in a global society. That includes one challenge on which we might be able to have an impact: climate change, which threatens the survival of our countries, economies, and future generations, especially in low-lying and third-world coastal communities. Pope Francis released a landmark encyclical on the

8 Personal communication/interview, November 17, 2014.

environment and humanity on June 18, 2015, called "On care for our common home." In it, the Pope warned of an "unprecedented destruction of ecosystems" and "serious consequences for all of us" if humanity fails to act on climate change (Pope Francis, 2015). The UN secretary general and the World Bank president, among other world leaders, welcomed the encyclical.

Responding to this challenge will require a moral transformation, according to His Holiness, driven by changes in how we steward our investments, manage businesses, and protect people and our ecology. Hinting at some answers, the Pope calls for policies that reduce planet-warming fuels, practices, and technologies and that, instead, develop sources of renewable energy. He gets very specific:

> Investments have ... been made in means of production and transportation which consume less energy and require fewer raw materials, as well as in methods of construction and renovating buildings which improve their energy efficiency. But these good practices are still far from widespread. (Pope Francis, 2015)

The Pope's landmark encyclical was aimed at the December 2015 climate change talks, the 21st UN Climate Change Conference of the Parties (COP21). While it is not a perfect document, representatives of 195 nations reached a landmark accord that will, for the first time, commit nearly every country to lowering planet-warming greenhouse gas emissions to help stave off the most drastic effects of climate change:

> The deal, which was met with an eruption of cheers and ovations from thousands of delegates gathered from around the world, represents a historic breakthrough on an issue that has foiled decades of international efforts to address climate change. (Davenport, 2015)

It is becoming clearer that we, as citizens and capital stewards, need to invest in ways that create good jobs and resilient growth. The "new normal"—financialization and short-termism—will not return our economy to balanced growth. Nor will it solve the retirement crisis. Rushing into new, unsafe, financially engineered investment products concocted on Wall Street will only make things worse.

Pension consultant Jack Marco remembers early discussions in the 1970s with public pension funds about economically targeted investments (ETIs).[9] He recalls that, in the beginning, there was stiff opposition to the concept of ETIs, and many pension fund principals were hostile to the idea. Along

9 Personal communication/interview, December 8, 2014.

the way, various federal administrations have either supported or hindered the ETI cause. Eventually, responsible multiemployer and public retirement funds, along with other like-minded investors, began investing in the triple bottom line, although adoption was slow to catch on. Some three decades later, many, many billions of dollars have now been invested profitably in ETIs, and progressive new global investment alliances, with much larger assets, are investing in the next wave of responsible investment.

Smart pension investment "aviators" such as Jack Marco and innumerable capital stewards cited in this volume (and many not cited) found a way to navigate the entrenched barriers and periodic political opposition to chart a new direction. It wasn't just investment innovation that won the day, it was hard work, sheer determination, and collective vision.

The model of short-term financial markets that mismanage our savings and assets must be scrapped, along with gridlock politics; both are starving the nation of vastly needed resources and depriving us of collaborative approaches to solving our problems. To change this model, capital stewards must be empowered to ask big questions and seek big solutions. The working families and citizens of the U.S.A. and its neighbors are clearly hungry and ready for the next big advances in progress, and we must be as audacious as the two pilots who are risking their lives to prove that we can have a cleaner world. One of the pilots asserted that their invention, its giant wings covered with 17,000 solar cells running four electric motors and its energy stored by lithium batteries, "Can fly a day and a night, it can fly a week, it can fly a month—theoretically it can fly a year" (Kermeliotis, 2014). It might be able to fly forever. Now that's long-term.

Trustees and capital stewards from many countries, inspired by aviators, are, today, gathering together and working across borders. These innovative trustee networks are creating peer-to-peer learning programs, working to democratize workers' capital, investing together in sustainable, cross-border enterprises and projects, and holding corporations and even countries more accountable.

Responsible investors could be robust partners in appropriately scaled capital strategies and partnerships to accelerate our shared progress in creating a more liveable, habitable, hopeful planet. Our hope is that this *Handbook* will help increase trustee knowledge around the why and how of aligning workers' retirement assets and savings with long-term, responsible investment practices so that we can, as a society, "pay it forward." Ultimately, we wish to spur active engagement and action, and elevate the responsible investment discussion into our national conscience and in conversations with a new generation of responsible investors.

References

Aalbu, K., Guha, A., & Swanston, K. (2011). *Responsible Investment in Infrastructure: A Compendium of Case Studies*. Retrieved June 21, 2016 from https://www.unpri.org/download_report/3784.

AFL-CIO (The American Federation of Labor and Congress of Industrial Organizations) (2014). Executive Paywatch 2014. Retrieved June 5, 2016 from http://www.aflcio.org/Corporate-Watch/Paywatch-2014.

AFL-CIO HIT (2016). Green Job Initiative. AFL-CIO HIT. Retrieved June 19, 2016 from http://www.aflcio-hit.com/wmspage.cfm?parm1=2674.

ASCE (American Society of Civil Engineers) (2014). *2013 Report Card for America's Infrastructure*. Retrieved June 4, 2016 from http://www.infrastructurereportcard.org.

Bivens, L.J. (2005, August 1). Truth and consequences of offshoring: recent studies overstate the benefits and ignore the costs to American workers. *Economic Policy Institute*. Retrieved June 5, 2016 from http://www.epi.org/publication/bp155/.

Bloomberg New Energy Finance (2016). *Sustainable Energy in America Factbook*. Retrieved June 21, 2016 from http://www.bcse.org/sustainableenergyfactbook.

Bloxham, E. (2011, April 13). How can we address excessive CEO pay? *Fortune*. Retrieved June 5, 2016 from http://fortune.com/2011/04/13/how-can-we-address-excessive-ceo-pay.

Burke, R. (2014, April 19). Rana Plaza: one year on from the Bangladesh factory disaster. *The Guardian*. Retrieved June 5, 2016 from http://www.theguardian.com/world/2014/apr/19/rana-plaza-bangladesh-one-year-on.

Carmichael, I. (2005). *Pension Power: Unions, Pension Funds, and Social Investment in Canada*. Toronto, Canada: University of Toronto Press.

Croft, T. (2009). *Up from Wall Street: The Responsible Investment Alternative*. New York, NY: Cosimo Books.

CWC (Committee on Workers' Capital) (2015). Global CEO Paywatch: trends in executive compensation. Retrieved June 5, 2016 from http://www.workerscapital.org/priorities/shareholder-activism/campaigns/trends-in-global-executive-compensation/.

Davenport, C. (2015, December 12). Nations approve landmark climate accord in Paris. *The New York Times*. Retrieved June 5, 2016 from http://www.nytimes.com/2015/12/13/world/europe/climate-change-accord-paris.html.

Denning, S. (2014, August 18). HBR: how CEOs became takers, not makers. *Forbes*. Retrieved June 5, 2016 from http://www.forbes.com/sites/stevedenning/2014/08/18/hbr-how-ceos-became-takers-not-makers/.

Doherty, P.C. (2013, January 9) A new U.S. grand strategy: why walkable communities, sustainable economics, and multilateral diplomacy are the future of American power. *Foreign Policy Magazine*. Retrieved June 5, 2016 from http://foreignpolicy.com/2013/01/09/a-new-u-s-grand-strategy/.

Evans, J. (2013). *Economic Briefing: A Review of the G20 Agenda on Tax Avoidance and on Long-Term Investment*. Retrieved June 5, 2016 from http://www.tuac.org/en/public/e-docs/00/00/0D/83/document_doc.phtml.

Fonds de solidarité (2016). Who we are. Retrieved June 20, 2016 from https://www.fondsftq.com/en/a-propos/qui-sommes-nous.aspx.

Hanin, F. (2010). Sécurité économique des emplois et stratégies collectives: l'exemple de Heartland Labor Capital Network [Jobs and economic security of collective action: the example of Heartland Labor Capital Network]. *Le capital au service du travail et du développement* [Capital in the Service of Work and Development], 1(2). Retrieved June 5, 2016 from http://www.eve.coop/?a=19.

Hargreaves, S. (2012, June 12). IEA calls for $36 trillion more in clean energy investments. *CNN Money*. Retrieved June 19, 2016 from http://money.cnn.com/2012/06/12/news/economy/iea-energy/.

Hawley, J.P. (2009) *An Exploration into the Corporate Governance, Risk Analysis and the Financial Crisis: What did Universal Owners Do, and Not Do, that Contributed to the Crisis?* PRI Academic Network Conference, Ottawa, Canada, October 1–3, 2009.

Hebb, T., & Sharma, R. (2012, January 1). New finance for America's cities. *Regional Studies*, 48(3), 485. Retrieved June 5, 2016 from http://ssrn.com/abstract=2391969.

Kay Review (2012). *The Kay Review of UK Equity Markets and Long-Term Decision Making*. Retrieved May 26, 2016 from https://www.gov.uk/government/uploads/system/uploads/attachment_data/file/253454/bis-12-917-kay-review-of-equity-markets-final-report.pdf.

Kermeliotis, T. (2014, April 15). Meet the pilots behind the sun-powered plan that can "fly forever." *CNN*. Retrieved June 5, 2016 from http://www.cnn.com/2014/04/15/tech/a-plane-that-flies-forever-solar-impulse/index.html.

LACERS (2011). *Report to Board of Administration. Los Angeles City Employees' Retirement System*. Retrieved June 20, 2016 from http://www.lacers.org/aboutlacers/board/BoardDocs/2011/board/20110426/ITEM%20VII-A%20%20TRAVEL%20AUTHORITY%20-%20RFK%20CENTER%20FOR%20JUSTICE%20&%20HUMAN%20RIGHTS%202ND%20ANNUAL%20COMPASS%20CONFERENCE.pdf.

Lazonick, W. (2009). *Sustainable Prosperity in the New Economy?: Business Organization and High-Tech Employment in the United States*. Kalamazoo, MI: WE Upjohn Institute for Employment Research.

——— (2014). Profits without prosperity. *Harvard Business Review*, September. Retrieved June 5, 2016 from https://hbr.org/2014/09/profits-without-prosperity.

Lublin, J.S. and Maher, K. (2010, April 21). Funds turn up heat on mine firm's CEO. *Wall Street Journal*. Retrieved June 5, 2016 from http://www.wsj.com/articles/SB10001424052748703763904575196323804098554.

Lund, S., Daruvala, T., Dobbs, R., Härle, P., Kwek, J., & Falcón, R. (2013). *Financial Globalization: Retreat or Reset?* New York, NY: McKinsey Global Institute.

McCormack, R. (2013). *ReMaking America*. Washington, D.C.: Alliance of American Manufacturing.

Murphy, D. (2012). *Toward Pension Sustainability: Principles for Pension Trustee Accountability*. Retrieved June 22, 2016 from http://hausercenter.org/iri/wp-content/uploads/2012/05/Pension-Investing-Principles-DM1.pdf.

NAPF (National Association of Pension Funds) (2013). *NAPF Responsible Investment Guide 2013*. Retrieved June 4, 2016 from http://www.plsa.co.uk/PolicyandResearch/DocumentLibrary/~/media/Policy/Documents/0308_NAPF_Responsible_Investment_guide_2013_DOCUMENT_2.ashx.

NECA (National Electrical Contractors Association) (2016). NECA Energy Conservation and Performance Platform (E-CAP). Retrieved June 5, 2016 from http://www.necanet.org/membership/member-benefits-services/tools-resources/neca-energy-conservation-and-performance-platform-(e-cap).

OECD. (2014, December). *Focus on Inequality and Growth: Does Income Inequality Hurt Economic Growth?* Retrieved June 19, 2016 from https://www.oecd.org/social/Focus-Inequality-and-Growth-2014.pdf.

Pisano, G., & Shih, W.C. (2009). Restoring American competitiveness. *Harvard Business Review*, July–August. Retrieved June 5, 2016 from https://hbr.org/2009/07/restoring-american-competitiveness.

Pope Francis (2015, June 18). The Earth, our home, is beginning to look like an immense pile of filth. *The Guardian.* Retrieved June 5, 2016 from http://www.theguardian.com/commentisfree/2015/jun/18/pope-francis-encyclical-extract.

Robert F. Kennedy Human Rights (2015, July). Robert F. Kennedy Human Rights Compass. Retrieved June 5, 2016 from http://rfkcenter.org/what-we-do/rfk-compass/.

Rossman, P., & Greenfield, G. (2006). *Financialization: New Routes to Profit, New Challenges for Trade Unions.* Retrieved June 5, 2016 from http://www.iufdocuments.org/www/documents/Financialization-e.pdf.

Schwartz, N.D. (2014, December 6) How Wall Street bent steel: Timken bows to activist investors, and splits in two. *The New York Times.* Retrieved June 5, 2016 from http://www.nytimes.com/2014/12/07/business/timken-bows-to-investors-and-splits-in-two.html.

Shah, J. (2013). *Creating Climate Wealth: Unlocking the Impact Economy.* Denver, CO: Icosa Media.

Stewart, L.A., & Atkinson, R. (2013). *The Greater Stagnation: The Decline in Capital Investment is the Real Threat to U.S. Economic Growth.* Washington, D.C.: ITIF.

Stokes, B. (2010, December 9) Act II for American manufacturing? *National Journal.* Retrieved June 5, 2016 from http://www.theatlantic.com/business/archive/2010/12/act-ii-for-american-manufacturing/426495/.

Stringer, S. (2015). Boardroom Accountability Project. Retrieved June 5, 2016 from http://comptroller.nyc.gov/boardroom-accountability/#sthash.jI5Fv60j.dpuf.

Trumka, R.L. (2014). Speech to U.N. Investor Summit on Climate Risk in New York, NY on January 15, 2014. Retrieved June 19, 2016 from http://www.aflcio.org/Press-Room/Speeches/U.N.-Investor-Summit-on-Climate-Risk.

Urry, J. (2014). *Offshoring.* Cambridge, UK: Polity Books.

USGBC (U.S. Green Building Council) (2013). The race to fortify our nation's infrastructure. Retrieved June 17, 2016 from http://www.usgbc.org/articles/race-fortify-our-nation's-infrastructure.

——— (2016). Benefits of green building. Retrieved June 21, 2016 from http://www.usgbc.org/articles/green-building-facts.

van der Zwan, N. (2011). *Contentious Capital: The Politics of Pension Investment in the United States and Germany, 1974–2003* (Unpublished doctoral dissertation). New School for Social Research, New School University, New York, NY.

——— (2014), Making sense of financialization. *Socio-Economic Review,* 12(1), 99-129.

Vitols, S., & Kluge, N. (2011). Introduction. In S. Vitols & N. Kluge (Eds.), *The Sustainable Company: A New Approach to Corporate Governance,* (vol. 1, pp. 4-14). Brussels, Belgium: ETUI.

Ward Jr., K. (2014, November 13). Longtime Massey Energy CEO Don Blankenship indicted. *West Virginia Gazette.* Retrieved June 5, 2016 from http://www.wvgazettemail.com/article/20141113/GZ01/141119629/2003041029.

Wharton School (2005, March 30). Why do so many mergers fail? *Knowledge @ Wharton.* Retrieved June 5, 2016 from http://knowledge.wharton.upenn.edu/article/why-do-so-many-mergers-fail/.

Williamson, J. (2015, July 28). Andy Haldane: shareholder primacy is bad for economic growth. *TouchStone.* Retrieved May 25, 2016 from http://touchstoneblog.org.uk/2015/07/andy-haldane-shareholder-primacy-is-bad-for-economic-growth/.

Wood, D., & Youngdahl, J. (2011). *Public Pension Fund Trustees and Fund Culture: Responsible Investment and the Trustee Leadership Forum.* Retrieved June 1, 2016 from http://hausercenter.org/iri/wp-content/uploads/2012/05/UNPRI-Youngdahl-Wood-Working-Paper.pdf.

Appendix A: Glossary

A

Active ownership. Voting company shares and/or engaging corporate managers and boards of directors in dialogue on environmental, social, and corporate governance (ESG) issues, as well as on business strategy issues. Investors increasingly pursue active ownership efforts to reduce risk and enhance long-term shareowner value.

Actuarial assumption. Factors actuaries use in estimating pension costs, such as the rate of interest on plan investments and the rate at which plan members are expected to leave the plan because of death or job termination.

Alternative investment. An investment that is not one of the three traditional asset types (stocks, bonds, and cash). Most alternative investment assets are held by pension funds and other institutional investors or accredited, high-net-worth individuals because of their complex nature, limited regulations, and relative lack of liquidity.

Asset allocation. A well-diversified portfolio is made up of a spectrum of asset classes as a means of spreading risk across classes. A fund's asset allocation policy is the targeted percentage of funds to be invested in an asset class as a percentage of total assets, assessed by the actual investment mix.

Asset churning. Excessive trading by a broker in a client's account largely to generate commissions. While there is no quantitative measure for churning, frequent buying and selling of securities that does little to meet the client's investment objectives may be construed as evidence of churning.

Asset targeting. Refers to the active targeting of investments, utilizing responsible investment principles and ETI methodologies.

B

Benchmark. A standard against which the performance of a security, index, or investment can be measured.

Best-in-class. Focusing investments in companies that have historically performed better than their peers within a particular industry or sector based on analysis of environmental, social, and corporate governance (ESG) issues. Typically involves positive or negative screening, or portfolio tilting.

Buyout funds. Specialize in acquiring a large or controlling stake in more companies, both mature and under-performing ones.

C

Capital gap. A capital gap results from inefficiencies in the financial markets linked to information asymmetries which occur when one party to the exchange, either the buyer or the seller, has more information about the investment. Smaller enterprises that seek capital are unable to secure affordable financing because sellers or owners know far more about the investment than the buyers (i.e., external investors). Due to this imbalance of knowledge, buyers are cautious and will either withdraw from the exchange or demand a higher risk premium for the investment to offset uncertainty.

Capital steward. Pension fund trustee; a fiduciary; a person entrusted to hold and invest other people's money, keeping their interest and principles in mind.

Carried interest. A share in the profits of a private equity fund. Typically, a fund must return the capital given to it by limited partners plus any preferential rate of return before the general partner can share in the profits of the fund. The general partner will then receive a 20% carried interest, although some successful firms receive 25–30%. Also known as "carry" or "promote."

Cleantech. A large and growing venture capital investment category representing a range of products, services, and processes that either directly reduce or eliminate ecological impacts or require lower resource inputs. Cleantech is an investment theme rather than an industrial sector as it may include investments in agriculture, energy, manufacturing, materials, technology, transportation, and water.

Climate risks. Risks stemming from climate change that have the potential to affect companies, industries, and whole economies. There are five key areas of business risk associated with climate change: regulatory, physical, litigation, competitiveness, and reputational.

Collateral benefits. Non-fiduciary benefits that may accompany financial benefits: the rule is that if risk and return are equal, the capital steward may choose the investment that provides the collateral benefit.

Collective bargaining agreement. The contractual agreement between an employer and a labor union that governs wages, hours, and working conditions for employees and which can be enforced against both the employer and the union for failure to comply with its terms.

Commercial mortgage-backed security. A security backed by a pool of mortgages. It is similar to a mortgage-backed security, but secured by loans with commercial property in addition to residential property.

Community investing. Directing investment capital to communities that are underserved by traditional financial services institutions. Generally provides access to credit, equity, capital, and basic banking products that these communities would otherwise lack.

Conflicts of interest. Transactions between the corporation and interested parties such as officers and directors.

Corporate governance. Procedures and processes according to which an organization (in this context, mainly a company) is directed and controlled. The corporate governance structure specifies the distribution of rights and responsibilities among the different participants in the organization—such as the board, managers, shareowners, and other stakeholders—and lays down the rules and procedures for decision-making.

Cost–benefit analysis. A comparison of the estimated costs of an action with the estimated benefits it is likely to produce.

Country risk. Risk to investments that stems from the conditions in the countries in which foreigners invest, such as labor rights abuses, political instability, and weak democratic institutions.

Cross-border capital stewardship. Applying the principles of capital stewardship to international investing, including through the adoption of specific international policies in seeking to build relationships with capital stewards in other countries.

Corporate social responsibility/corporate responsibility (CSR/CR). An approach to business which takes into account economic, social, environmental, and ethical impacts for a variety of reasons, including mitigating risk, decreasing costs, and improving brand image and competitiveness.

D

Defined benefit plan. A retirement plan which specifies the benefits or the method of determining the benefits; i.e., a specified amount per month at retirement (flat benefit), a stated percentage of compensation (fixed benefit), or a stated percentage of compensation multiplied by the years of service (unit benefit).

Defined contribution plan. A pension plan in which the contributions are fixed, but where the benefits are not fixed; i.e., a fixed amount is contributed for each hour of work or a fixed percentage of compensation is established. Examples include money purchase plans, profit-sharing plans, and 401(k) plans.

Delegation. Assigning responsibility to another; the person who delegated the responsibility still remains responsible if the task is not done.

Discretionary. The use of judgment in accomplishing a task.

Diversification. The spreading of risk by putting money into different types of investment or asset class.

Divestment. Selling or disposing of shares or other assets. Changes in corporate behavior or investment policies can lead investors to reduce or eliminate holdings in certain investments. Investors who practice active ownership often view divestment as the last resort. Divestment gained prominence during the boycott of companies doing business in South Africa, prior to the dismantling of apartheid. More recently, a campaign has focused on divestment from fossil fuel extraction companies.

Due diligence. The investigatory process performed by investors to assess the viability of a potential investment and the accuracy of the information provided by the target company.

E

Economically targeted investments (ETIs). Investments made by capital stewards that seek competitive rates of return but that also provide collateral benefits to communities and to society in general.

Emerging market. A less-developed country in which foreign investment is made, characterized by less-sophisticated capital markets and regulatory regimes.

Environmental, social, governance (ESG). An investment approach which incorporates environmental, social, and governance factors into the investment process. ESG terminology was developed and promulgated by the United Nations Principles for Responsible Investment (PRI).

ESG integration. The active investment management processes that include an analysis of environmental, social, and corporate governance risks and opportunism.

Exchange-traded fund (ETF). A security that tracks an index, a commodity, or a basket of assets like a mutual fund, but trades like a stock on an exchange. An ETF experiences price changes throughout the day as it is bought and sold (like a stock).

Ethical investing. Investment philosophy guided by moral values, ethical codes, or religious beliefs. This practice has traditionally been associated with negative screening.

Executive compensation. Compensation paid to corporate executives, including salary, cash, bonuses, long-term compensation, stock bonuses, stock options, incentive compensation, and retirement benefits.

Externality. Costs or benefits created by corporation's conduct that are paid for or enjoyed by third parties. Benefits are positive externalities. Costs are negative externalities.

Extra-financial factors. The factors that have the potential to have at least a long-term effect on financial performance but lie outside the usual span of variables that get integrated into investment decisions, irrespective of whether they are part of the research process. They include ESG factors but also traditional financial factors that are often ignored or underutilized, at least in terms of the alignment of investments with the interests of beneficiaries.

F

Fiduciary. A person who, by virtue of a relationship to another, is obligated to act solely in the interest of that person and exclusively for that person's benefit.

Fiduciary duties. The duties imposed on a person who exercises some discretionary power in the interests of another person in circumstances that give rise to a relationship of trust and confidence. Fiduciary duties are the key source of limits on the discretion of investment decision-makers in common law jurisdictions. The most important fiduciary duties are the duty to act prudently and the duty to act in accordance with the purpose for which investment powers are granted (also known as the duty of loyalty).

G

General partner (GP). A class of partner in a partnership. The general partner retains liability for the actions of the partnership. In the private equity world, the GP is the fund manager while the limited partners (LPs) are the institutional and high-net-worth investors in the partnership. The GP earns a management fee and a percentage of profits (see *Carried interest*).

H

Hedge fund. A private investment partnership that aggressively manages a portfolio of investments and uses advanced investment strategies such as leveraged, long, short, and derivative positions in both domestic and international markets with the goal of generating high returns (either in an absolute sense or over a specified market benchmark).

High-frequency trading. A program-trading platform that uses powerful computers to transact a large number of orders at very fast speeds. High-frequency trading uses complex algorithms to analyze multiple markets and execute orders based on market conditions. Typically, the traders with the fastest execution speeds will be more profitable than traders with slower execution speeds.

I

Impact investing. Investment strategies that provide capital to companies working to generate a financial return along with significant societal or environmental benefit.

Independent director. A director who has never been an employee of the corporation or its subsidiaries; is not related to an employee; provides no services to the corporation and is not employed by a firm which provides services to the corporation; and has received no compensation from the corporation other than directors' fees.

Institutional investors. Pension funds, banks, insurance companies, mutual funds, and other institutions that invest other people's money.

Investment advisor. An investment advisor monitors investment managers for the named fiduciaries and provides advice with regard to investment decisions.

Investment manager. A person who has the power to manage, acquire, or dispose of any asset of the plan; is registered as an investment advisor under the Investment Advisors Act of 1940; and has acknowledged in writing that he is a fiduciary with respect to the plan.

L

Leveraged buyout (LBO) fund. A leveraged buyout fund acquires another company using a significant amount of borrowed money (bonds or loans) to meet the cost of acquisition. Often, the assets of the company being acquired are used as collateral for the loans (in addition to the assets of the acquirer). The purpose of leveraged buyouts is to allow companies to make large acquisitions without having to commit a lot of capital, thus compounding the potential return (or loss).

Limited partner (LP). An investor in a limited partnership. The general partner is liable for the actions of the partnership while the limited partners are generally protected from legal actions and any losses beyond their original investment. The limited partner receives income, capital gains, and tax benefits.

Liquidity. The degree to which an asset or security can be bought or sold in the market without affecting the asset's price. Liquidity is characterized by a high level of trading activity. Assets that can be easily bought or sold are known as liquid assets. Liquidity also refers to the ability to convert an asset to cash quickly.

Low income. A term used to describe household income that does not exceed 80% of the area median income.

M

Management fee. A fee charged to the limited partners in a fund by the general partner. Management fees in a private equity fund typically range from 0.75% to 3% of capital under management, depending on the type and size of fund.

Merger. The combination of two corporations in which one corporation survives and the other disappears.

Minority- and female-owned and/or emerging manager (MFOE). Investment managers owned by minorities or females or have a relatively small amount of assets under management. The definition of "minority" manager can vary but commonly includes those firms majority owned by African-American, Native American, Asian-American, and Hispanic groups. In some cases, disabled or veteran owners also meet the definition for inclusion under an investor's policy in this area. The definition of "emerging" also varies but generally connotes a manager with between zero and several hundred million dollars in assets under management or that has a performance record of less than three years. A firm can be minority or female owned without being considered emerging, or vice versa. These managers would not ordinarily be included in a manager search and would benefit from an affirmative action program.

Moderate income. A term used to describe household incomes that range between 80% and 120% of the area median income.

Mortgage vehicle. An instrument engaged in the business of originating and/or funding mortgages for residential or commercial property. A mortgage is a loan collateralized by property.

Multiemployer plan. A pension or health and welfare plan to which more than one employer is required to contribute, which is maintained pursuant to a collective bargaining agreement (also called Taft–Hartley Fund).

N

Negative screening. A strategy of avoiding investing in companies whose products and business practices are harmful to individuals, communities, or the environment. It is a common mistake to assume that socially responsible investment (SRI) "screening" is simply exclusionary, or only involves negative screens. In reality, SRI screens are being used more and more frequently to identify and invest in companies that are leaders in adopting clean technologies, managing environmental impacts, and integrating exceptional social and governance practices.

P

Plan document. Documents that govern the conduct of the plan; including the trust agreement, the plan, the collective bargaining agreement, and the investment guidelines.

Plan sponsor. The employer or union that established the plan.

Pooled funds. Funds from many individual investors that are aggregated for the purposes of investment, as in the case here of pension funds, real estate funds, etc. Investors in pooled fund investments benefit from economies of scale, which allow for lower trading costs per dollar of investment, diversification, and professional money management.

Positive screening. Including strong corporate social responsibility (CSR) performers or otherwise incorporating CSR factors into the investment analysis process. Generally, socially conscious investors seek to own profitable companies that make positive contributions to society, and avoid those that do not. "Buy" lists may include enterprises with, for example, good employer–employee relations, strong environmental practices, products that are safe and useful, and operations that respect human rights around the world. See also *Qualitative analysis.*

Primogeniture. The right of succession belonging to the firstborn child, especially the feudal rule by which the whole real estate of an intestate passes to the eldest son.

Private capital. Traditionally invests in existing companies seeking to expand or to add new products. Private capital is generally employed as sizable privately placed debt and equity investments in SMEs in many industries, including manufacturing, transportation, distribution, communications, and technology.

Property development. Financing for the construction of new buildings and property.

Property redevelopment. Financing for improvements, upgrades, and expansions to existing real-estate stock.

Prospectus. The primary legal document offering securities or mutual fund shares for sale, required by the Securities Act of 1933. It must explain the offer, including the terms, issuer, investment objectives (if mutual fund) or planned use of the money (if securities), historical financial statements, and other information that could help investors decide whether the investment is appropriate for them.

Proxy voting. Entitled shareowners who do not attend shareholders' meetings delegate their proxy votes to others who vote on their behalf. Proxy voting allows shareholders to exercise their right to vote without committing the time involved in actually attending company annual meetings.

Proxy voting policy. The written policy which articulates how proxy voting decisions are to be made and executed. Proxy voting policies can include specific guidance on environmental, social, corporate governance, and ethical voting decisions.

Prudent man rule. A common rule pertaining to fiduciary duty in Anglo-Saxon countries. The Employee Retirement Income Security Act of 1974 (ERISA) outlines minimum standards for private pension plans that have since been adopted by many public pension plans.

Q

Qualified plan. A plan that meets the requirements of the Internal Revenue Code and, therefore, is entitled to preferential tax treatment.

Qualitative analysis. Analysis of company policies, practices, behaviors, and impacts which helps portfolio managers avoid undesirable companies and identify and invest in the best-managed organizations in each industry group. Often used interchangeably with *Positive screening*.

R

Responsible contractor policies. A policy signed as part of a construction project that requires all workers on the job, during and after construction, to be employed by a "responsible," i.e., an employer that pays prevailing wages and abides by workplace laws.

Responsible investment (RI). The integration of environmental, social, and corporate governance (ESG) considerations into investment management process and ownership practices in the belief that these factors can have an impact on financial performance. RI can be practices across all asset classes.

Responsible investment policy statement. A general (usually public) statement on RI adopted by boards of trustees or directors that directs investment staff practices and decisions. This can be included within a broader investment policy statement and/or developed as a stand-alone RI policy statement.

Responsible property investment. A property investment approach that includes the consideration of environmental, social, and corporate governance issues. Energy and resource efficiency, both in construction and ongoing operations, is a common consideration, as is social impact.

Restricted list. A list of securities that are not to be included in a portfolio by an investment manager. Typically facilitates implementation of negative screening.

Return on investment (ROI). The proceeds from an investment, during a specific time-period, calculated as a percentage of the original investment. Also, net profit after taxes divided by average total assets.

Risk-adjusted return. A measure of investment return in relation to the amount of risk. Often used to compare a high-risk, potentially high-return investment with a low-risk, lower-return investment.

S

Secondary market. A market for the sale of partnership interests in private equity funds. Sometimes limited partners choose to sell their interest in a partnership, typically to raise cash or because they cannot meet their obligation to invest more capital according to the takedown schedule. Certain investment companies specialize in buying these partnership interests at a discount.

Shareholder. A person or institution who owns a share of stock; a stockholder.

Shareholder activism. See *Active ownership.*

Shareholder engagement. The practice of monitoring corporate behavior and seeking changes where appropriate through dialogue with companies or through the use of share ownership rights, such as filing shareholder resolutions. Shareholder engagement is often employed in attempts to improve a company's performance on environmental, social, and corporate governance issues.

Shareholder proposal. A shareholder request that the company or its board of directors take particular action. Proposed by the shareholder, this request may be presented at a company's general shareholders' meeting and voted on by all shareholders. In some instances, shareholder proposals are withdrawn by shareholders or disallowed by regulators.

Short-termism. The bias some investors demonstrate for near- or immediate-term investment performance and share price appreciation instead of long-term investment performance. This bias may put pressure on corporate managers to make decisions that boost short-term accounting measures of profitability rather than long-term economic profitability.

Single-employer plan. A plan maintained by one employer.

Solvency ratio. A key metric used to measure an enterprise's ability to meet its debt and other obligations. The solvency ratio indicates whether a company's cash flow (a better determinant of solvency than net income) is sufficient to meet its short- and long-term liabilities. The lower a company's solvency ratio, the greater the probability that it will default on its debt obligations.

Special situations funds. A subset of buyout and turnaround funds that target financially distressed firms, even those in bankruptcy.

Socially responsible investment (SRI) mutual funds. SRI mutual funds integrate ESG analysis into the investment process, generally seeking to avoid owning companies with a harmful impact on society, and seeking to own the most responsible companies with the highest profit potential. Such funds may represent any asset class and many different investment strategies, including domestic and international investments. A growing range of products are available, including hedge funds and exchange-traded funds.

Stakeholders. The individuals or organizations with an interest in the actions and impacts of an organization. They may be employees, customers, suppliers, shareholders, communities, members of special interest groups, nongovernmental organizations, or regulators.

Stakeholder statute. Statute that allows a corporation to consider the interests of its stakeholders, including employees.

Sustainable development. The concept of meeting present needs without compromising the ability of future generations to meet their needs. It encompasses social welfare, protection of the environment, efficient use of natural resources, and economic wellbeing.

T

Taxable bonds. An obligation to which the income on an interest-bearing bond is taxable by the federal, state, and/or local governments.

Tax-exempt bonds. An obligation to which the interest income is exempt from the taxation of either federal or state governments. Municipal bonds issued by state or local governments are an example of these.

Thematic investment. The selected investment in companies with a commitment to chosen responsible business products and/or services, such as environmental technologies.

Total return. Return equal to income plus the change in value or market price of an asset.

Triple bottom line. A holistic approach to measuring a company's performance on environmental, social, and economic issues. The triple bottom line approach to management focuses companies not just on the economic value they add, but also on the environmental and social value they may add or compromise.

Trust agreement. The document that establishes the trust and sets out the trustees' authority and power.

U

Unfunded liabilities. Future payment obligations of the plan that are not fully funded.

Universal owner. A large investor that holds a broad selection of investments in different public companies as well as other assets and whose performance is, therefore, tied to the performance of markets or economies as a whole—not just to the performance of individual holdings. These investors have a vested interest in the long-term health of the economy, making public policy issues and cross-market ESG concerns particularly relevant.

V

Venture capital. Risk money; money invested in a risky company, usually a start-up company, for a greater-than-average rate of return.

Vesting (vested, adj.). The process by which an employee accrues nonforfeitable rights over employer-provided stock incentives or employer contributions made to the employee's qualified retirement plan account or pension plan. Vesting gives an employee rights to employer-provided assets over time, which gives the employee an incentive to perform well and remain with the company. The vesting schedule set up by the company determines when the employee acquires full ownership of the asset. Generally, nonforfeitable rights accrue based on how long the employee has worked there.

W

Wall Street Talk. Instead of selling an under-performing stock, the shareholder either meets with management to discuss ways to improve corporate performance, or files shareholder resolutions to accomplish the same results.

Wall Street Walk. A shareholder does the "Wall Street Walk" when, dissatisfied with the company's performance, the shareholder sells the stock.

Welfare plans. Welfare plans include benefits for medical, hospitalization, accidental death insurance, unemployment, legal service, day care, scholarships, and apprenticeships.

Appendix B: Important links

Below we provide a sample of responsible investment beliefs statements, responsible investment policies, responsible contractor polices, proxy voting guidelines, fund governance and investment implementation guidance, and responsible investment frameworks for readers' reference. Please note that these polices and frameworks vary greatly in scope and enforcement; however, they are intended to give trustees and other readers of this *Handbook* an idea of how to incorporate responsible investment goals in the management and investment of pension fund assets. Links were retrieved at the time of the writing of this book. As websites change, links may become obsolete.

Responsible investment beliefs statements

Australian Super. http://www.australiansuper.com/investments-and-performance/approach-and-holdings/our-investment-governance.aspx

CalPERS. https://www.calpers.ca.gov/docs/forms-publications/calpers-beliefs.pdf

NEPC, LLC. http://www.nepc.com/writable/research_articles/file/08_06_nepc_investment_belief_systems.pdf

New Zealand Superannuation Fund. https://www.nzsuperfund.co.nz/how-we-invest/beliefs

OMERS. http://www.omers.com/pdf/Statement_of_Investment_Beliefs.pdf

OTPP. http://www.otpp.com/documents/10179/20940/-/a2792268-6b8d-45b6-a152-2edb5af94406/Investment%20Beliefs.pdf

USS. https://www.uss.co.uk/en/how-uss-invests/investment-approach/investment-beliefs-and-principles

Responsible investment policies

Australian Super. http://www.australiansuper.com/investments-and-performance/approach-and-holdings/our-investment-governance.aspx#esg-policy

CalPERS. https://www.calpers.ca.gov/page/investments/governance/sustainable-investing/esg

CalSTRS. http://www.calstrs.com/sites/main/files/file-attachments/esg_policy_and_21_risk_factors.pdf

Hawaii ERS Investment Policy. http://ers.ehawaii.gov/wp-content/uploads/2012/10/ERS-Investment-Policy-Guidelines-Procedures-Manual-March-2016.pdf

LACERA. http://www.lacera.com/investments/inv_pdf/invest_policy_stmt.pdf

NEST. https://www.nestpensions.org.uk/schemeweb/NestWeb/includes/public/docs/statement-of-investment-principles,PDF.pdf

OTPP. https://www.otpp.com/documents/10179/20940/-/72ae966f-7aa9-40ae-b8fa-3642e76597df/Statement%20of%20Investment%20Policies%20&%20Procedures%202014.pdf

PGGM. https://www.pggm.nl/english/what-we-do/Documents/beliefs-and-foundations-for-responsible-investment_may-2014_pggm.pdf

Responsible contractor policies

AFL-CIO HIT. http://www.aflcio-hit.com/wmspage.cfm?parm1=151

ARA. http://www.americanreal.com/pdf/Corp%20Responsibility%20Brochure%202015.pdf

CalPERS. https://www.calpers.ca.gov/docs/policy-responsible-contractor-2015.pdf

CalSTRS. http://www.calstrs.com/general-information/responsible-contractor-policy

ISBI. http://www.illinois.gov/isbi/documents/investment-policy.pdf

LACERA. http://www.lacera.com/investments/inv_pdf/invest_policy_stmt.pdf

MEPT. http://www.mept.com/union/labor_req.php

OPERS. https://www.opers.org/pdf/investments/policies/Responsible%20Contractor%20Policy.pdf

TIAA-CREF. https://www.tiaa-cref.org/public/pdf/Real_Estate_Responsible_Contractor_Policy.pdf

ULLICO. Available on request from ULLICO

Proxy voting guidelines

AFL-CIO. http://www.aflcio.org/Corporate-Watch/Capital-Stewardship/Proxy-Voting

Glass, Lewis & Co., LLC. http://www.glasslewis.com/assets/uploads/2013/12/2015_GUIDELINES_United_States.pdf

ISS. http://www.issgovernance.com/policy-gateway/iss-global-voting-principles/

NYSCRF. http://www.osc.state.ny.us/pension/proxyvotingguidelines.pdf

OTPP. http://www.otpp.com/documents/10179/20940/TeachersCorpGovE.pdf/cfca9682-9368-4cf4-96ce-fe5381d5647e

Fund governance and responsible investment implementation guidance

Climate-Related Investing Across Asset Classes. http://hausercenter.org/iri/wp-content/uploads/2010/05/Handbook_ClimateRelatedInvesting.pdf

How to Construct an IPS. Boone, N., & Lubitz, L. (2004). *Creating an Investment Policy Statement.* Denver, CO: FPA Press.

How to Develop an Investment Beliefs Statement. http://hausercenter.org/iri/wp-content/uploads/2012/05/Investment-Beliefs-Statements-10-2011.pdf

How to Establish Strong Fund Governance Structures.

Woods, C., & Urwin, R. (2010). Putting sustainable investing into practice: a governance framework for pension funds. *Journal of Business Ethics*, 92(1), 1-19.

Stewart, F., & Yermo, J. (2008). Pension fund governance: challenges and potential solutions. *OECD Working Papers on Insurance and Private Pensions*, 18. Retrieved June 5, 2016 from http://www.oecd.org/finance/private-pensions/41013956.pdf.

Clark, G.L., & Urwin, R. (2007). *Best Practice Investment Management: Lessons for Asset Owners from The Oxford–Watson Wyatt Project on Governance.* doi:10.2139/ssrn.1019212.

Implementation Support Across Asset Classes. https://www.unpri.org/about/pri-teams/investment-practices

Responsible investment Across Asset Classes. http://hausercenter.org/iri/wp-content/uploads/2010/05/IRI_Responsible_Investment_Handbook_2008_2nd_Ed.pdf

Sample ESG-related questions for requests for proposals. See Appendix C in Ceres (2013). *The 21st Century Investor: Ceres Blueprint for Sustainable Investing.* http://www.calstrs.com/sites/main/files/file-attachments/21st_century_investor_-_ceres_blueprint_for_sustainable_investing.pdf

Sample human capital management-related questions to ask of companies. http://hausercenter.org/iri/wp-content/uploads/2012/05/HCM-Coalition-Questions.pdf

Additional resources

CalPERS Review of Investment Beliefs Implementation. https://www.calpers.ca.gov/docs/review-investment-beliefs-implementation.pdf

Ceres Principles. http://www.ceres.org/about-us/our-history/ceres-principles

Ceres Roadmap to Sustainability. http://www.ceres.org/roadmap-assessment/landing

G20/OECD High-Level Principles of Long-Term Investment Financing by Institutional Investors. http://www.oecd.org/daf/fin/private-pensions/G20-OECD-Principles-LTI-Financing.pdf

PRI. https://www.unpri.org/about/the-six-principles

Appendix C: Responsible investment support organizations

AFL-CIO Office of Investment.

http://www.aflcio.org/Corporate-Watch/Capital-Stewardship/

The AFL-CIO's Capital Stewardship Program enables workers to have a voice in the capital markets by leading corporate governance shareholder initiatives and advocating for legislative and regulatory reform. The AFL-CIO Proxy Voting Guidelines have been developed to serve pension fund trustees as a guide for voting their funds' shareholder proxies. The goal of the guidelines is to assist trustees in exercising their ownership rights in ways that achieve long-term value by supporting important shareholder initiatives on corporate accountability. These initiatives include board of directors' proposals, corporate governance, and proposals concerning employee relations, executive compensation, and corporate responsibility issues. The Proxy Voting Guidelines also provide an in-depth discussion of fiduciary duties of plan trustees described under the Employee Retirement Income Security Act (ERISA). As a complement to the guidelines, AFL-CIO's Key Votes Survey is designed to help pension fund trustees fulfill their fiduciary duty to monitor the proxy voting performance of investment managers. These proposals are assessed by the AFL-CIO Proxy Voting Guidelines and managers are ranked by the percentage of votes cast in accordance with the guidelines.

Aspen Institute. http://www.aspeninstitute.org

The Aspen Institute is an educational and policy studies organization based in Washington, D.C. Its mission is to foster leadership based on enduring values and to provide a nonpartisan venue for dealing with critical issues. These issue areas include community and family prosperity, culture and communication, economy, education, energy and environment, health, justice and equity, philanthropy and social enterprise, and security and global affairs. The Aspen Institute provides a document called *Long-Term Value Creation: Guiding Principles for Corporations and Investors*, a.k.a. the Aspen Principles, which is explicitly written as aspirational guidelines for good business practice. The document is available for download from https://www.aspeninstitute.org/publications/aspen-principles-long-term-value-creation-guiding-principles-corporations-investors/.

Business Ethics Magazine. http://business-ethics.com

Business Ethics is an online magazine working in the fields of ethics, governance, corporate responsibility, and socially responsible investing to "promote ethical business practices, to serve that growing community of professionals and individuals striving to work and invest in responsible ways."

California Public Employees' Retirement System (CalPERS). http://www.calpers.ca.gov

CalPERS is the largest public pension fund in the U.S.A. working to provide health and retirement benefits to public school, local agency, and state employers. Its mission is to provide responsible and efficient stewardship to improve long-term pension and health benefit sustainability (including taking account of environmental, social, and governance factors), to cultivate a high-performing, risk-intelligent, and innovative organization, and to engage state and national policy development to enhance the long-term sustainability and effectiveness of implemented programs. Each of these mission goals is broken down into specific objectives and initiatives, all related to CalPERS strategic themes (alignment of interest, human capital, and climate change) which can be found in the CalPERS 2012–17 Strategic Plan, available at https://www.calpers.ca.gov/docs/forms-publications/2012-17-strategic-plan.pdf.

CalPERS Sustainable Investment Research Initiative (SIRI). http://www.gsm.ucdavis.edu/project-overview

The SIRI was launched by CalPERS, in partnership with University of California, Davis to study the potential impacts of using ESG issues and sustainability factors to ensure long-term performance. The study hopes to bridge gaps in the global knowledge of how ESG factors, such as climate change, labor practices, human rights, and executive compensation, influence investment risk and return across asset classes.

Carbon Disclosure Project (CDP). https://www.cdp.net

CDP works to transform the way the world does business to prevent dangerous climate change and protect our natural resources. It uses the power of measurement and information disclosure to improve the management of environmental risk. By leveraging market forces, including shareholders, customers, and governments, CDP has incentivized thousands of companies and cities across the world's largest economies to measure and disclose their environmental information, and puts this information at the heart of business, investment, and policy decision-making. CDP holds the largest collection globally of self-reported climate change, water, and forest-risk data. Through its global system companies, investors and cities are better able to mitigate risk, capitalize on opportunities, and make investment decisions that drive action toward a more sustainable world.

Ceres. http://www.ceres.org

Ceres is a non-profit organization including a network of investors, companies, and public interest groups to mobilize investor and business leadership to build a sustainable global economy. The Ceres Coalition itself works with more than 130 member organizations and social, non-profit groups to engage with corporations and help advance the goal of building a sustainable global economy. Accessible from its website, Ceres also publishes a Company Network listing nearly 70 companies across a variety of sectors who are committed to improving their performance on social and environmental issues and disclosing strategies and progress publicly. It further provides an Investor Network, listing investors, including state treasurers, institutional investors, labor groups, and SRI funds, that are working to improve corporate strategies and public policies on environmental and social challenges. Ceres published *The 21st Century Investor: Ceres Blueprint for Sustainable Investment Summary*, which is available for download from http://www.ceres.org/resources/reports/the-21st-century-investor-ceres-blueprint-for-sustainable-investing-summary.

Committee on Workers' Capital (CWC). http://www.workerscapital.org
The CWC provides labor union organizations with vital connections to advance their global responsible investment agendas. The Committee's activities include educating union pension trustees, monitoring global trends and policy, and impacting corporate and financial markets. CWC members participate in various international organizations, such as the PRI, the ICGN, and the EURESA Institute, to work on issues of interest to the responsible investment of workers' capital.

Corporate Governance. http://www.corpgov.net
Corporate Governance (CorpGov.net) was founded in 1995 to provide news, commentary, and a network for those interested in transforming an arcane subject, discussed at a snail's pace in academia and by a few dozen practitioners, to a more practical discipline where knowledge is shared and put into practice by investors and corporations at much closer to the speed of light. The mission is to help share*holders* enhance the production of wealth by acting as long-term share*owners*. Engaged owners invest not just money, but ideas and actions.

Corporate Knights. http://www.corporateknights.com
Corporate Knights Inc. is a website and magazine that produces corporate rankings, research reports, and financial product ratings based on corporate sustainability performance. Based in Canada, its publication focuses on the built environment, clean technology, responsible investing, social enterprise, and natural capital.

CorpWatch. http://www.corpwatch.org
CorpWatch is a non-profit, independent group of investigative researchers and journalists working to expose corporate malfeasance and to advocate for multinational corporate accountability and transparency across a wide range of industries. Its mission includes fostering global justice, independent media activism, democratic control over organizations, and exposure of corporations that profit from war, fraud, environmental human rights, and other abuses. Its website provides an interactive research guide that takes you through the steps of researching a corporation's business strategy, operations, financial status, and environmental and social record.

Council of Institutional Investors (CII). http://www.cii.org
The CII is a non-profit organization of pension funds, employee benefit funds, endowments, and foundations. It works to educate its members and the public about effective corporate governance, shareowner rights, and other investment issues. It also advocates on behalf of its members for effective corporate governance and strong shareowners' rights. CII staff and members directly engage with corporate managers and directors, stock exchange officials, regulators, and policy-makers regarding CII policies.

CtW Investment Group. http://ctwinvestmentgroup.com/trustee-resources
The CtW Investment Group provides strategies and initiatives to pension funds sponsored by unions affiliated with Change to Win in order to enhance long-term shareholder returns through active ownership. The group aims to achieve corporate accountability and retirement security by ensuring independent and accountable directors, reasonable executive compensation, and sound environmental, human resource, and other business policies. Importantly, the CtW Investment Group's trustee resources include a report analyzing human capital management strategies currently practiced by U.S. public companies and their boards; it found a statistically significant and negative relationship between pay inequality within publicly traded companies and long-term shareholder returns.

Environmental Defense Fund (EDF). https://www.edf.org
EDF's "ESG Management Tool" for private equity is a self-assessment tool whereby a GP's current ESG-related management practices are benchmarked against current best practices. GPs will find this tool helpful in understanding how they are performing against current best practice areas and in identifying where they can improve.

Forum for Sustainable and Responsible Investment (U.S. SIF).
http://www.ussif.org
U.S. SIF is a membership association for investment management and advisory firms, mutual fund companies, research firms, financial planners and advisors, broker-dealers, banks, credit unions, community development organizations, pension funds, non-profit associations, and other asset owners engaged in sustainable, responsible, and impact investing. U.S. SIF and its members aim to advance investment practices that consider environmental, social, and corporate governance criteria to generate long-term competitive financial returns and positive societal impact. It is supported by the U.S. SIF Foundation, a non-profit organization that undertakes educational, research, and programmatic activities to advance the mission of U.S. SIF. It reports annually according to the Global Reporting Initiative Guidelines.

Global Impact Investing Network (GIIN). https://thegiin.org
The GIIN is a non-profit organization dedicated to increasing the scale and effectiveness of impact investing. Impact investments are those made into companies, organizations, and funds with the intention to generate social and environmental impact alongside a financial return. Impact investments can be made in both emerging and developed markets, and target a range of returns from below market to market rate, depending on the circumstances. The GIIN

builds critical infrastructure and supports activities, education, and research that help accelerate the development of a coherent impact investing industry.

Global Real Estate Sustainability Benchmark (GRESB). https://www.gresb.com
GRESB, an initiative of some of the world's largest institutional investors, leading academics, and industry bodies, provides a science-based sustainability benchmark for commercial property portfolios, acting as a tool for institutional investors to start a dialogue on social and environmental issues with their real estate managers. GRESB is committed to assessing the sustainability performance of real estate portfolios (public, private, and direct) around the globe. The dynamic benchmark is used by institutional investors to engage with their investments with the aim to improve the sustainability performance of their investment portfolio, and the global property sector at large.

Global Reporting Initiative (GRI). https://www.globalreporting.org
The GRI has specific guides and guidelines for reporting in different industries and sectors, and offers a wealth of sector-specific guidance on sustainability metrics and reporting. This includes a Sustainability Reporting Framework, with guidelines, templates, and checklists. The templates for sustainability reporting in different industries offer GPs an idea of the various issues which they may encounter at their portfolio companies.

Hermes Investment Management. https://www.hermes-investment.com
Hermes is the primary manager of the BT Pension Scheme and one of the largest institutional asset managers in the U.K. Public market capabilities include high active share equities, specialist credit, government bonds, and multi-asset. Private market expertise includes real estate, infrastructure, private equity, and private debt. Hermes EOS enables institutional shareholders around the world to meet fiduciary responsibilities and become active owners of public companies, based on the premise that companies with informed and involved shareholders are more likely to achieve superior long-term performance than those without.

InSight at Pacific Community Ventures.
http://www.pacificcommunityventures.org/reports-and-publications/
Pacific Community Ventures is a 501(c)(3) non-profit that was founded in 1998 by former Silicon Valley executives who believed that small businesses in underserved communities should have easier access to the high-caliber advice and capital that revolutionized the high-tech industry. PCV's services include advice and capital to help small businesses succeed, plus impact evaluation, research, and policy services to propel the impact economy forward.

Institutional Investor. http://www.institutionalinvestor.com
Institutional Investor is a leading international business-to-business publisher, focused primarily on international finance. It publishes magazines, newsletters, and journals as well as research, directories, books, and maps. It also runs conferences, seminars, and training courses and is a provider of electronic business information through its capital market databases and emerging markets information service.

Institutional Limited Partners Association (ILPA). http://ilpa.org
The ILPA Due Diligence Questionnaire Tool covers topics related to fund diligence with one section dedicated to governance and another section dedicated to risk/

compliance/ESG. This checklist gives GPs a clearer idea of LPs' ESG expectations during the fundraising period. The tool presents metrics which can be used to assess a GP on ESG, including an overview of the various ESG initiatives which GPs can join.

Interfaith Center on Corporate Responsibility (ICCR). http://www.iccr.org
The ICCR is a coalition of faith and values-driven organizations who view the management of their investments as a powerful catalyst for social change. Its membership comprises nearly 300 organizations, including faith-based institutions, socially responsible asset management companies, unions, pension funds, and colleges and universities, that collectively represent over $100 billion in invested capital.

International Corporate Governance Network (ICGN). https://www.icgn.org
An investor-led organization of governance professionals, ICGN's mission is to inspire and promote effective standards of corporate governance to advance efficient markets and economies worldwide. It does this through three core activities: (1) influencing policy by providing a reliable source of practical knowledge and experiences on corporate governance issues, thereby contributing to a sound regulatory framework and a mutual understanding of interests between market participants; (2) connecting peers and facilitating cross-border communication among a broad constituency of market participants at international conferences and events, via virtual networking, and through other media; and (3) informing dialogue among corporate governance professionals through the publication of policies and principles, exchange of knowledge, and advancement of education worldwide.

International Finance Corporation (IFC). http://www.ifc.org
The IFC has developed the Environmental and Social (E&S) Management Toolkit for Private Equity to operationalize its performance standards. It is designed to assist GPs in assessing and managing the environmental and social risks and opportunities of their investments. Organized into a three-phase investment cycle (screening, appraisal, management), the toolkit generates the main E&S issues to be addressed for each investment. An online assessment engine (the "ES-gine") offers resources and template to help tackle the identified E&S issues.

The IFC's FIRST for Sustainability portal provides financial institutions with guidance on how to manage environmental and social risks and opportunities in their investment activities. The portal covers ESG factors across different sectors and regions, and provides guidance on how to implement an environmental and social management system, how to conduct E&S due diligence for investment opportunities, and how to create a pipeline of new business opportunities which target specific environmental needs.

International Foundation of Employee Benefit Plans. http://www.ifebp.org
The IFEPB is a non-profit organization, dedicated to being a leading objective and independent global source of employee benefits, compensation, and financial literacy education and information. It delivers education, information, research, and networking opportunities to thousands of benefits and compensation professionals who have come to rely on it for objective, accurate, and timely information.

International Labor Rights Forum (ILRF). http://www.laborrights.org
The ILRF is a human rights organization that advocates for workers globally by working to hold global corporations accountable for labor rights violations in their supply chains; advance policies and laws that protect workers; and strengthen workers' ability to advocate for their rights. It works with a variety of groups, including trade unions, faith-based organizations, and community groups, to support workers and their families. It aims to achieve dignity and justice for workers worldwide and to ensure that workers have the power to speak out and organize to defend their rights and interests, free from discrimination.

International Labour Organization (ILO). http://www.ilo.org
Underlying the ILO's work is the importance of cooperation between governments and employers' and workers' organizations in fostering social and economic progress. The ILO aims to ensure that it serves the needs of working women and men by bringing together governments, employers, and workers to set labor standards, develop policies, and devise programs. The very structure of the ILO, where workers and employers together have an equal voice with governments in its deliberations, shows social dialogue in action. It ensures that the views of social partners are closely reflected in ILO labor standards, policies, and programs.

International Trade Union Confederation (ITUC). http://www.ituc-csi.org
The ITUC is the global voice of the world's working people. Its primary mission is the promotion and defense of workers' rights and interests, through international cooperation between trade unions, global campaigning, and advocacy within the major global institutions. Its main areas of activity include trade union and human rights; economy, society and the workplace; equality and nondiscrimination; and international solidarity. The ITUC has built the world's most comprehensive database of violations of workers' rights (http://survey.ituc-csi.org), where descriptive texts detailing facts on real-world violations faced by workers have been published since 1983. The ITUC Global Rights Index tracker annually releases numerical ratings, by nation, revealing the varying degree of collective labor rights enjoyed by workers.

Investor Network on Climate Risk (INCR). http://www.incr.com
A network of 100 institutional investors representing more than $13 trillion in assets, the INCR is committed to addressing the risks and seizing the opportunities resulting from climate change and other sustainability challenges. Its mission is to mobilize investor leaders to address climate and other key sustainability risks, while building low-carbon investment opportunities. The INCR includes the largest institutional investors in North America as well as leading religious and labor funds, asset managers, and socially responsible investment funds.

Labor and Worklife Program at Harvard Law School.
http://www.law.harvard.edu/programs/lwp/
Within the Labor and Worklife Program, the Pensions and Capital Stewardship Project was established to educate and inform workers, scholars, researchers, and practitioners on issues of retirement security, including employment-based retirement plans, and of pension fund governance, management, investment, and related matters.

Local Authority Pension Fund Forum (LAPFF). http://www.lapfforum.org
The LAPFF is the U.K.'s leading collaborative shareholder engagement group, bringing together local authority pension funds from across the country to ensure investments are made responsibly and to ensure returns are financially and environmentally sustainable over the long term. The LAPFF has adopted a high-profile, interventionist approach to shareholder engagement and stewardship, having publicly led investor criticism of accounting standards that misrepresent the capital position of financial institutions, and spoken out against poor standards and excessive salaries.

National Conference on Public Employee Retirement Systems (NCPERS).
http://www.ncpers.org
The NCPERS is the largest trade association for public-sector pension funds, representing more than 550 funds throughout the U.S.A. and Canada. It is a non-profit network of trustees, administrators, public officials, and investment professionals who collectively manage nearly $3 trillion in pension assets held in trust for approximately 21 million public employees and retirees—including firefighters, law enforcement officers, and teachers. Founded in 1941, NCPERS is the principal trade association working to promote and protect pensions by focusing on advocacy, research, and education for the benefit of public-sector pension stakeholders.

National Coordinating Committee for Multiemployer Plans (NCCMP).
http://www.nccmp.org
The NCCMP is an organization of national, regional, and local multiemployer pension and health and welfare plans, international and local unions, national and local employer associations, individual local employers, and multiemployer fund professionals. For more than 30 years, it has been representing the interests of multiemployer plan participants in the halls of Congress, in regulatory arenas, and in the courts. The NCCMP monitors, on a nonpartisan basis, legislative, regulatory, and legal developments from conception to implementation to enforcement, effectively representing the interests of multiemployer plans and participants every step of the way. By communicating with government officials, members of Congress, and staff about the unique characteristics of multiemployer plans, the NCCMP has saved multiemployer plans hundreds of millions of dollars in regulatory and administrative costs. These savings enable those plans to remain financially secure and healthy, while providing enhanced benefits to plan participants.

Organisation for Economic Co-operation and Development (OECD).
http://www.oecd.org
The mission of the OECD is to promote policies that will improve the economic and social wellbeing of people around the world. The OECD provides a forum in which governments can work together to share experiences and seek solutions to common problems, and works with governments to understand what drives economic, social, and environmental change. The OECD Guidelines are far-reaching recommendations addressed by governments to multinational enterprises operating in or from adhering countries. They provide voluntary principles and standards for responsible business conduct in areas such as

employment and industrial relations, human rights, environment, information disclosure, combating bribery, consumer interests, science and technology, competition, and taxation.

OECD Guidelines for Multinational Enterprises (MNEs).
http://www.oecd.org/corporate/mne/oecdguidelinesformultinationalenterprises.htm
The OECD Guidelines for MNEs are far-reaching recommendations for responsible business conduct that 44 adhering governments—representing all regions of the world and accounting for 85% of foreign direct investment—encourage their enterprises to observe wherever they operate. The Guidelines were updated in 2011 for the fifth time since they were first adopted in 1976.

OECD Principles of Corporate Governance.
http://www.oecd.org/corporate/oecdprinciplesofcorporategovernance.htm
First released in May 1999 and revised in 2004, the OECD Principles are one of the 12 key standards for international financial stability of the Financial Stability Board and form the basis for the corporate governance component of the Report on the Observance of Standards and Codes of the World Bank Group. In 2015, the OECD launched a review of the Principles to ensure their continuing high quality, relevance, and usefulness, taking into account recent developments in the corporate sector and capital markets.

Pensions & Investments. http://www.pionline.com
Founded in 1973, *Pensions & Investments* is an international newspaper of money management that consistently delivers news, research, and analysis to the executives who manage the flow of funds in the institutional investment market. Written for pension, portfolio, and investment management executives at the hub of this market, *Pensions & Investments* provides its audience with timely and incisive coverage of events affecting the money management business. Written by a worldwide network of reporters and correspondents, its coverage includes business and financial news, legislative reports, global investments, product development, technology, investment performance, executive changes, corporate governance, and other topics crucial to the people who drive the world of professional money.

Responsible Contractor Guide. http://www.responsiblecontractorguide.com
The Service Employees International Union, CTW, CLC, provides a guide that lists contractors who provide janitorial and security services by their responsibility ratings. The ratings are based on responsible employment practices, such as appropriate compensation and benefits; maximization of continuity at the workplace; prioritization of worker safety; encouragement of collective bargaining; provision of bona-fide complaint or grievance procedures; and support of environmental and energy efficiency policies. Contractors' ratings are displayed by color, where green indicates that the contractor follows responsible contracting policies, yellow indicates problems in a particular area of responsibility, and red indicates that the contractor has failed to follow responsible contracting practices.

Responsible Investor. https://www.responsible-investor.com
Focusing on business-critical news and data, *Responsible Investor* is the only dedicated news and events service covering responsible investment, ESG, and sustainable finance for institutional investors globally. *Responsible Investor* is read by pension funds, public and government funds, central banks, endowments, foundations, charities, faith groups, family offices, corporations, investment consultants, asset managers, research and data providers, insurance companies, commercial banks, private banks, investment banks, custodian banks, index providers, associations, governments, regulators, non-governmental organizations, trade unions, supranationals, lawyers, accountants, lobbyists, and the media.

Responsible Investor Association (RIA). http://www.riacanada.ca
The Responsible Investment Association is Canada's membership association for responsible investment (RI). Members include mutual fund companies, financial institutions, asset management firms, advisors, consultants, investment research firms, asset owners, individual investors, and others interested in RI. The RIA's purpose is to support RI activities of members, promote ESG factors into investment analysis, and promote the practice of responsible investing in Canada.

Shareholder Association for Research and Education (SHARE).
http://www.share.ca
SHARE is a Canadian leader in responsible investment services, research, and education for institutional investors. It works to advance responsible investment by encouraging and assisting asset owners to maximize long-term financial returns, "by promoting good corporate governance, respect for human rights, vibrant communities, and a healthy environment"; and to promote sustainable prosperity and realize enhanced returns by invoking responsibility for the impact of investments. Its clients include pension funds, mutual funds, foundations, faith-based organizations, and asset managers. SHARE is a signatory to the PRI and is a GRI Organizational Stakeholder.

SocialFunds. http://www.socialfunds.com
SocialFunds.com provides over 10,000 pages of information on socially responsible investing mutual funds, community investments, corporate research, shareowner actions, and daily social investment news. Its homepage has links to free investor guides including *Investing in Socially Responsible Mutual Funds, Community Investment Guide,* and *Working with Social Investment Professionals.*

Sustainability Accounting Standards Board (SASB). http://www.sasb.org
The SASB is developing industry-specific sustainability standards for the recognition and disclosure of material ESG impacts by companies which are traded on U.S. exchanges. It maps the relevant ESG issues for each of the sectors that it currently covers: healthcare, financials, technology and communications, nonrenewable resources, transportation, services, resource transformation, consumption, renewable resources and alternative energy, and infrastructure. For each of the industries in these sectors, the SASB identifies which ESG factors are likely to be material and provides associated accounting metrics. GPs can then use these standards to determine which ESG issues are likely to be material within different industries and the associated metrics which can be used for reporting.

top1000funds.com

http://www.top1000funds.com

Top 1000 Funds is the news and analysis site for the world's largest institutional investors. Focusing on investment strategy and implementation, it is populated by original news stories, case studies, and research that relate directly to the work of investment professionals at pension funds, endowments, and sovereign wealth funds. One of its defining characteristics is truly global editorial content that focuses on the investment strategies, portfolio construction, and implementation techniques used by major institutional funds. Its readers are the chief investment officers, chief executives, and their direct reports, of pension funds, endowments, and sovereign wealth funds in more than 50 countries. The website is run by editor Amanda White with weekly email updates sent to readers, in addition to Twitter alerts and RSS feeds.

Trades Union Congress (TUC) Member Trustee Network

https://www.tuc.org.uk/economic-issues/pensions-and-retirement/member-trustees

The TUC Member Trustee Network provides support to trustees to enable them to carry out their duties professionally and effectively. It provides regular updates on regulatory and investment issues, a quarterly newsletter, access to training and conferences, and the opportunity to meet and talk with fellow member trustees at other funds. The Network currently covers 1,000 participants.

Trustee Leadership Forum for Retirement Security at Harvard University (TLF).

http://hausercenter.org/iri/about/tlf

The TLF is an applied research collaboration that draws on the experiences of labor-affiliated trustees to identify problems in developing strategies for long-term sustainable wealth creation The TLF's goal is to support systematic thinking about responsible investment by trustees regarding long-term pension fund sustainability. It works toward this goal by conducting participatory action research with a self-defined group of labor-affiliated trustees and by soliciting input from a group of related stakeholders, including fund managers, lawyers and consultants, and academics.

UN Environment Programme Finance Initiative (UNEP FI).

http://www.unepfi.org

UNEP FI was established as a platform associating the United Nations and the financial sector globally bringing together banking, insurance, and investment—the three main sectors of finance—in a unique partnership. The need for such a partnership arose from the growing recognition of the links between finance and environmental, social, and governance (ESG) challenges, and the role financial institutions could play for a more sustainable world. UNEP FI works closely with over 200 members is continuously building its membership, which is made up of public and private financial institutions from around the world and is balanced between developed and developing countries.

UN Global Compact. http://www.unglobalcompact.org

The UN Global Compact is a strategic policy initiative for businesses that are committed to aligning their operations and strategies with 10 universally accepted principles in the areas of human rights, labor, environment, and anticorruption.

By doing so, business, as a primary driver of globalization, can help ensure that markets, commerce, technology, and finance advance in ways that benefit economies and societies everywhere. The Global Compact has shaped an initiative that provides collaborative solutions to the most fundamental challenges facing both business and society. It seeks to combine the best properties of the UN, such as moral authority and convening power, with the private sector's solution-finding strengths, and the expertise and capacities of a range of key stakeholders. The Global Compact is global and local; private and public; voluntary yet accountable.

UN Guiding Principles on Business and Human Rights.
http://www.ohchr.org/Documents/Publications/GuidingPrinciples BusinessHR_EN.pdf
In 2011, the United Nations Human Rights Council unanimously endorsed the UN Guiding Principles on Business and Human Rights, a set of guidelines for states and companies to prevent and address human rights abuses committed in business operations.

UN Principles for Responsible Investment (PRI). http://www.unpri.org
The United Nations-supported Principles for Responsible Investment (PRI) initiative is an international network of investors who are working to implement the six Principles for Responsible Investment. Its goal is to provide an understanding of sustainable investing's implications and support signatories to consider incorporating sustainable investing into their investment decision-making and ownership practices. The responsible investment process is tailored to each organization's resources and investment strategy. Under the six principles, the initiative aims to foster good governance, integrity, and accountability, and to address obstacles to a sustainable financial system that lie within market practices, structures, and regulation. The PRI is a leading global network for investors to publicly demonstrate their commitment to responsible investment.

West Coast Infrastructure Exchange (WCX). http://westcoastx.com
The WCX is a unique regional platform designed to serve as a translation point between the public and private sectors, and provide technical assistance regarding public–private partnerships to public-sector agencies in the three West Coast states of California, Oregon, and Washington. Formed in 2013, the WCX is an independent 501(c)(3) non-profit with a board composed of senior representatives of the governors and treasurers of the member states and the executive director of Partnerships British Columbia.

World Economic Forum. http://www.weforum.org
The World Economic Forum is an international institution comprised of political, business, academic, and other societal leaders whose goal is to utilize cooperation between public and private entities to improve the state of the world. The Forum aims to build, serve, and sustain communities through an integrated concept of meetings, research networks, task forces, and technological collaboration. Its website provides a number of links to reports, events, projects, issues, and communities working toward building sustained communities in the spirit of global citizenship.

About the authors

PHOTO: ANDREA BARTOSIEWICZ

Thomas Croft is the Managing Director of Heartland Capital Strategies and Executive Director of the Steel Valley Authority. His previous works include *Up from Wall Street: The Responsible Investment Alternative* (Cosimo Books, 2009; foreword by Richard Trumka); "Targeted responsible investments," a chapter in *The Next Generation of Responsible Investing*, edited by Tessa Hebb (2011, Springer Publishing); *Helping Workers' Capital Work Harder: A Report on Global Economically Targeted Investments (ETIs)* (2009), a report commissioned by the Global Unions Committee on Workers' Capital; "Collaboration between labor, academics and community activists to advance labor/capital strategies: the origins of the Heartland network," a chapter in *Money on the Line: Workers' Capital in Canada*, edited by Isla Carmichael and Jack Quarter (2003, Canadian Centre for Policy Alternatives); as well as numerous articles.

Heartland's Strategic Research Director **Annie Malhotra** began her career in the investment industry at Burgundy Asset Management Ltd in Toronto, Canada. There, she got deep exposure to the fundamental, value-based, long-term, and bottom-up investment principles and philosophy adhered to at the firm. Later, Annie joined the Social Innovation Generation (SiG) group at the MaRS Discovery District in Toronto—now the MaRS Centre for Impact

Investing—to lead the development of SVX, an intermediary whose aim is to democratize access to capital for micro, small, and medium-sized business and not-for-profit organizations. At SVX, Annie engaged in all aspects of developing this unique impact investment marketplace, itself a new social enterprise, taking the project from idea to implementation. Annie has also independently consulted in the areas of sustainability and impact investing. Annie has completed the Canadian Securities Course (CSC) and is a Chartered Financial Analyst (CFA).

Heartland Capital Strategies (HCS) fosters a "Community of Practice" for responsible investments. As a thought leader in responsible investment since 1995, Heartland's founders sought to bring together labor's capital stewards to advocate for the adoption and growth of responsible investments that achieve positive economic impacts. Thus, Heartland is working in a united front to rebuild our cities, renew our industrial commons, grow the clean economy, and make the "boss" more accountable. Along the way, Heartland has commissioned path-breaking books, toured and helped cities, and educated capital stewards and a new generation of responsible investors. Based in Pittsburgh, Pennsylvania, Heartland is a partnership launched by and housed at the Steel Valley Authority (SVA), an innovative regional organization that has been successfully restructuring troubled manufacturing firms for more than 30 years. Co-founders include the Steelworkers, the AFL-CIO HIT and the AFL-CIO IUC who created Heartland to bring together labor's capital stewards to explore ways to rebuild our economy and reclaim workers' capital. For more information, please visit http://www.heartlandnetwork.org and sign up for our Thursday *Espresso E-Journal.*

Index